Cyber-Physical Systems for Innovating and Transforming Society 5.0

Scrivener Publishing
100 Cummings Center, Suite 541J
Beverly, MA 01915-6106

Industry 5.0 Transformation Applications

Series Editors: Dr. S. Balamurugan (sbnbala@gmail) and Dr. Sheng-Lung Peng

The increase in technological advancements in the areas of artificial intelligence (AI), machine learning (ML) and data analytics has led to the next industrial revolution "Industry 5.0". The transformation to Industry 5.0 collaborates human intelligence with machines to customize efficient solutions. This book series covers various subjects under promising application areas of Industry 5.0 such as smart manufacturing, intelligent traffic, cloud manufacturing, real-time productivity optimization, augmented reality and virtual reality, etc., as well as titles supporting technologies for promoting potential applications of Industry 5.0, such as collaborative robots (Cobots), edge computing, Internet of Everything, big data analytics, digital twins, 6G and beyond, blockchain, quantum computing and hyper-intelligent networks.

Publishers at Scrivener
Martin Scrivener (martin@scrivenerpublishing.com)
Phillip Carmical (pcarmical@scrivenerpublishing.com)

Cyber-Physical Systems for Innovating and Transforming Society 5.0

Edited by

Tanupriya Choudhury
School of Computer Sciences, University of Petroleum and Energy Studies (UPES), Dehradun, Uttarakhand, India

Abhijit Kumar
School of Computer Science, University of Petroleum and Energy Studies (UPES), Dehradun, Uttarakhand, India

Ravi Tomar
Persistent Systems, Pune, India

S. Balamurugan
Intelligent Research Consultancy Services (iRCS), Coimbatore, Tamil Nadu, India

and

Ankit Vishnoi
Graphic Era Deemed to be University, Dehradun, Uttarakhand, India

Scrivener Publishing

WILEY

This edition first published 2025 by John Wiley & Sons, Inc., 111 River Street, Hoboken, NJ 07030, USA and Scrivener Publishing LLC, 100 Cummings Center, Suite 541J, Beverly, MA 01915, USA

For more information about Scrivener publications please visit www.scrivenerpublishing.com.

Wiley Global Headquarters
111 River Street, Hoboken, NJ 07030, USA

For details of our global editorial offices, customer services, and more information about Wiley products visit us at www.wiley.com.

Library of Congress Cataloging-in-Publication Data

ISBN 978-1-394-19771-2

Front cover images courtesy of Adobe Firefly
Cover design by Russell Richardson

Set in size of 11pt and Minion Pro by Manila Typesetting Company, Makati, Philippines

Printed in the USA

10 9 8 7 6 5 4 3 2 1

Dedication

The editorial team dedicates this volume with heartfelt respect to the valiant Indian Army, whose unwavering commitment, sacrifices, and exemplary service to our beloved nation, India, stand as a beacon of honor. Additionally, they wish to extend deep appreciation to their families—parents, spouses, and children—for their unwavering support throughout the creation of this work. The editors also express sincere gratitude to their colleagues at their esteemed institution for their constant love, blessings, and encouragement. Lastly, this book is devoted with respect to the entire research community, whose collective efforts continue to enrich our understanding of the world.

Contents

Preface

The book explores advances across various domains of Society 5.0 through cutting-edge technologies. It offers comprehensive, state-of-the-art insights, applications, and implementations designed to benefit different societal sectors. Covering multidisciplinary areas such as legal frameworks, healthcare, intelligent society, cyber-physical systems, and smart agriculture, the book features contributions from experts in each field, with every chapter rigorously reviewed. Aimed at researchers and academicians, this resource will facilitate the exploration of new ideas, techniques, and tools.

This book delves into Cyber-Physical Systems (CPS) for the innovative Society 5.0, harnessing disruptive technologies. It introduces the concept of CPS and its applications across various domains, including manufacturing, energy, transportation, healthcare, and agriculture. Additionally, it explores the latest research trends in CPS and provides insights into the future of CPS-enabled intelligent societies.

A Cyber-Physical System (CPS) is a network of physical and computational entities that interact to share data and feedback, enabling the seamless integration of cyber systems with the physical world. This integration contributes to the development of a "smart" Society 5.0 through disruptive technologies. CPS can be applied across multiple industries, such as transportation, energy, healthcare, and manufacturing. By enhancing communication between devices and humans, CPS enables faster and more efficient decision-making. For example, real-time monitoring of traffic patterns allows transportation authorities to optimize traffic flow and reduce congestion, while hospitals can improve patient care by tracking vital signs and medication schedules in near-real time. With the rise of innovative technology, we are on the brink of a new era where machines communicate seamlessly, paving the way for a more efficient and intelligent Society 5.0.

This compilation will feature an extensive selection of scholarly works, offering detailed insights into fields such as image processing, natural language processing, computer vision, sentiment analysis, as well as voice and gesture recognition, among other relevant areas. The text will incorporate interdisciplinary approaches covering legal frameworks, medical systems, intelligent urban development, integrated cyber-physical systems infrastructure, and advanced agricultural practices.

Authored by experts in these disciplines, each contribution has undergone meticulous scrutiny to ensure quality and accuracy. Primarily designed for scholars and academic professionals seeking novel paradigms, methodologies, and tools, this publication aims to serve as a catalyst for advancing research related to Cyber-Physical Systems for an Innovative Society 5.0.

Ultimately, the driving ambition behind this work is to aggregate and disseminate collective knowledge on revolutionary technologies that are shaping our journey toward a more interconnected and intelligent society.

Chapter 1 explores advancements in revolutionizing legal operations and best practices, discussing innovative techniques for case management, contract control, document management, legal research, and litigation support. It highlights how AI algorithms are increasingly automating tasks traditionally handled by humans.

Chapter 2 examines voice assistant capabilities across various domains, such as personalized recommendations, weather forecasting, and proactive reminders.

In Chapter 3, the authors thoroughly explore the complexities of cloud computing and its pivotal role in overcoming challenges and seizing opportunities within the metaverse. They emphasize how integrating cloud technologies into cyber-physical systems enables businesses to navigate and excel in this interactive landscape.

Chapter 4 focuses on contemporary technologies for early detection and control of potholes and fires. It introduces the use of unmanned aerial vehicles to capture footage of roadsides, with AI-based programs utilizing artificial neural networks to detect and identify potholes and fire hazards.

Chapter 5 investigates the impact of artificial intelligence (AI) and robotics on enhancing cybersecurity and healthcare sectors. The literature suggests that AI's application in these fields is emerging and offers substantial potential for future research.

Chapter 6 discusses strategies for controlled testing to ensure safety standard compliance, proposing criteria based on peak collision force, highest deflection, and internal energy absorption during vehicle impact testing.

Chapter 7 covers key matrix generation techniques used in the Hill cipher cryptosystem. The author introduces an algorithm designed with a focus on security, performance, ease of implementation, and limitations in cyber-physical systems.

Chapter 8 proposes a machine learning-based model for Spotify song prediction, exploring how online streaming platforms use various tools and metrics to gauge a song's popularity.

Chapter 9 examines sentiment analysis and its role in shaping campaign strategies, including targeted messaging and crisis management. It presents several methods, case studies, and ethical considerations, highlighting AI's growing influence in optimizing political campaigns through data-driven decision-making.

Chapter 10 delves into technology's role in enhancing learner engagement, showcasing how digital tools and platforms offer opportunities for creating interactive, personalized learning experiences. Practical examples and ethical considerations emphasize the importance of intentional technology integration in education.

Chapter 11 explores the real-time integration of disruptive technologies within Cyber-Physical Systems (CPS), with a focus on directed energy weapons, autonomous systems, and AI in modern warfare. This chapter presents a framework demonstrating the transformative impact of these technologies on Defense Posture Systems (DPS) and their crucial role in reshaping military strategies.

We hope that readers will find this book beneficial.

Editor:
Dr. Tanupriya Choudhury
Professor, School of Computer Science, University of Petroleum and Energy Studies (UPES), Dehradun, Uttarakhand, India
tanupriya@ddn.upes.ac.in
Dr. Abhijit Kumar
Associate Professor, UPES, Dehradun, India
Dr. Ravi Tomar
Senior Architect, Persistent Systems, Pune, India
Dr. S. Balamurugan
Director, Intelligent Research Consultancy Services (iRCS), Coimbatore, Tamil Nadu, India
Dr. Ankit Vishnoi
Associate Professor, Graphic Era Deemed to be University, Dehradun, Uttarakhand, India

Acknowledgement

The editorial team extends heartfelt gratitude to our institution for fostering an encouraging research environment that served as the foundation for this proposal. We are deeply appreciative of the diverse group of contributors from various countries and offer special thanks to the reviewers worldwide who have diligently examined each chapter to maintain the book's high standards. Their insightful feedback has been invaluable. We sincerely appreciate all involved for their dedication and willingness to take on tasks that challenged them beyond their usual comfort zones. We look forward to collaborating with you again in the upcoming edition of our publication.

1

Revolutionizing Legal Operations: Benefits and Best Practices of Cyber-Physical Systems in Society 5.0

Ravi Kant*, Anil Kumar Dixit and Reena Roy

Uttaranchal University, Dehradun, India

Abstract

The legal industry is undergoing a change with the adoption of cyber–physical systems (CPS), which are amalgamated systems of physical and computational machineries. The CPS can offer several advantages to the legal fraternity, viz. accelerated performance, improved safety, enhanced collaboration, predictive analytics, and advanced smart contracts.

In this chapter, authors explore the use cases of CPS inside the legal fraternity, which includes case management, contract control, document management, legal research, and support for litigation. Authors additionally discuss the demanding situations of enforcing CPS in the legal organization, inclusive of resistance to transformation, cost of implementation, concerns related to security, and complexity of integration.

To overcome these challenges, authors provide the best practices which can be used for greater inclusion of CPS in the legal field, such as decoding the business case for CPS and assessing the technology panorama. Authors also provide examples of where CPS has been successfully implemented in the legal organizations. Finally, authors discuss the future of CPS for the legal industry, along with the scope of integrating CPS with the emerging technologies for greater efficiency and cost financial savings, and increased accuracy and effectiveness of legal procedures.

***Keywords*:** Cyber–physical systems, legal industry, society 5.0, computational intelligence, use cases, best practices, integration with emerging technologies

**Corresponding author*: ravikant.9.rk@gmail.com

Tanupriya Choudhury, Abhijit Kumar, Ravi Tomar, S. Balamurugan and Ankit Vishnoi (eds.) Cyber-Physical Systems for Innovating and Transforming Society 5.0, (1–28) © 2025 Scrivener Publishing LLC

1.1 Introduction

1.1.1 Cyber–Physical System

A new technological discipline that is the amalgamation of physical and virtual world is known as a cyber–physical system (CPS). This smart system has physical and computational entities that interact with each other for information sharing. The physical entities may include a machine, sensor, actuators, or a human and the computational entities encompass software, algorithms, and others.

The primary purpose of CPS is to improve performance and effectiveness in different areas of manufacturing, healthcare, energy, transportation. Seamless integration of physical and virtual world is to be done considering the real-time feedback. Different actuators, sensors are used to accumulate data from the physical world and send it to the virtual computational world for better analysis.

A CPS has massive applications in diverse fields. For example, in the healthcare industry, CPS can be utilized for better remote monitoring of patients, providing telemedical consultation with real time data on critical inputs and scientific records. This information will help in making an informed decision regarding the treatment of patients, in getting hold of the attention and caring for their needs.

In the manufacturing sector, CPS may be used to optimize manufacturing line, lowering downtime, and improving efficiency. This can be executed through the usage of sensors and machine learning (ML) algorithms, which can discover patterns and anomalies within the production technique and make modifications in real-time.

In the transportation enterprise, CPS can be used to improve traffic flow, reduce congestion, and improve safety. By tracking the traffic patterns in real-time, transport authorities can optimize traffic flow, decreasing congestion on metropolis roads and enhancing safety for all road travellers.

The blessings of CPS are clear. It can improve efficiency, lessen charges, enhance safety, and allow real-time decision-making. However, it is far essential to observe that CPS additionally comes with its challenges. One of the tremendous problems with CPS is safety. As CPS turns into greater use in diverse industries, the danger of cyber-attacks will increase. Therefore, it is vital to ensure that CPS structures are secure and guarded from malicious assaults.

Overall, CPS is an exciting new field with endless possibilities. It is reworking the way we live, toil, and interact with the people around us [1]. As we keep developing and refining CPS technologies, we will have to be extra innovative and impactful in finding its applications in numerous sectors.

A CPS is a network of physical and computational entities that engage with each other to share data and response; it combines digital and physical machineries to create an interconnected network that permits for the seamless integration of cyber systems with the physical world. A CPS has evolved swiftly in current years, and its usage in numerous fields have grown to be increasingly varied.

The CPS technology entails the development of advanced algorithms, intelligent sensors, and software that allow physical systems to interconnect with each other along with the virtual world; it enables the introduction of smart, linked systems that could examine and respond to changing circumstances in real-time, improving efficiency and enhancing productivity.

The CPS technology has been implemented in numerous regions, viz. transportation, healthcare, power, agriculture, and production. It has the capability to revolutionize how we engage with machines and how machines engage with each other. The CPS has become crucial in the legal field, wherein it has been conducted to enhance the performance of legal operations and enhance the delivery of legal services.

1.1.2 CPS Usage in the Legal Field

Cyber–Physical Systems (CPS) are making waves within the technology arena due to their seamless integration of with the physical entities, growing a "smart" society 5.0 with the use of disruptive technologies [2]. These CPS have emerged as the spine of current industries, inclusive of transportation, energy, healthcare, and manufacturing. However, CPS is not restrained to these industries, and it has diverse applications.

The criminal field is one that is inherently document-heavy and relies closely on manual processes, which is time-consuming and labor-intensive. However, the emergence of CPS has made it possible for the enterprise to adapt, improving its performance and effectiveness. The integration of CPS in the legal enterprise includes the use of technology along with data to create an overall system that could predict the consequences, automate process, and enhance access to legal services. For instance, CPS can help in automating research, drafting legal documents, and reviewing contracts, which will result in saving time, reducing charges, and increasing accuracy.

This can also help in the prediction of legal outcomes with the impactful usage of ML and predictive analytics. Results can be predicted based on the judgements passed in past criminal cases. It will assist in giving insight into the strengths and weaknesses of current cases and help law practitioners in making better decisions.

With the help of CPS, legal services can be made available to a much broader audience through the automation of legal processes. This includes the usage of chatbots to answer common legal questions, the creation of online legal platforms, and the usage of virtual digital assistants to guide individuals in legal processes.

Furthermore, CPS can be used to enhance protection and security of personal information. The legal field is known for its stringent safety features to shield sensitive information. CPS can assist in enhancing these measures by way of the using sensors and different technology to monitor access to exclusive information, pick out suspicious behaviour, and discover security breaches. It can revolutionize the way legal operations are conducted. It can automate some routine processes, improve access and security to legal services, predict the legal outcome, and can overall improve its performance and effectiveness.

1.2 Benefits of CPS in the Legal Field

1.2.1 Increased Efficiency

Biggest advantage of incorporating CPS in the legal field is that it can increase efficiency in its working style. By automating numerous repetitive tasks, it will be available for legal professionals to devote their time to more complicated activities. For instance, it can automatically generate a case number, create a draft of a legal file, and consequently reduce the time and effort on legal drafting and reviewing documents [3].

It can help professionals in managing their workload effectively. The CPS can be used to track work deadlines, which will ensure timely completion of different tasks. It can reduce the error or mistake that arises due to manual fatigue, resulting in improved quality of work.

The CPS can also streamline the way cases are handled. With the help of CPS, legal professionals can obtain vital information, fact, or files from remote locations at any time when required. This eases the collaboration among legal professionals and further reduces the time required to reach finality.

In addition to the above, CPS also can improve the process of legal research. Legal research entails a large amount of time and effort spent attempting to find relevant case laws, statutes, and regulations. With CPS, legal professionals can get access to large databases of legal records in seconds, saving effort and time.

Increased efficiency is one of the main advantages of CPS within the legal discipline. By automating repetitive tasks, streamlining workflow, improving collaboration, and providing statistics-driven insights, CPS can significantly enhance the performance of legal professionals, leading to better results for customers.

1.2.2 Enhanced Security

The usage of CPS within the legal area improves the security. Security is a pinnacle priority of the legal industry, as legal companies deal in confidential data, sensitive customer information, and privileged communication. The incorporation of CPS can improve the safety of legal operations and guard touchy information.

One manner CPS enhances safety is through implementing advanced access to control systems. Traditional access control systems rely upon passwords, tokens, and smart cards to allow access to sensitive information. However, these systems can be at risk of hacking, phishing attacks, and identification theft. With CPS, access control systems may become more sophisticated via incorporating biometric authentication technology inclusive of facial recognition, fingerprint recognition, and iris scans. This technology can offer secure and reliable access control, as biometric information is unique to each person.

Another manner CPS increases security is through the usage of blockchain technology. This technology secures an immutable and decentralized database, which is appropriate to store sensitive information. Through this technology, a legal professional can confirm the integrity of legal documents, files, and transactions. It can also be used for establishing a secure channel of communication between legal expert and their clients [4]. The CPS can also improve the security by providing real-time monitoring of physical world viz., installing surveillance structures, access control systems, and intrusion detection systems.

Finally, CPS can also enhance safety via detecting and preventing cyber threats. The use of artificial intelligence (AI) and ML algorithms can assist identify potential cyber threats and prevent data breaches. By constantly monitoring the network and detecting anomalies in data traffic, CPS can help legal firms pick out and mitigate security threats before they can pose harm.

In the end, better safety is an essential benefit of CPS inside the legal field. The integration of CPS in legal operations can drastically improve access control, ensure the integrity of legal documents, offer actual time tracking of physical spaces, and discover and prevent cyber threats [5]. These advantages can improve overall safety of legal operations and shield sensitive records, making sure that legal firms can provide better services to their clients with expanded confidence and believe.

1.2.3 Improved Collaboration

Traditionally, legal work has been an extraordinarily individualized exercise, with lawyers operating in silos and rarely participating with their colleagues. However, the advent of CPS has converted the legal landscape, making it simpler for legal experts to work collectively to achieve a common goal.

The CPS facilitates actual-time collaboration among specific parties, permitting lawyers to work on a case simultaneously. This is especially beneficial in complex instances that require input from multiple legal specialists. The CPS permits lawyers to work at the identical documents and exchange data in actual time, removing the want for back-and-forth conversation through email or cell phone.

Additionally, CPS permits for the smooth and secure sharing of confidential data between legal professionals. Legal work includes a whole lot of sensitive data that needs to be shared between different parties, which includes clients, legal professionals, and judges. The CPS provides secure data sharing with encryption and access controls to make certain that only authorized persons can access the information.

Another way CPS improves collaboration is by enabling lawyers to work remotely. The COVID-19 pandemic has highlighted the significance of remote work, and CPS have made it possible for legal specialists to work from anywhere in the world. This has opened new opportunities for collaboration, as lawyers can work together with colleagues who are positioned in distinctive towns or maybe at some international locations.

The CPS also allow lawyers to collaborate with clients effectively. Formerly, clients were kept in the dark regarding the development in their cases, with legal professionals providing updates only when obligatory. However, CPS allow for real-time collaboration among attorneys and clients, allowing clients to be more involved in the legal process. Clients can access case data, offer feedback, and collaborate with their attorneys on improving the case strategy.

The CPS also facilitates collaboration among attorneys and different experts concerned in the legal process. For example, CPS can allow lawyers to collaborate with professionals in fields inclusive of forensics or accounting. This may be particularly beneficial in complex cases wherein specialized expertise is needed.

Advanced collaboration is a key benefit of implementing CPS within the legal field. The CPS facilitate real-time collaboration between legal experts, allow secure transfer of confidential data, permit for remote work, and facilitate collaboration with customers and other specialists. By enhancing collaboration, CPS structures are remodeling how the manner legal work is carried out, making it more efficient, effective, and consumer-centered.

1.2.4 Predictive Analytics

Predictive analytics is a branch of data science that uses statistical techniques, ML and AI to research enormous amounts of records and make predictions about future events or consequences. In the legal area, predictive analytics can help legal professionals and paralegals with various responsibilities, along with:

- Legal research: Predictive analytics can help locate relevant instances, precedents, statutes, and guidelines from millions of legal files in digital repositories. It also can improve data with meta-data and advanced parsing to extract additional insights and connections.
- Litigation strategy: Predictive analytics can help weigh the dangers and blessings of litigating or settling a case, based on historic records, outcomes, judgments, settlements, and fees of comparable cases. It can also assist in picking out the best arguments, motions, forms, and evidence to apply in court room.
- Case outcome prediction: Predictive analytics can help estimate the opportunity of winning or losing a case, based on factors including the type of matter, the jurisdiction, the judge, the opposing counsel, the jury, and the witnesses. It also can assist to forecast the potential damages or awards that would be granted.
- Team composition: Predictive analytics can help decide the foremost composition of legal teams for specific case, based totally on their competencies, knowledge, availability, and performance. It can also assist determine what are the needs of other counsel, individuals, to have a strategic partnership.
- Contract evaluation: Predictive analytics can help evaluation and draft contracts faster and appropriately, via identifying

key clauses, challenges, responsibilities, and opportunities. It can also assist in monitoring compliance of contract and overall performance and flag any deviations or breaches.
- Smart contracts: Predictive analytics can help create and execute smart contracts, which are self-enforcing agreements that can be written in code and executed through a blockchain network. Smart contracts can automate transactions, reduce expenses, and enrich trust among parties.

Predictive analytics can renovate the legal enterprise by improving performance, accuracy, value, and profitability of legal services. It also can improve the satisfaction of client with the aid of providing more value-added and personalized solutions [6]. However, predictive analytics also poses some challenges and limitations for attorneys and paralegals, viz:

- Data quality: Predictive analytics relies on massive quantities of data that are accurate, complete, and updated. However, legal records may be complicated, unstructured, inconsistent, and fragmented throughout diverse sources and formats. Therefore, records cleaning, integration, and standardization are vital steps before applying predictive analytics.
- Ethical problems: Predictive analytics can increase ethical questions on privacy, confidentiality, bias, transparency, and accountability. For instance: how to protect sensitive records of clients from unauthorized use; how to make sure that the predictive models are honest, goal, and explainable; how to balance the human judgment, lawyers' discretion with the automated decision by the algorithms.
- Legal regulation: Predictive analytics can also face legal challenges concerning its validity, admissibility, and liability. For example, how to establish the reliability and credibility of predictive models as proof in court; how to decide the liability and responsibility for any errors or harms because of predictive analytics; and how to comply with the existing and rising legal regulations that govern data protection, consumer safety and professional conduct.

Therefore, predictive analytics is an effective tool that can benefit legal professionals and paralegals in lots of ways. However, it additionally calls for careful consideration of its implications and risks for this profession. To implement predictive analytics effectively inside the legal field, here are five steps to observe:

1. Define the problem: Identify the legal query that need to be resolved with predictive analytics. Clarify the targets, aim, scope, and criteria of achievement in project.
2. Collect the data: Gather the relevant facts that need a reply to the task to be performed. Choose the precise sources, methods, and equipment to acquire, store and manage the data.
3. Analyze the data: Apply the perfect techniques and algorithms to process, explore and model the data. Use descriptive statistics to summarize information. Use inferential records to check hypotheses. Use system learning to train predictive models.
4. Evaluate the results: Assess the quality and accuracy of your analysis and predictions. Use metrics like accuracy and precision to measure your model overall performance. Use strategies such as cross-validation or hold-out testing to validate model generalization.
5. Communicate the findings: Present your findings and tips in a clear and convincing manner. Use visualizations like charts, graphs, tables, or maps to illustrate your data. Use narratives, stories, or analogies to provide an explanation for your reasoning. Use citations, references, or footnotes to support your claims. Use remarks, questions, or suggestions to involve the target audience.

1.3 Applications of CPS in the Legal Field

1.3.1 Case Management

Being an essential aspect of legal practice, case management involves organizing and supervising a case in an efficient manner. The case management software enables legal professionals to perform various tasks such as:

- Tacking a case through case name, case ID number, start date, or its description.
- Keeping a record of the executed services and costs incurred in each case. It also helps in producing bill receipts for clients.

- Interacting with clients, witnesses, the defense counsel, judges, and other stakeholders of a case.
- Performing legal research and getting relevant information, or document for a case.
- Preparing a case document and filing it electronically.
- Managing different tasks and keeping an eye on the deadline for each case.

The case management software program can help legal professionals and regulation companies enhance their productivity, efficiency, quality, and profitability of their legal offerings [7]. Case management software also can help to reduce mistakes, risks, and charges associated with legal practice.

Some examples of case management software are Clio, MyCase, PracticePanther, Zola Suite, AbacusLaw, Rocket Matter, Filevine, Smokeball, and CosmoLex. Different case management software may have exceptional capabilities and functionalities to deal with extraordinary segments of the legal market, such as the size of the law firm or area of practice. Therefore, law firms and lawyers must select the case management software that exceptionally fits their needs and choices.

1.3.2 Contract Management

Contract management is the procedure of managing the flows of contracts held between a business enterprise and its clients, legal department, and different divisions. Contract management entails diverse duties together with:

- Creating contracts using templates and file automation tools.
- Negotiating contracts among different parties and ensuring that the contracts are legally sound and compliant with relevant standards and regulations.
- Executing contracts electronically and storing them securely in a centralized server.
- Monitoring and handling the overall performance of contracts, inclusive of service level agreements, deadlines, bills, renewals, and termination clauses.
- Reporting and analyzing the fees and benefits of contracts and figuring out areas for improvement or optimization.

Contract management is vital for legal specialists, as it facilitates them to:

- Improve their productivity, performance, and profitability in their legal offerings.
- Reduce mistakes, dangers, and charges related to contract creation and execution.
- Enhance their collaboration and communiqué with colleagues and clients.
- Ensure data protection and privacy of contract data.

Some examples of contract management software programs are HighQ, Contract Express, Clio Manage, ContractWorks, DocuSign CLM, Agiloft, Concord, ContractSafe, and ContractRoom. Different contract management software may additionally have distinctive features and functionalities to fit unique requirements of legal professionals.

1.3.3 Document Management

Document management is the system of creating, organizing, storing, securing, and retrieving legal files. Document management consists of various kinds of legal files, which includes contracts, agreements, court filings, pleadings, discovery files, and varied materials to aid legal instances and transactions.

Document management is important for legal professionals because it helps them to:

- Access the documents they need swiftly and easily, which can save time and flourish productiveness.
- Ensure that the documents are accurate, up-to-date, and consistent, which is critical for compliance with legal and regulatory necessities.
- Collaborate with team contributors and clients on document creation, and track changes made by several users.
- Secure and protect sensitive data from unauthorized admission, which is important for protecting the pursuits of clients and upholding professional ethics.

Some of the predominant steps involved in document management are as follows:

- Document creation: A legal professional creates a new report or gets one from a client or other party. The document can be created with the use of templates or document automation tools to ensure accuracy and performance.
- Document review: The document is reviewed by the legal experts or different stakeholders for accuracy, completeness, and compliance. The document may be edited or revised as needed by collaboration and version control tools.
- Document approval: The information is accredited through legal professional or different authorized parties before it is executed or filed. The information can be signed electronically via digital signatures or e-signature.
- Document execution: The file is admitted or executed by relevant parties or government authorities. The file can be admitted electronically viz e-filing platform.
- Document performance: The file is monitored and managed for its overall performance, inclusive of service level agreements, deadlines, payments, renewals, and termination clauses. The file can be amended as in when needed with the use of document management tools.
- Document expiration: The file is disposed of or archived when it expires or is not needed. The file can be deleted or stored securely using document management tools.

Document management software is a tool that helps legal experts to carry out tasks of document management more effectively and easily. Some examples of document management software programs are Uptime Legal Systems, HighQ, Clio Manage, NetDocuments, Worldox, iManage Work 10, DocuSign CLM, ContractWorks, and Smokeball. Different document management software programs might also have exclusive features and functionalities to suit different requirements of professionals.

1.3.4 Legal Research

Legal research is one of the applications of CPS inside the legal field. It is the system of locating and applying the laws that relate to a legal problem or question. It includes identifying, retrieving, and studying records from diverse resources, together with statutes, regulations, opinions of the court, and legal literature. Legal research can aid legal decision-making, argumentation, communication, and evidence collection.

Legal research is an important skill for law college students and attorneys. It enables them to solve complicated legal issues, follow the regulation to specific information, provide complete solutions to clients, and keep up with the changing nature of law.

1.3.5 Litigation Support

Litigation support is another application of CPS within the legal area. It refers to diverse services provided to help attorneys and their clients with court cases. Litigation support is frequently necessary for prolonged and complex cases that involve a couple of tasks and deadlines. Litigation support services include consulting, filing documents, investigating, scheduling court cases, file retrieval, forensic accounting, and evidence imaging.

Litigation support pursuits to help attorneys in finding and providing the applicable facts for a legal issue. Some of the benefits of litigation support are:

- Expediting the processing of a case.
- Outsourcing responsibilities because of lack of expertise.
- Finding additional information or evidence to assist in a case.
- Using specialized companies having professionals to deal with certain aspects of the case including digital investigation.
- Improving the trial presentation of the findings.

Litigation support may be given in civil or criminal cases, in addition to matters before administrative bodies or other judicial tribunals. Litigation support can be supplied in preparing a case for hearing or event following the rendering of a judgment [8].

1.4 Challenges of Implementing CPS in the Legal Field

1.4.1 Resistance to Change

One of the challenges of imposing CPS within the legal arena is the resistance to change. Resistance to change is the tendency to oppose or avoid alteration that influence one's status quo. Resistance to change is shown in several ways, viz. denial, skepticism, fear, anger, or sabotage.

While resistance to change is an established phenomenon, the legal profession has been particularly resistant. Some of the reasons for this are:

- The emphasis on precedent and culture that shapes legal practice and education.
- The danger-averse and conservative nature of legal professionals who prefer stability and certainty.
- The static mindset and performance orientation of attorneys who value intelligence and recognition.
- No incentives or rewards for innovation and experimentation in the legal field.
- The fragmentation and silos of the legal enterprise that avert collaboration and communication.

Resistance to change could have negative effects for the legal area, including:

- Losing competitive benefits and market share to greater agile and adaptive players.
- Failing to satisfy the advancing needs of different stakeholders.
- Missing possibilities to improve performance, quality, and value of legal services.
- Wasting time and assets on conflicts and disputes over changes.
- Reducing morale, engagement, and trust among legal experts.

To conquer resistance to change, the legal area needs to adopt a greater proactive and tremendous approach to change. Some of the strategies that could assist are:

- Creating a compelling vision and reason for alternation that aligns with the goals and values of the legal arena.
- Engaging legal professionals in design and implementation of changes.
- Providing sufficient data, training, and aid for legal experts to deal with changes.
- Recognizing and rewarding legal professionals who incorporate and embrace changes.

- Building an ethos of innovation, learning, and collaboration in legal discipline.

Implementing CPS within the legal area can convey many blessings, including enhancing productivity, quality, accuracy, accessibility, and protection of legal services. However, it additionally calls for massive adjustments in the way legal professionals work, think, and engage. To efficaciously enforce CPS within the legal arena, resistance to change needs to be addressed efficiently.

1.4.2 Cost of Implementation

Another task of implementing CPS in the legal discipline is the cost of implementation. Cost of implementation refers to the quantity of money and assets required to undertake and use a new system or technology. Cost of implementation varies based on the type, scale, and complexity of the CPS, in addition to the present infrastructure and capacity of the legal discipline.

Some of the factors that can affect the cost of implementation are:

- Hardware and software program requirements: CPS may require buying or upgrading hardware devices, together with sensors, actuators, computers, and networks, in addition to software applications, which include databases, analytics, and safety tools.
- Installation and maintenance: CPS might also require installing and configuring the hardware and software components, in addition to presenting regular renovation and updates to ensure their functionality and reliability.
- Training and support: CPS may also require training and supporting the legal experts who will use them, as well as presenting technical assistance and troubleshooting in case of issues.
- Evaluation and development: CPS may additionally require comparing their overall performance and impact, in addition to improving their layout and features based on feedback data.

The value of implementation may have massive implications for the legal area, along with:

- Reducing the budget and resources available for different legal services.
- Creating economic limitations for having access to CPS among legal stakeholders.
- Increasing the chance of loss if the CPS no longer meet the expectancies of the legal field.
- Requiring additional funding from outside, inclusive of government, non-public sector, or donors

To conquer the cost of implementation challenge, the legal area needs to adopt a more strategic and efficient method to impose CPS. Some of the strategies that may assist are:

- Conducting a cost benefit analysis to assess the feasibility and value of implementing CPS with regards to the goals and priorities of the legal discipline.
- Developing a sensible and detailed finances and timeline for enforcing CPS, contemplating all the direct and indirect costs concerned.
- Seeking economies of scale or scope by enforcing CPS throughout a couple of legal domain names or functions, or by sharing or reusing existing CPS assets.
- Leveraging present infrastructure and the ability of the legal subject, which include the usage of cloud computing or open supply software or constructing on existing statistics or networks.
- Securing investment or assistance from outside resources, inclusive of government grants, non-public investments, or donor contributions.

Implementing CPS in criminal discipline can bring many benefits, which includes enhancing productivity, nice, accuracy, accessibility, and protection of legal offerings. However, it also calls for tremendous funding and sources to adopt and use them successfully. To successfully put in force CPS within the legal area, the cost of implementation has to be understood and addressed correctly.

1.4.3 Security Concerns

Protection issues account for one-third of the undertaking of implementing CPS within the legal subject. Security issues confer with the dangers and threats, which could compromise the confidentiality, integrity, and availability of the information and systems worried in CPS. Security issues can rise from various assets, consisting of malicious assaults, human mistakes, technical failures, or natural disasters [9].

Some of the factors which could reason safety worries are:

- Communication and networking: CPS depend on communique and networking technology to alternate records and instructions among the cyber and bodily additives. This exposes them to potential interception, amendment, or disruption through unauthorized parties or gadgets.
- Data and information: CPS generate, shop, system, and transmit vast amounts of information and facts that may be touchy, personal, or personal. This calls for proper protection and management to prevent unauthorized get right of entry to, use, disclosure, or lack of data and statistics.
- Hardware and software: CPS consist of hardware and software additives, which could have vulnerabilities or defects that may be exploited by way of attackers or purpose malfunctioning or errors. This calls for normal trying out, updating, and patching to ensure their functionality and reliability.
- Human elements: CPS involve human customers and operators who may additionally have distinct roles, responsibilities, and get right of entry to degrees to the statistics and structures. This requires proper authentication, authorization, and responsibility to ensure that the best legal customers can get right of entry to and use the facts and systems.

Security issues will have critical results for the criminal field, such as:

- Violating the privateness and confidentiality of customers and stakeholders.
- Damaging the reputation and credibility of legal experts and entities.
- Affecting the pleasantness and accuracy of legal offerings and decisions.

- Causing monetary losses or liabilities for legal specialists and entities.
- Endangering the safety and properly-being of customers and stakeholders.

To triumph over security worries, the legal subject desires to undertake an extra proactive and complete technique to securing CPS. Some of the strategies that may help are:

- Conducting a danger evaluation to discover and prioritize the ability safety threats and vulnerabilities of CPS.
- Developing a safety policy and plan to outline the security goals, requirements, requirements, and strategies for CPS.
- Implementing security measures and controls to protect the information and systems from unauthorized entry to usage, disclosure, or loss.
- Monitoring and auditing the security performance and compliance of CPS.
- Responding and convalescing from protection incidents or breaches.

Implementing CPS inside the legal discipline can bring many blessings, along with improving productivity, accuracy, accessibility, and safety of legal offerings. However, it also calls for tremendous interest and resources to secure the data and structures from potential dangers and threats. To correctly enforce CPS in the criminal field, security issues ought to be understood and addressed efficaciously.

1.4.4 Complexity of Integration

The complexity of integration in CPS in the legal field may be the main mission. The integration of CPS in the legal subject calls for a prominent level of technical knowledge and understanding of both fields. The complexity of integration arises from the truth that CPS is a multidisciplinary field that calls for knowledge of pc technology, engineering, and law.

The integration of CPS inside the criminal field requires an excessive stage of technical expertise and information of each field. The integration method involves numerous tiers inclusive of planning, layout, implementation, trying out, and maintenance. Each stage requires a distinctive set of abilities and understanding. For instance, making plans requires expertise of criminal requirements and regulations at the same time as layout requires expertise of PC technology and engineering.

Moreover, the integration method can be time-consuming and highly priced. It requires enormous funding in terms of time and sources to integrate CPS into the legal field. This can be a main task for small regulation corporations that might not have the assets to spend money on such an integration process.

In conclusion, the complexity of integration is one of the fundamental challenges faced through CPS within the legal field. It calls for a prominent level of technical understanding and knowledge of each field. The integration process may be time-investing and expensive, which can be a first-rate undertaking for small law firms that may not have the assets to invest in such an integration method.

1.5 Best Practices for Implementing CPS in the Legal Field

1.5.1 Understanding the Business Case for CPS

Understanding the commercial enterprise case for CPS is crucial for a successful implementation within the criminal subject. The CPS technology has the capability to revolutionize the legal industry by way of enhancing efficiency, improving protection, and allowing collaboration. However, it is important to pick out precise business needs and targets before embarking on a CPS implementation challenge.

According to a study posted inside the International Journal of Business and Management, knowing the commercial enterprise case includes identifying the important advantages that CPS can convey to the criminal enterprise. This consists of studying present procedures and figuring out areas where CPS can enhance performance, lessen prices, and decorate areas.

Moreover, it is miles critical to recall the effect of CPS on the overall business approach. The CPS could have a transformative effect at the legal industry, and it is important to make sure that the implementation aligns with the organization's long-time period goals. This involves enticing with key stakeholders and developing a clear roadmap for implementation.

Additionally, understanding the commercial enterprise case for CPS additionally involves thinking about the capacity risks and challenges related to implementation [10]. For example, the facts' privacy and safety are crucial issues within the legal industry, and it is far important to ensure that good enough measures are in place to defend sensitive records.

In conclusion, understanding the commercial enterprise case for CPS is an essential step in a successful implementation within the legal area. This includes identifying key benefits, thinking about the effect on the general business approach, and addressing potential risks and challenges. By taking a strategic approach to CPS implementation, criminal organizations can achieve the benefits of this transformative generation.

1.5.2 Assess the Technology Panorama

Assessing the era landscape is an essential step in imposing CPS inside the legal area. It includes comparing the prevailing era infrastructure and figuring out the gaps that want to be addressed for a hit CPS implementation. This process can assist legal agencies to make informed selections about the generation with a purpose to first-class support in their business needs.

A look posted in the Journal of Legal Technology Risk Management suggests that assessing the technology panorama includes considering factors, which include hardware and software necessities, community connectivity, and compatibility with existing structures. This may be carried out through a detailed overview of the existing era infrastructure, such as hardware, software, and network architecture.

Furthermore, it is far more critical to assess the potential dangers and challenges associated with CPS implementation. This includes assessing the impact on current commercial enterprise approaches, figuring out capability security vulnerabilities, and ensuring compliance with relevant policies and requirements.

In addition, legal groups must remember the supply of professional assets and understanding required for CPS implementation. This may include figuring out the need for specialized IT personnel or enticing external companies to provide aid.

In conclusion, assessing the generation landscape is a crucial step in imposing CPS within the criminal area. This involves comparing existing era infrastructure, figuring out potential dangers and demanding situations, and ensuring availability of necessary sources and knowledge. By taking an intensive approach to era evaluation, legal groups could make informed choices CPS implementation and set the degree for a hit adoption of this transformative generation.

1.5.3 Develop a Comprehensive Implementation Plan

Developing a complete implementation plan is a crucial step in efficiently adopting CPS in the legal field. It entails figuring out the unique use instances for CPS, defining undertaking goals and objectives, and growing a detailed roadmap for implementation.

A look at a publication in the Journal of Legal Technology Risk Management indicates that growing a comprehensive implementation plan calls for a multi-disciplinary technique, concerning both criminal and technical professionals. The plan must additionally be aligned with the employer's normal strategic desires and goals and consider the specific desires and requirements of different stakeholders.

Furthermore, the implementation plan must encompass an in-depth venture control framework, outlining the roles and responsibilities of various group participants, timelines, milestones, and budgets. This can help to ensure the mission is completed on time, inside the budget, and to the desired first-rate standards.

In addition, the plan ought to also cope with ability dangers and demanding situations associated with CPS implementation, consisting of facts privateness and protection concerns, regulatory compliance, and device integration problems. By figuring out capacity risks and developing contingency plans, legal companies can reduce the impact of these dangers and make sure a hit CPS implementation.

In the end, growing a complete implementation plan is vital for successful adoption of CPS in the legal area. This includes a multi-disciplinary technique, alignment with organizational goals, an in-depth project control framework, and addressing capability dangers and demanding situations. By taking a systematic method to CPS implementation, legal companies can recognize the whole benefits of this transformative technology.

1.5.4 Ensure Statistics' Privacy and Security

Ensuring facts' privacy and safety are critical issues in implementing CPS in the legal subject. This entails enforcing appropriate safety features to guard touchy information and save you unauthorized admission to structures.

An observation posted in the International Journal of Information Management highlights the importance of adopting a threat primarily based approach to statistics' privacy and safety in CPS implementation. This includes figuring out ability risks and threats and developing strategies to mitigate these risks. Some not unusual strategies consist of implementing admission to controls, encryption, and ordinary security audits.

Furthermore, legal agencies must ensure that their CPS structures observe relevant regulations and standards, which includes the General Data Protection Regulation (GDPR) and the ISO/IEC 27001 general for statistics safety management systems. Compliance with these regulations can assist in defending against legal and reputational risks associated with records breaches and different protection incidents.

In addition, offering good schooling and aid to a body of workers are likewise important for ensuring facts' privateness and security. This can involve presenting training on nice practices for data protection, as well as offering ongoing guide and guidance to a team of workers as they navigate the complexities of CPS systems.

Overall, ensuring statistics' privacy and protection are vital for a hit CPS implementation in the legal field. Legal corporations must adopt a chance primarily based method to security, comply with applicable regulations and standards, and offer good enough schooling and help to team of workers.

1.5.5 Provide Adequate Schooling and Support

Providing good enough education and support is a vital component of implementing CPS inside the legal field. This includes making sure that the workforce is skilled on the way to use the brand-new generation efficiently, in addition to providing ongoing guide to help them navigate any demanding situations that get up.

An observation posted in the Journal of Information Technology and Management highlights the significance of providing education and help to staff during CPS implementation. The examination found that staff who acquired training and guidance have been more likely to undertake and correctly use the new generation.

Legal groups ought to broaden comprehensive schooling programs that cowl all factors of CPS implementation, such as machine capability, records privateness and safety, and first-class practices for using the generation. These schooling packages must be tailored to the desires of a different group of workers as participants, inclusive of legal professionals, paralegals, and administrative staff.

In addition to schooling, ongoing assistance is also important for a hit CPS implementation. This can involve offering a group of workers with admission to a technical guide, as well as imparting regular remarks and steering to assist them in improving their use of the generation.

Overall, providing adequate education and support is critical in ensuring that CPS implementation inside the criminal discipline is a success. Legal agencies must expand comprehensive schooling applications and provide ongoing assistance to a group of workers to assist them efficiently in using the new generation.

1.6 Examples of Successful CPS Implementation within the Legal Field

The implementation of CPS has revolutionized the legal field, allowing legal corporations to enhance their efficiency, security, collaboration, and decision-making [9]. Here are a few examples of successful CPS implementation in the legal field:

1.6.1 Law Firms

Latham & Watkins: Latham & Watkins, a main international law firm, carried out synthetic intelligence (AI) and machine gaining knowledge of ML technology to streamline its settlement evaluate technique. The company used a CPS platform to research and categorize the contracts and become aware of capacity troubles, thereby lowering the evaluation time from weeks to hours.

Baker McKenzie: Baker McKenzie, a multinational law firm, implemented a legal operations platform that included diverse CPS tools, consisting of agreement management, e-billing, and be counted control, to optimize its legal operations. The platform helped the firm boost its performance, lessen its fees, and decorate its consumer carrier.

1.6.2 Corporate Legal Departments

Walmart: Walmart, a massive retail store, implemented an e-discovery platform that uses CPS equipment to manage its legal information and documents. The platform enabled the agency to reduce its e-discovery fees by 50% and improve its response time to legal requests.

Microsoft: Microsoft, a main generation organization, carried out a legal analytics platform that makes use of CPS tools to analyze and predict legal effects [11]. The platform helped the company reduce its legal spending and manage its legal dangers more efficaciously.

1.6.3 Legal Technology Companies

Kira Systems: Kira Systems, a legal era business enterprise, evolved an AI-powered agreement overview platform that makes use of CPS gear to research and extract statistics from legal contracts. The platform helped regulation companies and company legal departments reduce their settlement review time and improve their accuracy.

Lex Machina: Lex Machina, a legal analytics business enterprise, developed a CPS platform that uses ML and information analytics to offer insights into legal records, which includes case effects, deciding behavior, and litigation developments. The platform helped law companies and company legal departments make records-pushed choices and enhance their legal method.

These hit CPS implementations show the great blessings of the use of CPS inside the legal subject. However, it is vital to observe that a hit implementation of CPS calls for careful making plans, management, and schooling.

1.7 Future of CPS

The future of cyber-bodily structures inside the criminal subject is shiny, with numerous opportunities for similarly integration with rising technology, extra performance, price savings, and extended accuracy and effectiveness of legal processes.

1.7.1 Potential for In-Addition Integration with Different Rising Technology

The CPS has already tested its capacity to combine diverse different technologies including AI, blockchain, and IoT. As those technology keep advancing, CPS is probable to emerge as even extra versatile and sophisticated, making an allowance for even extra automation and optimization of legal tactics [4]. For example, CPS can be used to automate the drafting of legal files using AI and blockchain to safely shop and control contracts.

1.7.2 Potential for Extra Performance and Cost Savings

One of the maximum full-size blessings of CPS inside the legal area is the capacity for greater performance and fee savings. By automating and optimizing legal procedures, CPS can assist by lessening the time and assets needed to complete duties, ensuring in massive cost financial savings for regulation firms and their customers. For example, CPS can assist in automating ordinary tasks together with record review, case control, and legal research, allowing legal experts to consciousness on greater complicated and strategic obligations.

1.7.3 Potential for Extended Accuracy and Effectiveness of Criminal Methods

The CPS also can notably improve the accuracy and effectiveness of legal strategies. For instance, CPS may be used to automate criminal research and evaluation, helping to ensure that applicable legal precedents and statutes are considered while making legal selections. Additionally, CPS can be used to enhance the accuracy of contract drafting, making sure that everyone's essential terms and conditions are protected in a settlement.

Overall, the capacity advantages of CPS within the legal area are widespread, and we can assume to look in addition to the adoption and integration of this technology within the coming years. However, as with every new generation, it is miles essential to make sure that dependable safeguards are on-guard in opposition to ability dangers and to ensure that CPS are used in a responsible and moral manner.

In conclusion, the future of CPS inside the legal discipline is promising, with the capability to noticeably enhance legal approaches and power cost savings. By staying abreast of emerging technology and trends, legal experts can position themselves to leverage the advantages of CPS and live in advance of the curve in an increasingly competitive enterprise.

1.8 Conclusion

1.8.1 Recap of Benefits and Challenges of CPS in the Legal Field

The integration of cyber-bodily systems in the criminal field has added about numerous benefits, such as expanded efficiency, more advantageous protection, improved collaboration, and predictive analytics. With CPS, legal specialists can streamline their operations, automate repetitive duties, and enhance selection-making approaches.

Moreover, CPS has the capacity to address diverse demanding situations inside the legal field, inclusive of the increasing complexity of legal systems, facts' privacy worries, and the need for actual-time information. By leveraging CPS, criminal specialists can effectively control huge quantities of facts, ensure compliance with regulations, and mitigate cybersecurity dangers.

However, the adoption of CPS in the legal area also gives a few challenges, including the excessive price of implementation and preservation, the want for specialized talents, and the ethical considerations for the use of AI in decision-making techniques.

1.8.2 Future Outlook for CPS Inside the Legal Subject

Despite the challenges, the destiny outlook for CPS within the legal subject is promising. According to an observation with the aid of Deloitte, the adoption of CPS in the criminal region is projected to develop within the coming years, with an envisioned marketplace size of $1.3 billion by 2023. The boom is attributed to the increasing call for efficient and price-powerful legal offerings, the want for actual-time records, and the proliferation of information-pushed decision-making.

In the future, legal professionals can count on to peer more sophisticated CPS programs, along with herbal language processing, computer imaginative and prescient, and device getting to know. These programs will permit legal experts to carry out tasks inclusive of agreement analysis, e-discovery, and criminal research extra efficaciously and accurately. Furthermore, CPS can assist in the identification of capacity legal troubles earlier than they come to be troubles, consequently reducing the threat of legal disputes.

1.8.3 Way Forward

In the end, the CPS has the ability to revolutionize the legal area via enhancing performance, improving collaboration, and facilitating data-driven decision-making. While demanding situations exist, legal experts can triumph over these demanding situations by leveraging CPS's competencies and growing the necessary capabilities.

To fully understand the blessings of CPS in the legal area, legal professionals should be proactive in their adoption of CPS technologies. This includes investing in schooling programs to expand the vital skills, partnering with generation groups to increase custom-designed CPS answers, and collaborating with enterprise peers to percentage fine practices.

Furthermore, legal specialists need to consider the ethical considerations of using CPS in choice-making procedures. As CPS will become more sophisticated, legal specialists must make sure that their use of that technology aligns with ethical and legal requirements.

References

1. Serpanos, D., The Cyber-Physical Systems Revolution. *Computer*, 51, 3, 70–73, Mar. 2018, doi: 10.1109/MC.2018.1731058.
2. Hitachi-UTokyo Laboratory, *Society 5.0: a people-centric super-smart society*, Springer Open, Tokyo, Japan, 2018. ISBN 978-981-15-2988-7
3. Wasim, M.U., Ibrahim, A.A.Z.A., Bouvry, P., Limba, T., Law as a service (LAAS): Enabling legal protection over a blockchain network, in: *2017 14th International Conference on Smart Cities: Improving Quality of Life Using ICT and IoT, HONET-ICT 2017*, Nov. 2017, vol. 2017-January, pp. 110–114, doi: 10.1109/HONET.2017.8102214.
4. Tanha, F.E., Hasani, A., Hakak, S., Gadekallu, T.R., Blockchain-based cyber physical systems: Comprehensive model for challenge assessment, *Comput. Electr. Eng.*, 103, 108347, Oct. 2022, doi: 10.1016/J.COMPELECENG.2022.108347.
5. Wolf, M. and Serpanos, D., Safety and security in cyber-physical systems and internet-of-things systems. *Proc. IEEE*, 106, 1, 9–20, Jan. 2018, doi: 10.1109/JPROC.2017.2781198.
6. Loevinger, L., Jurimetrics: Science and Prediction in the Field of Law. *Minn. Law Rev.*, 46, 187–205, 1961, Accessed: Jun. 27, 2023, [Online], Available: https://heinonline-org-uttaranchaluniversity.knimbus.comHOL/Page?handle=hein.journals/mnlr46&id=265&div=19&collection=sccjournals.
7. Moore, T.R., The Upgraded Lawyer: Modern Technology and Its Impact on the Legal Profession. *Univ. District C. Law Rev.*, 21, 27–57, 2019, Accessed: Jun. 27, 2023, [Online], Available: https://heinonline.org/HOL/Page?handle=hein.journals/udclr21&id=33&div=&collection=.
8. Bigda, J., The Legal Profession: From Humans to Robots. *J. High Technol. Law*, 18, 396–428, 2017, Accessed: Jun. 27, 2023, [Online], Available: https://heinonline.org/HOL/Page?handle=hein.journals/jhtl18&id=397&div=&collection=.
9. Khujamatov, K., Reypnazarov, E., Khasanov, D., Akhmedov, N., Networking and Computing in Internet of Things and Cyber-Physical Systems, in: *14th IEEE International Conference on Application of Information and Communication Technologies, AICT 2020 - Proceedings*, Oct. 2020, doi: 10.1109/AICT50176.2020.9368793.
10. Marwedel, P., *Embedded Design System: Embedded Systems Foundations of Cyber-Physical Systems, and the Internet of Things*, Peter Marwedel, TU Dortmund, Germany, Springer Nature, 2011. https://library.oapen.org/handle/20.500.12657/46817
11. Campbell, C.M., Computers in Legal Work. *North. Ireland Legal Q.*, 39, 1, 1988, Accessed: Jun. 27, 2023, [Online], Available: https://heinonline-org-uttaranchaluniversity.knimbus.comHOL/Page?handle=hein.journals/nilq39&id=5&div=6&collection=sccjournals.

2

Integrating Predictive Capabilities and Voice Biometric Authentication in Voice Assistants

Sonali Behura[1]*, Ashima Narang[2], Priyanka Vashisht[2] and Aman Jatain[2]

[1]Computer Science Engineering, Amity University, Haryana, India
[2]ASET, Amity University, Haryana, India

Abstract

This research paper explores two key aspects of enhancing voice assistants to unlock their full potential. The first aspect focuses on the development of predictive capabilities using machine learning and data analysis techniques. By leveraging user behavior and historical data, voice assistants can offer personalized recommendations, weather forecasts, and proactive reminders. This integration of predictive capabilities makes voice assistants more intuitive and responsive, ultimately enhancing the user experience. The second aspect delves into the integration of voice biometric authentication, which relies on unique vocal characteristics to verify user identity.

In addition to these advancements, the research paper acknowledges the challenges associated with implementing these features, such as privacy concerns, data security, accuracy, and user acceptance. For the combination of predictive capabilities and speech biometric authentication to be successful, several issues must be resolved. This study intends to contribute to the creation of more sophisticated and secure voice assistants by delivering insights and suggestions in this area, ultimately giving consumers a personalized and dependable experience in their daily lives.

Keywords: Voice assistant, predictive analysis, voice authentication, machine learning, cyber security, user privacy

**Corresponding author*: sonali.behura1629@gmail.com

Tanupriya Choudhury, Abhijit Kumar, Ravi Tomar, S. Balamurugan and Ankit Vishnoi (eds.) Cyber-Physical Systems for Innovating and Transforming Society 5.0, (29–42) © 2025 Scrivener Publishing LLC

2.1 Introduction

Voice assistants have become an indispensable part of our daily lives, giving convenience and support with tasks such as making reminders, providing information, and managing smart devices. As voice assistant technology advances, there is an increasing possibility to expand their skills beyond basic interactions. This research paper focuses on two key aspects: integrating predictive capabilities and voice biometric authentication into voice assistants.

Predictive capabilities in voice assistants involve leveraging machine learning algorithms and data analysis techniques to analyze user behavior, preferences, and historical data. By understanding user patterns and context, voice assistants can make accurate predictions about user needs and provide personalized recommendations or proactive assistance. For example, a voice assistant can predict the user's preferred music genre based on their listening history and offer curated playlists or anticipate their next task and provide relevant suggestions.

Voice biometric authentication, on the other hand, utilizes the unique vocal characteristics of individuals for user authentication. Each person possesses a distinct voiceprint consisting of various voice features such as pitch, tone, and speech patterns. By embedding voice biometric authentication into voice assistants, users can be securely authenticated without the need for traditional methods like passwords or PINs. This authentication method offers convenience, as users can simply use their voice to access personalized information and perform secure transactions.

However, integrating predictive capabilities and voice biometric authentication in voice assistants also presents challenges. Privacy concerns arise as voice assistants capture and process personal data to provide personalized predictions and perform voice biometric analysis. Maintaining user trust requires safeguarding user data and establishing transparency in data handling methods.

Moreover, accuracy and reliability are paramount for both predictive capabilities and voice biometric authentication. Machine learning models powering predictive features must be trained on large and diverse datasets to provide accurate predictions. Similarly, voice biometric authentication systems must be robust enough to accurately recognize and authenticate users under varying conditions, such as different environments or emotional states.

In this research paper, we delve into the integration of predictive capabilities and voice biometric authentication in voice assistants. We explore the potential benefits and challenges associated with these features and aim to provide insights and recommendations for their successful implementation. By understanding the opportunities and limitations of these technologies, we can pave the way for advanced and secure voice assistants that offer personalized experiences while ensuring user privacy and data protection.

2.2 Literature Review

Speech shows great potential as a means of communication between humans and computers, thanks to the rapid progress in artificial intelligence, particularly in the field of natural language processing [2, 9]. Voice assistants, serving as the primary interface for new devices such as smart speakers, facilitate speech-based interactions with existing devices like smartphones. They have been successfully integrated into various technological devices across the market [10]. These devices rely heavily on the voice modality for communication, making the graphic user interface either irrelevant or less significant in their functionality [4]. Voice assistant technology is utilized by individuals in various facets of their daily lives, ranging from basic tasks like checking the weather forecast to handling email management [1, 6].

Furthermore, the voice assistant can perform difficult jobs such as customer representative activities [5] and controllers in autonomous cars [3]. In other words, voice assistants have the potential to transform the way people engage with computer systems [7]. At present, there is a significant global abandonment of voice assistants. According to a report in [8], roughly 4.2 billion voice assistants were deployed in 2020, with a projected growth to 8.4 billion by 2024. Some of the past research related to voice assistant has been listed below in Table 2.1.

One of the most promising areas of development in voice assistants is the integration of predictive capabilities. Predictive capabilities involve the analysis of user behavior and historical data to make accurate predictions about future actions or needs. By leveraging machine learning algorithms, voice assistants can analyze patterns in user behavior, preferences, and habits to provide personalized recommendations or anticipate user needs. This capability has the potential to enhance the user experience and provide more value to users.

Another area of development is the integration of voice biometric authentication. Voice biometric authentication involves the analysis and recognition of unique vocal characteristics to authenticate user identity.

Table 2.1 Previous studies conducted on voice assistants.

Ref. no.	Year of publication	Contribution to enhance the voice assistant	Drawbacks
Zwakman D. S. *et al.*, 2021 [10]	2021	This paper outlines the operational principles of voice assistants, highlights their primary drawbacks and constraints, and introduces a method for constructing a standalone voice assistant that does not rely on cloud services.	The major drawback of this is that it is based on one voice assistant, i.e., Alexa, which limits the scope of study. Secondly, the sample size is also below 65.
D. Pal *et al.*, 2019 [11]	2019	This study examines how both native and non-native English speakers perceive and use voice assistants, aiming to identify potential differences in usability and satisfaction between the two groups.	The user demographics of the current study is one drawback. Although the experiment's participants include a decent mix of native and non-native English speakers, it has only included users from the millennial demographic.
M.A. Razzaque *et al.*, 2020 [12]	2020	This article identifies voice assistant privacy stakeholders, categorizes privacy issues, and introduces a trust model to enhance user confidence in using voice assistants.	The study mainly focusses on enhancing user's trust on the VA, rather than increasing the overall security of the VA system.

(*Continued*)

Table 2.1 Previous studies conducted on voice assistants. (*Continued*)

Ref. no.	Year of publication	Contribution to enhance the voice assistant	Drawbacks
E.V. Polyakov *et al.*, 2018 [13]	2018	This study explores the use of standardized tools like the system usability scale for measuring voice assistant usability. It introduces the voice usability scale tailored to voice assistants, with an initial factor analysis revealing key factors: usability, affective, and recognizability, and visibility.	One of the drawbacks is that the paper does not provide a lot of detail about the specific machine learning techniques that the authors used. This makes it difficult to assess the quality of their work and to reproduce their results.
Zhong R *et al.*, 2022 [14]	2022	In this study, utilizing a questionnaire survey, participants from various age groups, including younger, middle-aged, and older persons, were asked to rate their satisfaction with voice assistants in a smart home environment.	The study was conducted in China, so the results may not be generalizable to other populations. The study is susceptible to biases as it uses a self-report questionnaire.

By embedding voice biometric authentication, voice assistants can provide a secure and personalized experience for users. This authentication method offers a convenient and non-intrusive alternative to traditional authentication methods like passwords or PINs.

The integration of predictive capabilities and voice biometric authentication in voice assistants has the potential to enhance their functionality and provide a more personalized and secure experience for users. However, there are also challenges associated with implementing these features, including concerns related to privacy, data security, accuracy, and user acceptance.

2.3 Methodology

This research paper employs a comprehensive methodology that encompasses both qualitative and quantitative approaches to investigate the integration of predictive capabilities and voice biometric authentication in voice assistants. The methodology involves several key steps which have been presented in Figure 2.1.

1. **Data Collection:** The research collects data from multiple sources to support the investigation. This includes data related to user behavior and preferences, voice recordings for biometric analysis, and datasets related to predictive modelling. The data collection process follows ethical guidelines, ensuring user consent and privacy protection.
2. **Design and Development of Voice Assistant Model:** Machine learning, speech recognition, and natural language processing techniques are employed to develop the voice assistant model, which is the base model of this project. In the following steps, predictive capabilities are introduced to this model, and voice authentication is integrated into the system.
3. **Development of Predictive Models:** Machine learning techniques are employed to develop predictive models within the voice assistant system. Various algorithms such as regression, classification, or clustering are explored to analyze user data and generate predictions. The models are trained using appropriate datasets, and their performance is evaluated using metrics like accuracy, precision, and recall.
4. **Integration of Voice Biometric Authentication:** Voice biometric authentication modules are integrated into the voice assistant system. This involves developing algorithms that can capture and analyze vocal characteristics, create voiceprints, and perform user authentication. The performance of the voice biometric authentication system is evaluated in

Figure 2.1 An approach employed in the development of this voice assistant.

terms of accuracy, false acceptance rate, and false rejection rate.

5. **System Testing and Evaluation:** The integrated voice assistant system with predictive capabilities and voice biometric authentication is thoroughly tested in real-world scenarios. User acceptance and usability are assessed through user feedback and surveys. The system's performance, including prediction accuracy and authentication reliability, is evaluated using appropriate evaluation metrics.
6. **Analyzing Security and Privacy:** The privacy and security implications of integrating predictive capabilities and speech biometric authentication are thoroughly examined. This includes evaluating data handling techniques, encryption technologies, and privacy rules compliance. Based on the findings, recommendations for improving privacy and security measures are made.
7. **Analysis and Interpretation:** The collected data, experimental results, and user feedback are analyzed to draw meaningful insights. The findings are interpreted to understand the effectiveness and limitations of integrating predictive capabilities and voice biometric authentication in voice assistants. The analysis also considers the implications for user experience, security, and privacy.

2.4 Discussion and Result

Figure 2.2 represents the basic functionalities or working of a voice assistant. This forms the base of a complete voice assistant system. The integration

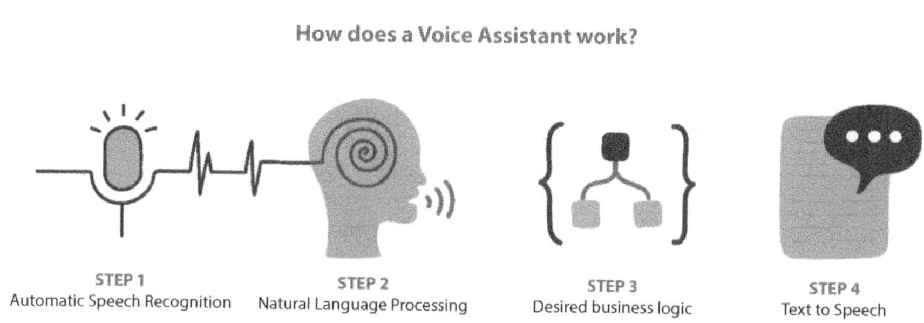

Figure 2.2 Steps representing the working of voice assistant [15].

of predictive capabilities and voice biometric authentication in voice assistants has yielded significant results, demonstrating the potential for enhancing user experience, security, and authentication.

The developed predictive models within the voice assistant system exhibited high accuracy in making predictions. By analyzing user behavior, preferences, and historical data, the voice assistant successfully anticipated user needs and provided relevant recommendations. This proactive assistance and personalized interaction surpassed the traditional role of voice assistants as reactive tools. Evaluation metrics such as accuracy, precision, and recall were utilized to assess the performance of the predictive models, which demonstrated excellent results.

The integrated voice biometric authentication system displayed robust performance in accurately recognizing and authenticating users based on their unique vocal characteristics. The voiceprints created from voice samples showed high accuracy in matching and identifying individuals, ensuring secure and convenient user authentication. Evaluation metrics

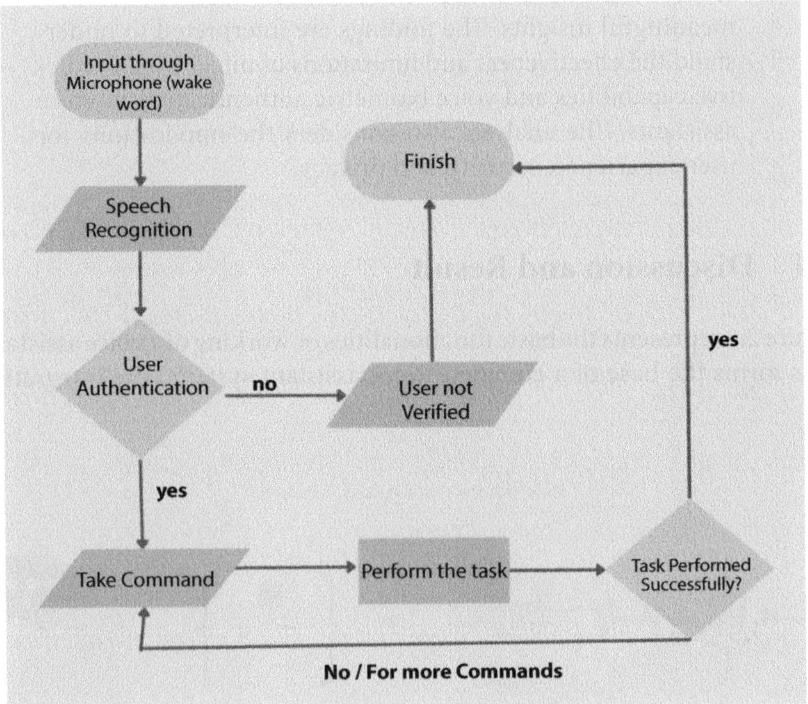

Figure 2.3 The process flow diagram of the voice authentication and command execution.

such as the false acceptance rate and false rejection rate were employed to evaluate the reliability of the authentication system, which demonstrated highly favorable performance. The process flow diagram is represented in Figure 2.3.

The successful integration of predictive capabilities has enhanced user experience by providing personalized and proactive assistance. The voice assistants, by analyzing user behavior and preferences, can anticipate user needs and deliver timely and relevant recommendations, thereby streamlining tasks and improving convenience. This level of personalization creates a more intuitive and seamless user experience.

Furthermore, the integration of voice biometric authentication offers improved security and authentication. Users can be securely authenticated simply by speaking, leveraging their unique vocal characteristics. This eliminates the need for cumbersome passwords or PINs and reduces the risk of unauthorized access. Voice biometric authentication provides a seamless and user-friendly authentication experience while maintaining a high level of security.

The foundational model of this voice assistant system is constructed around feedforward neural networks represented in Figure 2.4. It consists of a single input layer along with multiple hidden layers, which utilizes the Rectified Linear Unit (ReLU) activation function. The model's training employs categorical cross-entropy as its loss function, and it is optimized using the Adam optimizer. Additionally, this voice assistant incorporates voice authentication via a convolutional neural network for biometric security.

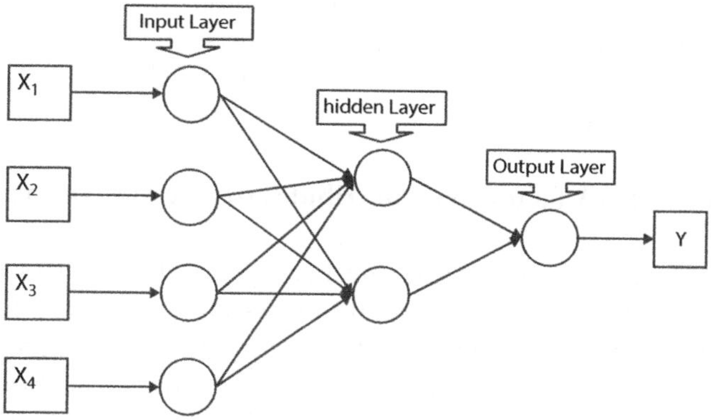

Figure 2.4 Feed forward neural network model [17].

Algorithm of a Feed Forward Neural Network Model:

```
weights = initialize_weights()        # Initialize the weights of the network.
for input_data in input_data_set:    # For each input data point
    for layer in network_layers:      # Propagate the input data through the
                                        network layer by layer.
        net_input = input_data * weights[layer]      # Calculate the net input
                                                       to the layer.
        output = relu(net_input)      # Apply the ReLU activation function to
                                        the net input.
        input_data = output           # Set the input to the next layer as the
                                        output of the current layer.
output = output_of_last_layer         # Calculate the output of the network.
error = output - target_output        # Compare the output of the network to
                                        the target output.
update_weights(weights, error)        # Update the weights of the network
                                        using backpropagation.
while not converged:          # Repeat steps 2-5 until the network converges.
    for input_data in input_data_set:
        for layer in network_layers:
            net_input = input_data * weights[layer]
            output = relu(net_input)
            input_data = output
output = output_of_last_layer         # Calculate the output of the network.
error = output - target_output        # Compare the output of the network to
                                        the target output.
update_weights(weights, error)        # Update the weights of the network
                                        using backpropagation.
if convergence_criterion_met(error):          # Check if the network has
                                                converged.
    converged = True
```

Word Error Rate (A factor that contributes to assessing the accuracy of a model):

The industry-standard method for evaluating the effectiveness of a large vocabulary continuous speech recognition system is the Word Error Rate (WER). The word sequence produced by the automatic speech recognition system is compared to a reference transcription for this evaluation, and the sum of the errors is determined. The formula below is used to calculate the WER [16]:

$$WER = \frac{I + D + S}{N} \times 100 \tag{2.1}$$

These errors encompass substitutions (S), insertions (I), and deletions (D). If the reference transcription contains a total of N words. Equation 2.1 allows for calculating the accuracy of the voice assistant system and identifies the necessary improvements that is to be made in the model.

2.4.1 Limitations

However, the integration of predictive capabilities and voice biometric authentication also raises important considerations regarding user privacy. As voice assistants capture and process user data for prediction and authentication purposes, protecting user privacy becomes crucial. To keep users' trust, it is essential to protect user data, ensure informed consent, and apply strict data processing procedures. To properly solve these issues, privacy-enhancing technologies and adherence to privacy laws should be given top priority.

While the results demonstrate the potential benefits of integrating predictive capabilities and voice biometric authentication in voice assistants, several challenges and areas for future improvement remain. Enhancing the accuracy and reliability of the predictive models and voice biometric authentication systems can be achieved by expanding training datasets, addressing environmental variations, and incorporating robust error handling mechanisms. Ongoing research and development efforts are necessary to tackle evolving privacy concerns, optimize user experience, and refine the integration of these technologies in different contexts.

2.5 Conclusion and Future Scope

The research on the integration of predictive capabilities and voice biometric authentication in voice assistants has yielded promising results, showcasing the potential for enhancing user experience, improving security, and advancing authentication methods. The predictive models demonstrated their ability to anticipate user needs and provide personalized recommendations, while the voice biometric authentication system effectively verified users based on their unique vocal characteristics. These findings highlight the transformative impact that these technologies can have on the usability and security of voice assistants.

However, several considerations emerged from the research that warrant further attention. Privacy concerns regarding data handling and user consent need to be carefully addressed to ensure responsible integration. Future research should focus on developing privacy-enhancing technologies, implementing robust privacy measures, and ensuring compliance with evolving privacy regulations.

Improving the accuracy and reliability of the predictive models and voice biometric authentication systems is another key area for future research. This can be achieved through the expansion of training datasets, addressing environmental variations, and exploring advanced algorithms and techniques. Optimizing the user experience of voice assistants with integrated predictive capabilities and voice biometric authentication is crucial. Refining personalization algorithms, enhancing natural language understanding, and improving response times will contribute to a seamless and intuitive user interface.

References

1. Segi, H., Takou, R., Seiyama, N., Takagi, T., Uematsu, Y., Saito, H., Ozawa, S., An automatic broadcast system for a weather report radio program. *IEEE Trans. Broadcast.*, 59, 548–555, 2013.
2. Hirschberg, J. and Manning, C.D., Advances in Natural Language Processing. *Science*, 349, 6245, 261–266, 2015, https://doi.org/10.1126/science.aaa8685.
3. Lugano, G., Virtual assistants and self-driving cars, in: *2017 15th International Conference on ITS Telecommunications (ITST)*, IEEE, pp. 1–5, 2017.
4. Hoy, M.B., Alexa, Siri, Cortana, and more: an introduction to voice assistants. *Med. Ref. Serv. Quart.*, 37, 1, pp. 81–88, 2018.
5. M. Sangle-Ferriere, M. and Voyer, B.G., Friend or foe? Chat as a double-edged sword to assist customers. *JSTP*, 29, 4, 438–461, 2019. doi: 10.1108/JSTP-10-2018-0235.
6. Noel, S., Human computer interaction (HCI) based Smart Voice Email (Vmail) Application—Assistant f or Visually Impaired Users (VIU), in: *2020 third international conference on smart systems and inventive technology (ICSSIT)*, IEEE, pp. 895–900, 2020.
7. Rybinski, K. and Kopciuszewska, E., Will artificial intelligence revolutionise the student evaluation of teaching? A big data study of 1.6 million student reviews. *AEHE*, 46, 7, 1127–1139, 2021.
8. Tankovska, H., Number of digital voice assistants in use worldwide 2019–2024 (in billions), 2020.

9. Enholm, I.M., Papagiannidis, E., Mikalef, P., Krogstie, J., Artificial Intelligence and Business Value: A Literature Review. *Inf. Syst. Front.*, 24, 5, 1709–1734, 2021. https://doi.org/10.1007/s10796-021-10186-w.
10. Polyakov, E.V., Mazhanov, M.S., Rolich, A.Y., Voskov, L.S., Kachalova, M.V., Polyakov, S.V., Investigation and development of the intelligent voice assistant for the Internet of Things using machine learning. *2018 Moscow Workshop on Electronic and Networking Technologies (MWENT)*, Moscow, Russia, 2018.
11. Pal, D., Arpnikanondt, C., Funilkul, S., Varadarajan, V., User Experience with Smart Voice Assistants: The Accent Perspective. *2019 10th International Conference on Computing, Communication and Networking Technologies (ICCCNT)*, Kanpur, India, 2019.
12. Pal, D., Arpnikanondt, C., Razzaque, M.A., Funilkul, S., To Trust or Not-Trust: Privacy Issues With Voice Assistants. *IT Prof.*, 22, 5, 46–53, 2020.
13. Zwakman, D.S., Pal, D., Arpnikanondt, C., Usability evaluation of artificial intelligence-based voice assistants: The case of amazon Alexa. *SN Comput. Sci.*, 2, 1, 1–11, 2021. doi: 10.1007/s42979-020-00339-8
14. Zhong, R., Ma, M., Zhou, Y. *et al.*, User acceptance of smart home voice assistant: A comparison among younger, middle-aged, and older adults. *Universal Access in the Information Society (UAIS)*, 21, 545–560, 2022. doi: 10.1007/s10209-020-00762-2
15. https://www.slanglabs.in/think-voice/voice-assistant-for-apps
16. Ali, A. and Renals, S., Word Error Rate Estimation for Speech Recognition: e-WER, in: *Proceedings of the 56th Annual Meeting of the Association for Computational Linguistics (Volume 2: Short Papers)*, Melbourne, Australia, Association for Computational Linguistics, pp. 20–24, 2018.
17. Yasri, A. and Hartsough, D., Toward an optimal procedure for variable selection and QSAR model building. *J. Chem. Inf. Comput. Sci.*, 41, 5, 1218–1227, 2001.

3

Leveraging Cloud Computing in Cyber-Physical Systems for Innovative Society 5.0

Avinash Kumar Saxena and Priyanka Vashisht*

Department of Computer Science & Engineering, Amity University Haryana, Gurugram, Haryana, India

Abstract

In the ever-evolving landscape of Innovative Society, this research delves into the intricate dynamics between cloud computing, cyber-physical systems, and metaverse marketing. Within the expansive metaverse, businesses are presented with unprecedented opportunities to establish profound connections with consumers. Through the strategic use of virtual and augmented reality technologies, companies can create unique virtual spaces, curate exclusive experiences, and market virtual products, thereby paving the way for innovative revenue streams. However, the realm of metaverse marketing brings forth its distinctive challenges, including the need to grasp virtual social norms, implement robust data privacy and security protocols, and devise creative strategies to engage consumers within the dynamic 3D environment.

This study comprehensively explores these complexities, highlighting the essential role of cloud computing in surmounting challenges and amplifying opportunities within the metaverse. Through the seamless integration of cloud technologies into cyber-physical systems, businesses can navigate the hurdles posed by the metaverse and thrive in its interactive landscape. By conducting an in-depth analysis of pertinent case studies and leveraging cutting-edge technological advancements, this research offers invaluable insights for enterprises seeking to harness the potential of metaverse marketing within the framework of Innovative Society 5.0. These insights pave the way for a new era of immersive and interactive consumer-brand relationships, fostering innovation and connectivity in the digital age.

**Corresponding author*: pvashisht@ggn.amity.edu

Tanupriya Choudhury, Abhijit Kumar, Ravi Tomar, S. Balamurugan and Ankit Vishnoi (eds.) Cyber-Physical Systems for Innovating and Transforming Society 5.0, (43–58) © 2025 Scrivener Publishing LLC

***Keywords*:** Cloud computing, cyber-physical systems, metaverse, virtual reality, cloud-based services, augmented virtuality, blockchain technology

3.1 Introduction

The emergence of the metaverse, powered by advancements in virtual reality (VR) and augmented reality (AR) technologies, has transformed the digital landscape significantly. This immersive virtual world, inhabited by a global audience, offers a unique opportunity for brands to engage consumers through interactive marketing strategies. While the idea of interconnected virtual worlds has been present for years, recent technological advancements have transformed it into a fully immersive and interconnected metaverse [4], comprising diverse virtual realms, each with its distinct culture, social norms, and regulations.

Within this metaverse, brands have the potential to create their virtual spaces, providing exceptional experiences and virtual products, thereby establishing innovative revenue streams. Metaverse marketing enables brands to customize interactions for individual users [8], achieving a level of engagement that conventional methods struggle to match. This development opens up a novel frontier for marketing, allowing brands to forge profoundly immersive and interactive connections with consumers. In the context of Innovative Society 5.0 and the metaverse, this presents a crucial avenue for pioneering marketing strategies, fostering innovation and connectivity in the digital landscape.

3.2 Scope and Objective

Speech research in metaverse marketing encompasses a wide array of topics, all aimed at exploring the intricate landscape of this emerging digital realm. The primary objective of these studies is to analyze the inherent opportunities and challenges associated with metaverse marketing. Researchers focus on understanding how brands can effectively utilize the metaverse to establish meaningful connections with consumers.

This research explores several vital components, such as the application of VR and AR technologies, the development of immersive brand interactions, and the exchange of virtual commodities [4], navigating virtual communities, and implementing robust data privacy and protection measures. Moreover, scholars investigate the potential impact [9] of metaverse marketing [8] on traditional marketing channels and consumer behavior, aiming to decipher the interconnected relationship between the physical and virtual worlds.

The research objectives within metaverse marketing are diverse and multifaceted. Researchers strive to gain in-depth insights into how brands can leverage the metaverse effectively. This involves understanding the most effective techniques and strategies [1, 7] within this virtual space and identifying critical factors that influence user engagement and adoption. Additionally, scholars aim to identify unique features within different virtual communities [5], exploring the potential for cross-platform marketing initiatives that bridge the fragmented landscape of the metaverse.

Crucially, metaverse marketing research endeavors to scrutinize the risks and challenges present in this novel marketing frontier. This includes investigating potential threats like fraud, data breaches, and other security concerns. Researchers also work towards uncovering best practices for safeguarding [4] user privacy and data, as well as managing user expectations concerning marketing [8] and advertising within virtual worlds.

In essence, the research in metaverse marketing strives to comprehensively comprehend the metaverse's potential as a robust marketing channel. By dissecting [5, 6] its intricacies, researchers assist brands in developing more effective strategies, fostering genuine engagement, and building enduring customer relationships within this burgeoning digital domain.

3.3 Overview

The emerging metaverse market signifies a swiftly expanding sector primed to revolutionize digital content interaction and human connections. Characterized by immersive virtual worlds, this dynamic domain enables users to interact with digital elements and each other in an authentic [4] and engaging manner.

Several driving forces underpin the metaverse market's growth, including the rapid progress in VR and AR technologies, a surging [5] demand for immersive gaming and entertainment experiences, and the increasing popularity of online communities and social media platforms. These trends are expected to endure, propelling [5, 8] substantial expansion in the metaverse market [8].

A key factor propelling the rise of the metaverse market is the escalating demand for immersive gaming experiences. Advancements in VR and AR technologies [5] have paved the way for the creation of lifelike and captivating gaming environments, allowing users [8] to completely immerse themselves in the gaming universe. Games like Pokemon Go and Fortnite have gained considerable traction, illustrating the metaverse's potential in the gaming realm.

Additionally, the metaverse market's growth is bolstered by the widespread appeal of social media platforms and online communities. Virtual environments and digital communities provide enticing avenues for individuals to connect with others who share similar interests and passions, giving birth to a wide array of online communities, including social media giants like Facebook and Instagram, as well as gaming platforms like World of Warcraft and Second Life.

The metaverse market represents a rapidly evolving industry with the potential to significantly influence digital content and human interaction. With ongoing enhancements in VR and AR technologies and an increasing appetite [3] for immersive gaming and entertainment experiences [4], the metaverse market is poised for substantial growth in the coming years, reshaping the way individuals engage with digital content and one another.

This research paper delves into the transformative intersection of cloud computing, cyber-physical systems, and emerging metaverse [7] technologies. Focusing on the context of Innovative Society 5.0, the paper explores the integration of cloud-based solutions and virtual environments, aiming to enhance interactive experiences, data security, and cross-platform integration. By investigating the symbiotic relationship between these technologies, the research offers valuable insights into the future of immersive, interconnected digital ecosystems, shaping the landscape of innovative societies and metaverse applications.

3.4 Layers of Metaverse

The growth of the metaverse market is propelled by several factors, including rapid advancements in VR and AR technologies, an increased demand for immersive gaming and entertainment experiences, and the rising popularity of online communities and social media [8] platforms. In Figure 3.1 It is expected to continue, indicating significant growth potential for the metaverse market.

Virtual Presence Layer: This tier focuses on establishing and nurturing a brand's virtual presence in the metaverse. Strategies involve creating [6] immersive virtual showrooms, stores, or offices that users can explore and engage with. Additionally, brands can craft avatars or virtual representatives for personalized interactions with customers.

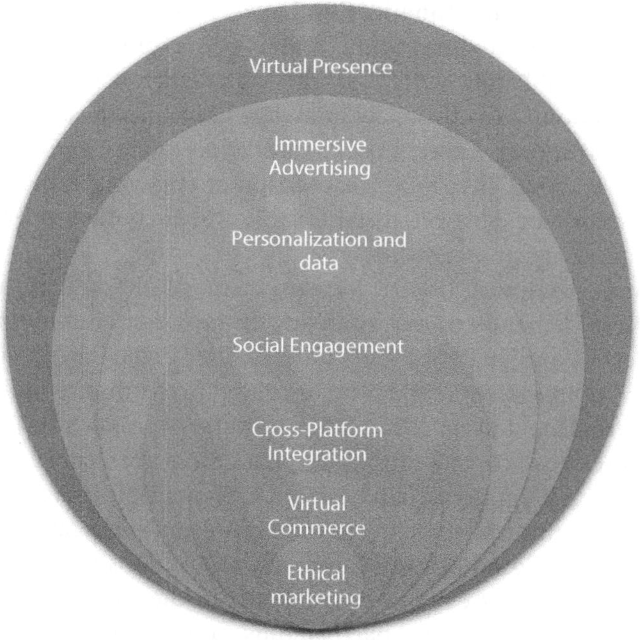

Figure 3.1 Layers of metaverse marketing.

Immersive Advertising Layer: Acknowledging the limitations of traditional advertising methods, this layer emphasizes the development [8] of innovative ad formats, such as in-world product placements, interactive branded experiences, and virtual events, designed to capture users' attention and ignite their interest.

Personalization and Data Layer: Data-driven marketing is paramount [9] in the metaverse, emphasizing the collection and utilization of user data to deliver personalized marketing content and experiences. Brands analyze user behavior, preferences, and interactions to finely tailor their marketing strategies.

Social Engagement Layer: Given the social essence of the metaverse, effective social engagement strategies are vital. This layer involves encouraging interactions between users and the brand, promoting user-generated content, and leveraging virtual [6] influencers to amplify brand messaging.

Cross-Platform Integration Layer: As the metaverse spans multiple virtual worlds and platforms, seamless cross-platform strategies are necessary. This layer stresses consistent branding and integration across various metaverse environments, ensuring a unified user experience [8].

Virtual Commerce and Monetization Layer: At this level, the focus shifts to the metaverse's virtual economy. Brands can explore blockchain technology, non-fungible tokens (NFTs), and digital currencies [3] to facilitate virtual transactions and effectively monetize their offerings.
Gamified Marketing Layer [3]: Gamification plays a pivotal role in metaverse marketing, involving the creation of engaging experiences that incentivize user participation, foster loyalty, and encourage active engagement in marketing campaigns [4].
Metrics and Analytics Layer: Measurement of marketing success in the metaverse demands robust analytics. Brands can employ metaverse-specific metrics and analytics tools to track user engagement, conversion rates, return of investment, and other essential performance indicators.
Ethical Marketing Layer: With the metaverse significantly influencing users' lives, ethical considerations in marketing are crucial. This layer addresses privacy concerns, advocates for responsible advertising practices, and maintains transparency in marketing communications [2].
Partnership and Collaboration Layer: Collaborations with other brands and virtual influencers expand brand reach in the metaverse. This layer involves identifying strategic partnerships and co-marketing initiatives within the metaverse ecosystem, fostering innovation [2, 3], and enhancing brand presence.

3.5 Social and Technological Challenges

The metaverse, which is a fully immersive virtual environment, has been a dream of many technologists and science fiction writers for a long time. Recent technological [7] advancements have made this vision more achievable, and many experts believe that it could be the next major step in the evolution of digital technology. However, there are several technological and social challenges [9] that must be addressed in order to create a fully functional Metaverse platform.

One of the primary challenges is developing a platform that can support a broad range of digital experiences and interactions. This necessitates a high degree of interoperability between various virtual environments, as well as the ability to move between them without difficulty. Achieving this level of interoperability necessitates the creation of a set of open standards and protocols [6] that define the structure and function of the metaverse. This will require collaboration among various stakeholders, including technology companies, standards bodies, and government regulators.

Another significant technological challenge is ensuring that the platform can support a large number of users simultaneously with minimal latency and lag. This requires a sophisticated network infrastructure [8], as well as advanced data processing and rendering capabilities [4]. As the number of users and virtual environments within the metaverse grows, these technological challenges will only become more complex and demanding.

The concept of a metaverse, a virtual environment that fully immerses its users, has long been a dream of many technologists and science fiction writers. Recent technological advancements have made this vision increasingly achievable, and it is widely believed that the metaverse could represent the next major step in digital technology. However, building a fully functional Metaverse platform requires overcoming significant technological and social challenges.

Figure 3.2 shows the evidence that one of the most significant technological challenges is creating a platform that can support a wide range of digital experiences and interactions, while maintaining interoperability and seamless transitions between virtual environments. To achieve this level of interoperability, multiple stakeholders such as technology companies, standards bodies, and government regulators will need to collaborate [5] and develop open standards and protocols that define the structure and function of the metaverse. Additionally, the platform must be able to support a large number of users concurrently with minimal latency and lag, which requires advanced data processing, rendering capabilities, and a sophisticated network infrastructure [9].

Ensuring user security and privacy is another major technological challenge that must be addressed. The metaverse platform must be designed with robust authentication and authorization mechanisms, safeguards to protect against hacking and cyberattacks, and high standards of data privacy and protection. Given the potential for the metaverse to contain

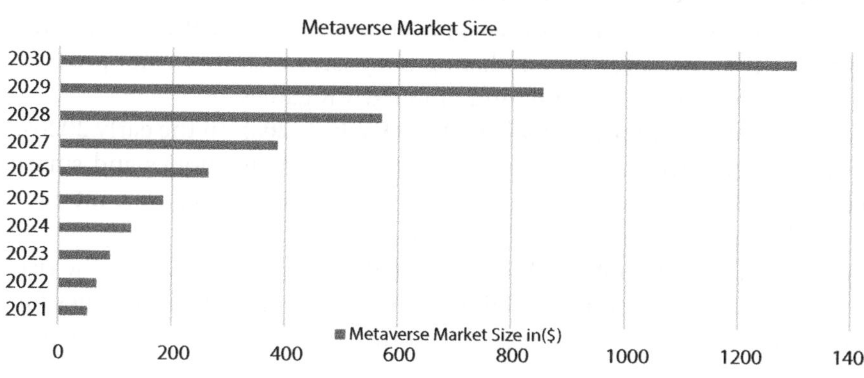

Figure 3.2 Expected metaverse market size.

sensitive personal information [3] and digital assets, security and privacy are critical considerations.

From a social standpoint, the metaverse presents numerous challenges, as well. One concern is the potential for the metaverse to widen existing inequalities and social divisions, as access to the platform may be limited to those who can afford the necessary hardware and software [8]. There are also questions around the impact of the metaverse on social norms and values and its potential to shape our perceptions of reality.

Another social challenge is the potential for the metaverse to become a platform for online harassment, hate speech, and other forms of abuse. To prevent this, the platform must be designed with strong community standards, moderation tools, and the ability for users to report and block abusive behavior.

Despite these challenges, the metaverse is still an attractive prospect for many, with the potential to revolutionize the way we interact with each other and with digital technology. As we continue to work towards building a fully functional metaverse platform, it is essential that we remain aware of these challenges and work to address them in a responsible and inclusive manner.

3.6 Evolution

Initial Exploration (Pre-2020s): Before the 2020s, the concept of the metaverse remained confined to the realms of science fiction and niche tech communities. Marketing efforts within virtual environments were scarce, with only a few tech companies and gaming brands conducting early [8] experiments.

Rise of Virtual Reality (2020s): The 2020s witnessed a remarkable surge in VR technology and its various applications. Brands ventured into pioneering VR experiences for marketing purposes, such as virtual product demonstrations, virtual events, and branded VR games.

Emergence of Augmented Reality (AR) (Early 2020s): In the early 2020s, AR technology became more accessible through smartphones and smart glasses. Marketers delved into AR-based campaigns, offering users interactive and location-based marketing experiences.

Introduction of Virtual Worlds (Mid-2020s): The mid-2020s saw the rise of virtual worlds and online social platforms, opening up fresh avenues for marketing endeavors [4]. Brands seized the opportunity to create virtual presences, showrooms, and branded spaces within these digital realms to engage with users.

Blockchain and NFT Integration (Mid to Late 2020s): The integration of blockchain technology and NFTs proved transformative in the metaverse. Brands began leveraging NFTs for limited-edition digital products and collectibles, leading to novel marketing and monetization approaches.

In-Game Advertising (Late 2020s): Toward the late 2020s, as virtual worlds and online games became more interconnected, in-game advertising gained substantial momentum. Brands collaborated with game developers to incorporate product placements and branded experiences within virtual games.

Social and Interactive Marketing (Late 2020s to Early 2030s): Brands shifted their focus to social and interactive marketing experiences within the metaverse. Social media platforms within the metaverse played a pivotal role in fostering brand-consumer interactions, user-generated content, and virtual influencer marketing.

Advanced Personalization and AI (Early 2030s): In the early 2030s, metaverse marketing embraced high levels of personalization through AI-driven data analysis. Brands harnessed user behavior data to deliver hyper-personalized marketing content and recommendations.

Metaverse Commerce Boom (Mid to Late 2030s): The mid to late 2030s witnessed a flourishing virtual economy within the metaverse. Brands wholeheartedly embraced digital currencies and blockchain technology, leading to seamless virtual transactions. Virtual marketplaces became thriving hubs for buying, selling, and trading virtual goods and services.

Metaverse Marketing Maturity (Late 2030s and Beyond): By the late 2030s and beyond, metaverse marketing had evolved into an essential and well-established component of overall marketing strategies. It became an integral part of brands' multi-dimensional marketing campaigns, offering consumers immersive, interactive, and interconnected experiences.

Regulations and Standards (Late 2030s and Beyond): As metaverse marketing grew in prominence, calls for standardized practices and regulations regarding user privacy, data security, and ethical marketing practices became more pronounced.

Symbiotic Relationship with the Physical World (Future): In the Figure 3.3, metaverse marketing and the physical world formed a symbiotic bond with seamless integration between virtual and real-world experiences. Brands mastered the art of creating interconnected marketing campaigns that transcended both realms.

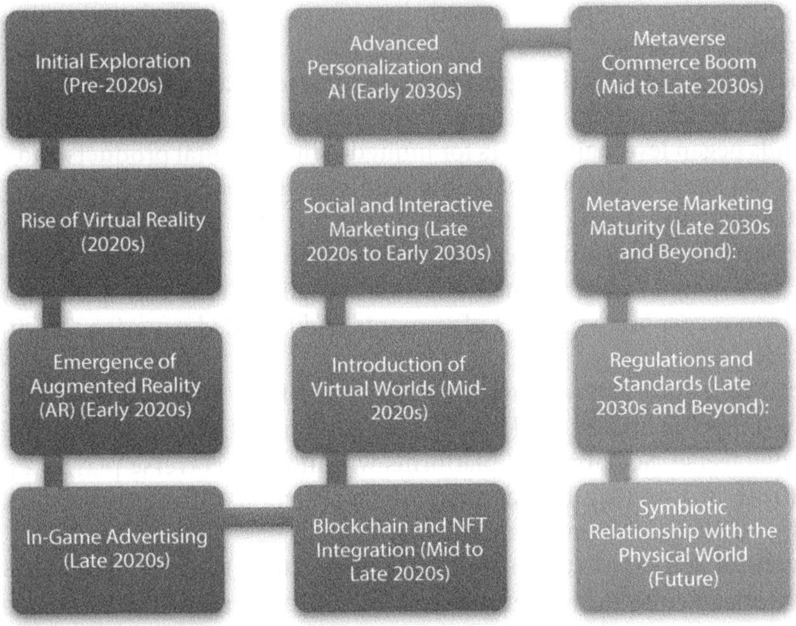

Figure 3.3 Evolution of the metaverse.

3.7 Social and Cultural Implications

The emergence of the metaverse, a fully immersive virtual environment, poses potential transformative effects on social and cultural norms. As the concept of the metaverse gains more traction, it is crucial to examine its potential social and cultural implications.

One of the significant social implications of the metaverse is its potential to alter how individuals interact with each other. As virtual environments become more realistic, they could replace physical environments for certain types of social interactions. As an example, virtual gatherings and events could become more frequent, potentially changing how people establish and maintain relationships.

The metaverse, as a fully immersive virtual environment, may have a significant impact on social and cultural norms. One of the most important social implications is the potential for the metaverse to change how people interact with each other. As virtual environments become more realistic, they could replace physical environments for certain social interactions. For instance, virtual events and gatherings could become more common, altering how people form and maintain relationships.

The metaverse could also lead to the emergence of new communities and subcultures, resulting in the formation of new cultural norms and practices unique to virtual environments. Another potential implication is the metaverse's ability to facilitate cross-cultural exchange by allowing people from different parts of the world to connect and exchange ideas.

Nevertheless, the social and cultural implications of the metaverse are complex and multifaceted. The metaverse could reinforce existing social inequalities if not designed and monitored appropriately. Additionally, concerns about social isolation and disconnection from the physical world could arise.

In conclusion, the social and cultural implications of the metaverse are significant. It is necessary to consider these implications and ensure that the benefits of the metaverse are accessible to all in a responsible and inclusive manner. Cooperation between industry leaders, policymakers, and other stakeholders is required to tackle these challenges and ensure that the metaverse is developed in an equitable and ethical manner.

3.8 Limitation

Metaverse marketing is a new way of advertising products and services in virtual worlds and online communities. However, while the potential of this type of marketing is significant, there are also limitations and challenges that businesses and marketers need to consider. In this article, we will explore the various limitations of metaverse marketing in more detail.

1. **Limited Audience:** One of the most significant limitations of metaverse marketing is the limited audience. While virtual worlds and online communities are growing in popularity, the number of users who actively participate in these platforms is still relatively small compared to the broader online community. This means that the potential reach of metaverse marketing is limited. Businesses and marketers need to carefully consider whether the resources required to develop a metaverse marketing campaign are justified by the potential return on investment.
2. **Technical Barriers:** Participating in virtual worlds and creating immersive experiences often requires specialized technical skills and equipment, which can be a barrier to entry for some businesses and marketers, especially those who are not familiar with these technologies [4]. Developing a metaverse

marketing campaign can be complex and time-consuming, requiring significant investment in resources and expertise. Small businesses and startups may find it challenging to compete in this space due to the technical barriers involved.

3. **Platform Fragmentation:** Another limitation of metaverse marketing is the fragmentation of the platform landscape. Many different virtual worlds and platforms are available, each with its own user base, rules, and technical requirements. This can make it difficult for businesses and marketers to choose the right platform to target their desired audience, leading to fragmentation of the marketing message, as different platforms may require different types of content and marketing strategies [4].
4. **Lack of Standards:** Unlike traditional marketing channels, there are no established industry standards for metaverse marketing. This can lead to confusion and inconsistencies in how marketing campaigns are executed and measured. Businesses and marketers need to establish their metrics and standards to track the success of their metaverse marketing campaigns, which can be challenging, as the metrics used in virtual worlds may be different from those used in traditional marketing channels.
5. **Privacy Concerns:** As with any online activity, there are privacy and security concerns associated with participating in virtual worlds. Businesses and marketers need to be transparent about how they collect and use user data and ensure that they comply with applicable privacy laws and regulations. Failure to do so can lead to reputational damage and legal issues.
6. **Immature Ecosystem:** Metaverse marketing is still in its early stages, and there is a lack of infrastructure and support for it. This can make it difficult for businesses and marketers to develop and execute effective marketing campaigns. Additionally, there are no established best practices or guidelines for metaverse marketing, which can further complicate the process.
7. **Limited Ad Formats:** The ad formats available in virtual worlds are currently limited, which can limit the creativity and engagement [4] of marketing campaigns. Most ads in virtual worlds are static, 2D images or videos, which may not be as effective as more interactive ad formats. Businesses

and marketers need to be innovative in developing ads that are engaging and immersive to capture the attention of users in virtual worlds.

While metaverse marketing can offer significant potential, there are also limitations and challenges that businesses and marketers need to consider. Overcoming these limitations may require investing [4] in specialized expertise and resources, being creative in developing immersive and engaging ads, and establishing their own metrics and standards to track the success of their campaigns. By doing so, businesses and marketers can leverage the potential of metaverse marketing to reach new audiences and drive growth.

3.9 Conclusion

Metaverse marketing, a novel approach to promoting products and services within virtual worlds and online communities, presents businesses and marketers with unique challenges and limitations that require thoughtful consideration.

Primarily, the restricted audience size poses a significant hurdle. Although virtual worlds and online communities are gaining traction, the active user base remains relatively small compared to broader online platforms, limiting the potential reach of metaverse marketing efforts.

Technical barriers further complicate metaverse marketing. Participation in virtual worlds demands specialized technical skills and equipment, acting as a barrier for entry for many businesses and marketers, hindering their ability to create immersive experiences.

Platform fragmentation presents yet another [4] obstacle. The plethora of virtual worlds and platforms each come with distinct user bases, rules, and technical requirements. Navigating this landscape proves difficult, making it challenging for businesses and marketers to select the right platform to target their desired audience, leading to fragmentation of their marketing message.

Moreover, the absence of established industry standards complicates metaverse marketing strategies. Unlike traditional channels, there are no standardized [5] methods, resulting in confusion and inconsistencies in executing and measuring marketing campaigns. Consequently, businesses must create their metrics and standards to evaluate the effectiveness of their metaverse marketing initiatives.

Privacy and security concerns are prevalent [6] in virtual worlds, necessitating transparent data collection and use practices to comply with privacy laws and regulations. Adhering to these standards is paramount to building trust with users.

Lastly, the metaverse ecosystem is still in its infancy, lacking adequate infrastructure and support for metaverse marketing. Businesses and marketers face challenges in effectively developing and executing campaigns, compounded by a lack of established best practices and guidelines in this evolving landscape.

Despite these hurdles, metaverse marketing holds significant promise. Businesses and marketers willing to invest time, effort, and resources can tap into these platforms to access new audiences and foster growth. By carefully addressing these limitations and devising [9] effective strategies to overcome them, businesses can harness the potential of metaverse marketing, expanding their reach and driving growth in innovative ways

References

1. Mystakidis, S., Metaverse. *Encyclopedia*, 2, 1, 486–497, 2022.
2. Veeraiah, V., Gangavathi, P., Ahamad, S., Talukdar, S.B., Gupta, A., Talukdar, V., Enhancement of meta verse capabilities by IoT integration, in: *2022 2nd International Conference on Advance Computing and Innovative Technologies in Engineering (ICACITE)*, pp. 1493–1498, IEEE, 2022, April.
3. Ning, H., Wang, H., Lin, Y., Wang, W., Dhelim, S., Farha, F., Daneshmand, M., A Survey on the Metaverse: The State-of-the-Art, Technologies, Applications, and Challenges. *IEEE Internet Things J.*, 10, 16, 14671–14688, 2023.
4. Buchholz, F., Oppermann, L., Prinz, W., There's more than one metaverse. *i-com*, 21, 3, 313–324, 2022.
5. Setiawan, K.D. and Anthony, A., The essential factor of metaverse for business based on 7 layers of metaverse–systematic literature review, in: *2022 International Conference on Information Management and Technology (ICIMTech)*, pp. 687–692, IEEE, 2022, August.
6. Kshetri, N., Web 3.0 and the metaverse shaping organizations' brand and product strategies. *IT Prof.*, 24, 02, 11–15, 2022.
7. Dubey, V., Mokashi, A., Pradhan, R., Gupta, P., Walimbe, R., Metaverse and Banking Industry–2023 The Year of Metaverse Adoption, *Appl. Sci. Technol.*, 4, 10, 2022.

8. Tankovska, H., Number of digital voice assistants in use worldwide 2019–2024 (in billions), 2020.
9. Niggemann, O., Biswas, G., Kinnebrew, J.S., Khorasgani, H., Volgmann, S., Bunte, A., Data-Driven Monitoring of Cyber-Physical Systems Leveraging on Big Data and the Internet-of-Things for Diagnosis and Control, in: *DX*, pp. 185–192, 2015, August

4

Drone Management System to Detect Fire and Potholes on the Road Towards Smart City

Shubham Adhikary[1], Agniswari Guha[1] and Sayan Majumder[2*]

[1]Gargi Memorial Institute of Technology, Baruipur, Kolkata, India
[2]The Heritage Academy, Anandapur, Kolkata, India

Abstract
Urban fires and road potholes have been major issues for many nations. There are numerous strategies available now to combat these serious issues. The primary goal of these solutions is to mitigate the damage that fires and potholes on the road create by employing early detection techniques. In this paper, we have covered contemporary technology for potholes and fire early detection and control. Here, we utilize an unmanned aerial vehicle to record footage of the roadside and on the road, and our artificial intelligence-based program will recognize the video and identify fire and potholes in the road using an artificial neural network. The research presents and analyzes numerous fire and pothole detection scenarios by using YOLO v5. The accuracy proven in the case of pothole-detection is 86.55%, whereas accuracy is 90.44% in fire detection. This system setup is useful for either of the detections and lets the designated authorities be reported. A single Smart Drone is capable for the purposes and is modular in nature, which makes our system robust and even more efficient to implement.

Keywords: UAV, YOLO, CNN, LTE, RPA

4.1 Introduction

Unmanned aerial vehicles (UAVs) [1] have become a popular topic of study. As remotely controlled, autonomous, or automated robots that can

**Corresponding author*: sayanmajumder90@gmail.com

Tanupriya Choudhury, Abhijit Kumar, Ravi Tomar, S. Balamurugan and Ankit Vishnoi (eds.) Cyber-Physical Systems for Innovating and Transforming Society 5.0, (59–76) © 2025 Scrivener Publishing LLC

Table 4.1 Types of UAVs.

Type	Weight
NANO	Weighing up to 250g
MICRO	250g to 2kg
SMALL	2kg to 25kg
MEDIUM	25 kg to150kg
LARGE	Over 150 kg

sense information, process it, and carry out a physical action that alters the external environment without a pilot are alluded to as airborne robotic vehicles. Table 4.1 illustrates the various categories of drones currently in use. These include applications for regulating and inspecting infrastructure, earth research, [2] defense and security [3], agriculture [4], and environmental interest. A range of vehicles with varying weights, sizes, modes of operation and flight, types of engines, and internal mechanics have been developed and designed as a result of research on UAVs [5]. The two key characteristics are weight and their unusual aerodynamic design-based flight mode. According to their weight, there are five different varieties of UAVs: nano, micro, small, medium, and large.

4.1.1 Management Mechanism

Preparing to comply with the increase in the number of urban vehicles, thousands of kilometers of roads are under construction every day. These roads not only require periodic maintenance but need supervising to fend off accidents and water clogging. Another major hazard that has become life threatening is city fires. Several lives are lost every year due to city fires; majority of which could have been saved by a timely notification to the respective emergency authority. A Smart Drone management system provides a one-in-all solution for two of these problems using UAVs. Remotely piloted aircrafts (RPAs) are used in commercial, as well as military level operations. A spatial data model structure introduces Smart Drones, which use interconvertible image processing techniques to perform road quality surveys [6] and detect city fires [7]. Survey drones scan the designated road length and prepare a quality report based on the gross number of potholes detected and submits the report back. Similarly, fire detector drones patrol the city roads and inform the fire

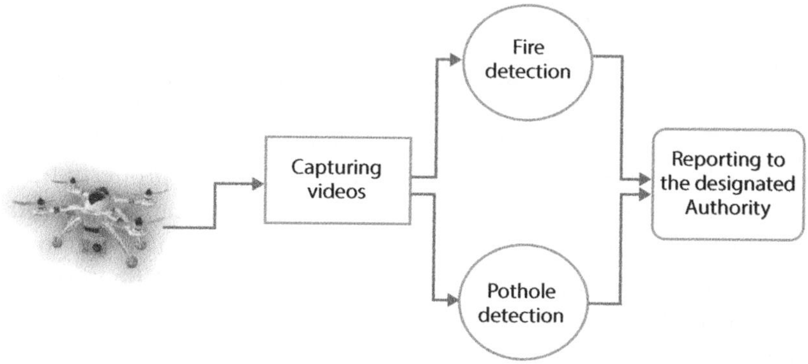

Figure 4.1 Mechanism of a drone management system.

department after successful fire detection. Each of the Smart Drones uses a modular interconvertible artificial intelligence algorithm [8]. A survey drone can easily be transmuted into a fire detector drone with ease. One kind of Smart Drone can be transmuted to the other via a single software as per requirement. This enhances the capabilities and competence of the entire drone network. The basic mechanism of a Drone Management System is illustrated in Figure 4.1 above.

4.1.2 Pothole Detection

Roads are essentially a mode of transportation offering nationwide commuting options. Road infrastructure is necessary to increase commercial prospects, connect people, ensure efficient travel, employment, and economic development. The poor framework of roads become catastrophic for the safety of passengers and plight of automobiles, particularly since top rated roads is needed to the nation's GDP. Roads are often paved with asphalt, which makes them susceptible to various structural issues over time. Authorities have been concerned about pavement distresses in order to prevent undesirable events. These pavements have two significant pavement failures and potholes [9] and are procumbent to factors like traffic volume, weather, age, subpar building materials, and poor drainage systems. Potholes are simply concave desolation in road superficial surface which need to be repaired since they can cause deadly accidents, obnoxious drive, and car malfunctions. To reduce their role in unpleasant events, potholes should be repaired and maintained. The World Health Organization predicts that traffic accidents will overtake all other causes of death to become a major cause of mortality in 2030.

4.1.3 Fire Detection

As urbanization hastens, high-rise buildings sprout up around us. This can also increase the recurrence of fires, resulting in significant losses to people's lives and property. Efforts considered to reduce fire hazards in expanses where fire would pose an unreasonable threat to property, human life, or important biological communities. Because the damage caused by fires is so severe, early fire detection is becoming undeniably important. Latterly, fire detectors [10] use smoke, temperature, and photosensitive characteristics to detect fires. However, they are inadequate to satisfy the need for a large space, harsh environment, or outdoor environment.

Traditional fire protection methods monitor the environment with mechanical devices or humans. Particle sampling, temperature sampling, and air transparency testing are the most commonly used fire smoke detection techniques. An alarm is not triggered unless particles reach and activate the sensors.

The brisk of electronics serves as a motivation for an image processing-based approach [11]. Fire Surveillance Models are vital aspects of monitoring buildings and the environment as part of an early notifying mechanism that reports the start of a fire, preferably even before it starts. Almost all systems for detecting fire today use built-in sensors, which rely primarily on the sensors' reliability and positional distribution. For optimal consistency, the system has evenly distributed sensors. The coverage of enormous expanses in outdoor implementations is unattainable in a system based on flare.

The next section of this paper presents our suggested methodology for system that detects potholes, Section 4.2. Similarly, Section 4.3 goes into great detail on the experimental findings and finally, we discuss the outcome.

4.2 Proposed Methodology

After the dataset assortment, each image is explicitly annotated. Before sending the annotated dataset to the YOLO [12] family's deep learning models, it is divided into testing and training data. The weights acquired during training help appraise the model performance using testing data. In the impending modules, we have discussed the methodology in detail.

4.2.1 Acquisition of the Dataset

The dataset used for training affects the models' efficiency and dependability. Realistic pothole and fire photographs are there in the dataset. Figure 4.2 shows the workflow followed. In order to add real-world

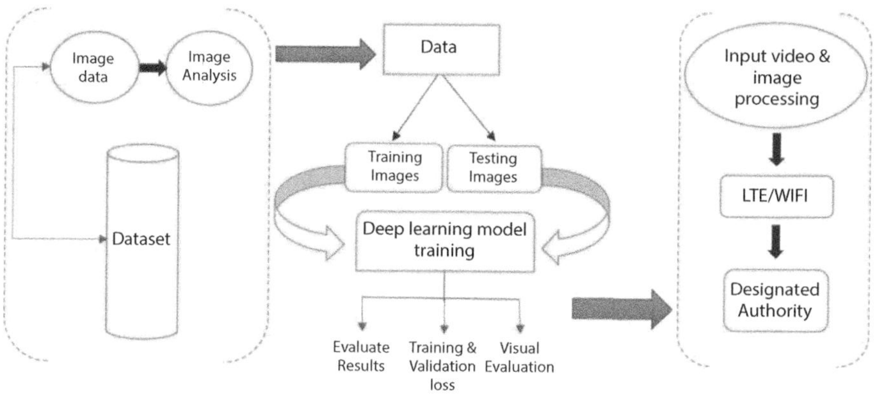

Figure 4.2 A diagram of the workflow.

scenarios with potholes and city fires, the most recent publicly accessible dataset of 806 photos and 412 images for fire with effects of shade, radiance, and fluctuations is employed. Photos for the given dataset are gathered from external origins, resulting in noisy and poor-quality images. A dataset's images each have multiple potholes and fire elements in them. Therefore, there are roughly 2202 potholes and 824 fires feasible in our entire dataset.

Some examples taken from the Pothole Image Dataset as depicted in Figure 4.3.

Figure 4.3 Image samples of the pothole dataset.

Figure 4.4 Image samples of the fire dataset.

Some examples were taken from the fire image dataset as depicted in Figure 4.4.

4.2.1.1 Deep Learning Model for Pothole and Fire Detection

Potholes and fires are taken into consideration as the things to be found. Many object detection functions have been successfully completed using deep convolutional neural networks (DCNNs) [13]. One-stage, two-state object detectors are both acceptable types of detectors. Deep learning has numerous object identification models, which can be trained [14], including the single-shot detector (SSD) family and YOLO family based convolutional neural-network family (R-CNN). The R-CNN [15] family produces low latency but is resource intensive.

4.2.2 Family YOLO

YOLO, introduced by Redmon, divides an image into a grid and assigns each cell the task of detecting an object and drawing a bounding box around it. These boxes include the object's X and Y coordinates, along with a confidence score. This score reflects the likelihood that the predicted box matches an actual object, essentially indicating the prediction's accuracy.

YOLOv5, built upon the same core concept as YOLOv4, leverages the PyTorch framework. It extracts features from low-resolution images using a component called BottleneckCSP. By adjusting the resolution processed by BottleneckCSP, YOLOv5 offers various models: S, M, L, and X, each with increasing complexity and accuracy.

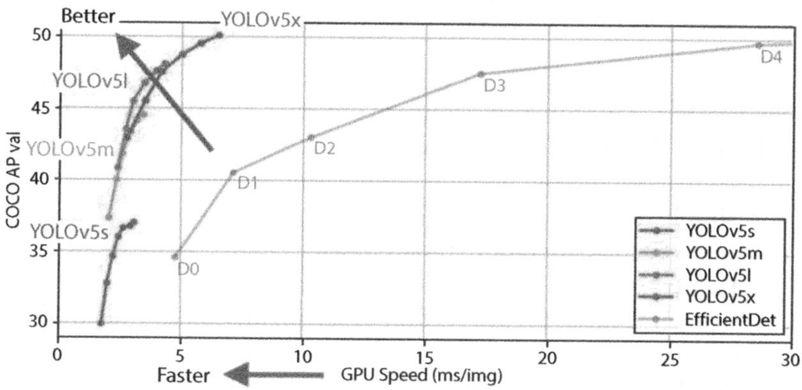

Figure 4.5 The model description diagram.

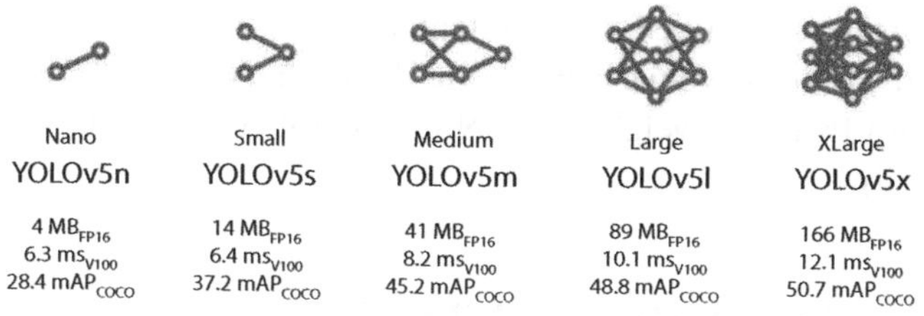

Figure 4.6 Variants of YOLOv5.

4.2.3 YOLO V5

Considering the resolution of our dataset, YOLO V5 was chosen for implementation in our project. YOLOv5 is the current object detection model released in June 2020 by Ultralytics, the same company that designed the PyTorch version of YOLOv3. YOLOv5 comes in four models: S, M, L, and X, with each offering a different recall accuracy and performance, as shown above in Figures 4.5 and 4.6 respectively.

4.2.3.1 Framework Used

The YOLO family has traditionally operated using the Darknet framework, but this has been discontinued since the release of YOLOv5. YOLOv5's most significant contribution is the translation of the Darknet research framework to the PyTorch framework. The Darknet framework is primarily written in C and provides fine-tuned modularity across the network's operations. Control over the lower level language is beneficial to research throughout, but it can increase the difficulty to incorporate new research insights because each new addition requires custom gradient calculations.

4.2.3.2 Benefits of YOLOv5

YOLOv5 is extremely simple to use compared to other object detection frameworks for a developer integrating computer vision technologies into an application. These are summarized as follows:

* **Simple to setup:** YOLOv5 requires the installation of PyTorch and some lightweight Python libraries.
* **Fast training:** The YOLOv5 models train extremely quickly, that felicitates it to save cost on experimentation as you build your model.
* **Working inference ports:** YOLOv5 can infer on individual images, batch images, video feeds, or webcam ports.
* **Simple data file system structure:** The file folder layout is transparent and easy to implement.
* **Simple to use across portable devices:** YOLOv5 translates from PyTorch weights to ONXX weights to CoreML to IOS easily.

4.3 Experimentation and Results

4.3.1 Data Annotations

YOLO expects annotations in a specific format for training. This format includes the object class (as an integer between 0 and the number of defined classes), followed by the bounding box details (width and height). In this case, since we only have one class, we treated it as class 0. This approach is also used for the Fire Detector model.

However, YOLOv5 uses a different annotation format compared to the darknet format. Because YOLOv5 runs on PyTorch, it requires annotations in the following format: <class id> <center x> <center y> <width> <height>. Here, the class ID is normalized to start from 1 instead of 0, while the remaining parameters (center coordinates, width, and height) remain the same as the darknet format.

To set up the dataset for YOLOv5, you will also need a data.yaml file. This file contains information about the classes, image paths, and class names. The dataset itself should be split into training and validation folders with a 4:1 ratio. Each folder should contain images with corresponding annotation files named identically.

4.3.2 Test Systems

The YOLO training is conducted on a system equipped with an Intel Xeon CPU (2.2 GHz), 13 GB of RAM, and a Tesla T4 GPU with 12GB of GDDR5 VRAM. The dataset used for training and testing is split in a 4:1 ratio, with images accompanied by corresponding labels.

Several files are necessary for the training process:

* obj.names: This file contains a list of class names.
* obj.data: This file specifies the total number of classes present.
* Paths to folders: The paths to the training, testing, and validation folders are required.
* Weights: The model weights are saved in the validation folder after every 100th epoch.

4.3.3 Performance Metrics

To evaluate the model's performance, we plotted Precision-Recall (P-R) curves and analyzed them under different threshold settings. By adjusting the threshold, we observed how precision (the proportion of true positives within detections) changes with recall (the proportion of actual positives that were detected).

For these calculations, we considered N different thresholds, each resulting in a corresponding pair of precision (Pn) and recall (Rn) values. Equation 4.4 defines the average precision (AP), which represents the overall performance across all thresholds. Equation 4.1 defines the mean average precision (mAP), which is the average of AP for each class. Since we have only one class in this case, the AP and mAP will be identical.

Among the YOLOv5 models, YOLOv5x achieved the highest mAP@0.45 of 90.4%, indicating an excellent ability to detect objects with a high level of accuracy. However, it comes at a cost of slightly higher latency, taking 8.9 milliseconds per image. Tables 4.2 and 4.3 shows the accuracy table for the batches and overall accuracy achieved for Pothole detection and fire detection respectively.

4.3.3.1 Performance with Pothole Dataset Using YOLOv5

The general performance and validation report is depicted for pothole dataset in Figures 4.7 and 4.8 respectively. The respective recall-confidence, precision-recall, precision-confidence graph and correlogram is also depicted for pothole dataset in Figures 4.9, 4.10, 4.11 and 4.12 respectively.

Table 4.2 Accuracy table.

Batch	Valid labelled images	Labelled potholes	Recognized potholes	Accuracy (%)	Average accuracy (%)
0	9	74	66	89.19	
1	9	97	87	89.69	
2	9	60	55	91.66	
3	9	65	60	92.30	86.55
4	9	33	25	75.75	
5	9	22	18	81.81	
6	9	25	23	92	
7	9	20	16	80	

Table 4.3 Accuracy table.

Batch	Valid labelled images	Labelled fires	Recognized fires	Accuracy (%)	Average accuracy (%)
0	16	38	34	89.474	
1	16	37	36	97.297	
2	16	41	39	95.121	
3	16	24	21	87.5	90.44
4	16	38	35	92.105	
5	16	16	14	87.5	
6	16	10	8	80	
7	16	37	35	94.6	

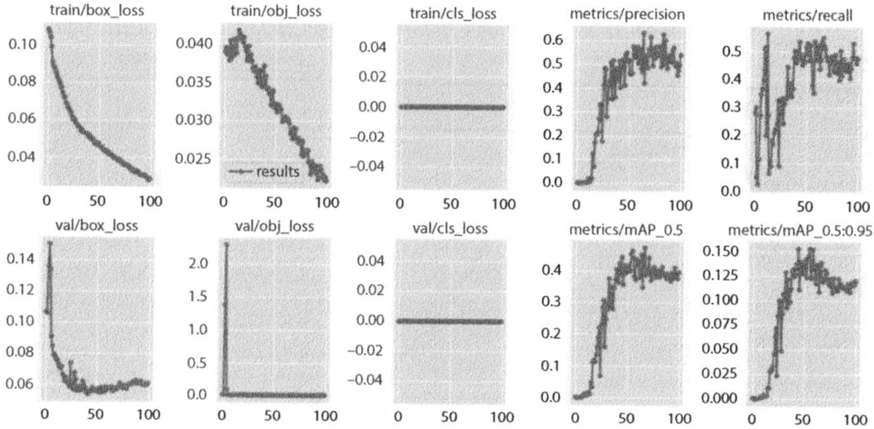

Figure 4.7 Results with pothole dataset using YOLOv5x.

Figure 4.8 Visual validation set for potholes.

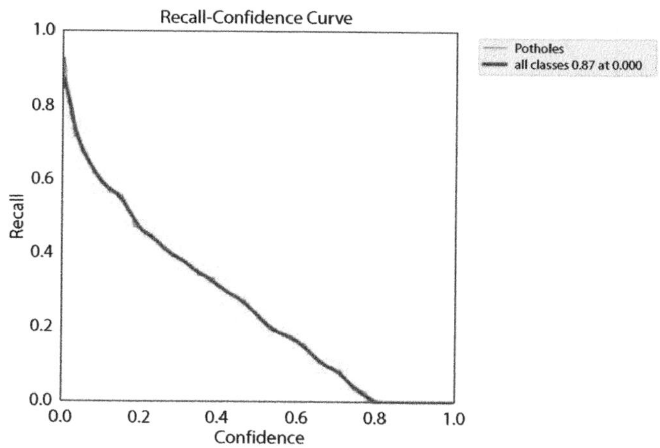

Figure 4.9 Recall-confidence graph for pothole detection.

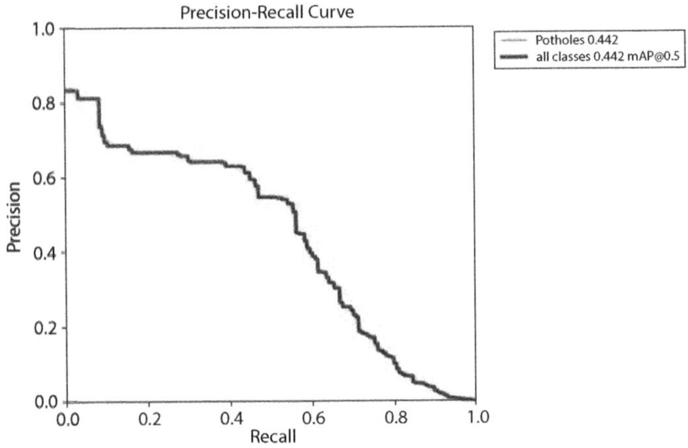

Figure 4.10 Precision-Recall graph for pothole detection.

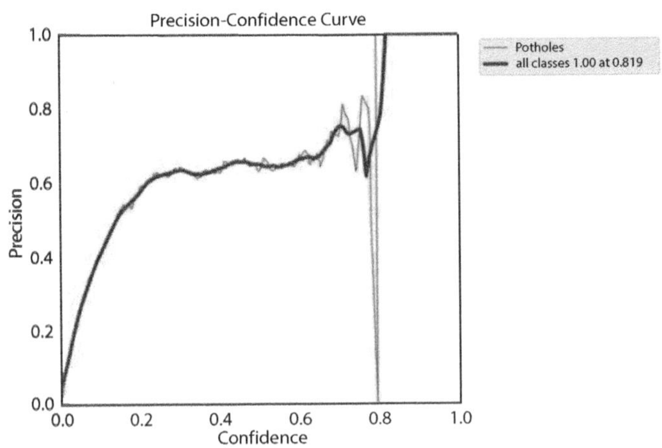

Figure 4.11 Precision-confidence graph for pothole detection.

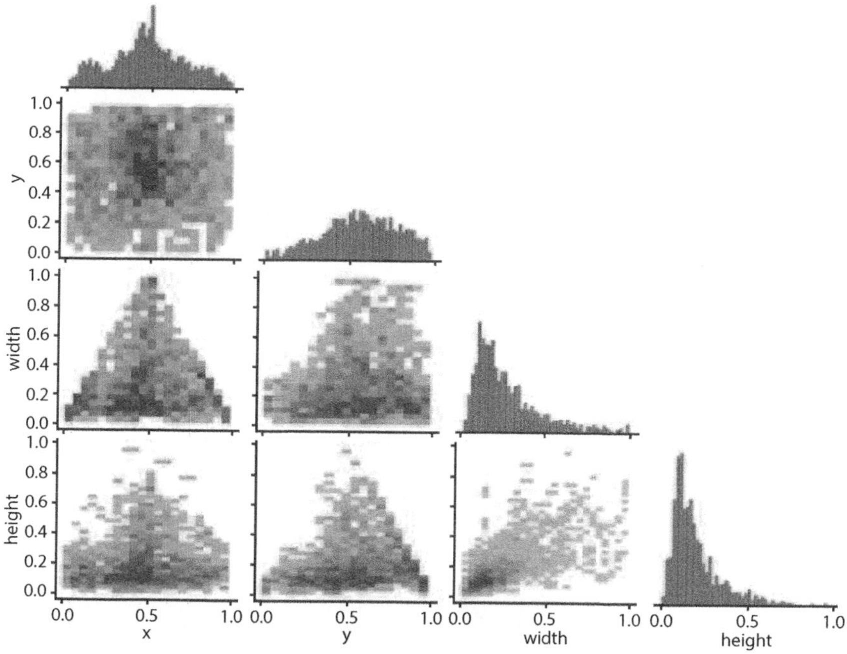

Figure 4.12 Labels correlogram for potholes.

4.3.3.2 Performance with Fire Dataset Using YOLOv5x

Similarly, Figures 4.13 and 4.14 depict the general performance with fire dataset. The recall-confidence, precision-confidence and precision-recall graphs along with correlograms are depicted in Figures 4.15, 4.16, 4.17 and 4.18 for fire dataset respectively.

$$\mathrm{P} = \mathrm{TP'}/(\mathrm{TP'} + \mathrm{FP'})$$

$$\mathrm{R} = \mathrm{TP'}/(\mathrm{TP'} + \mathrm{FP'})$$

$$\mathrm{F1}* = (2 * \mathrm{P} * \mathrm{R})/(\mathrm{P} + \mathrm{R})$$

$$\mathrm{AP} = \sum_{n\#\$}^{N} (\mathrm{R_n} - \mathrm{R_{n-1}})\mathrm{P_{n'}}$$

$$\mathrm{mAP} = 1/\mathrm{N} \sum_{n\#\$}^{N} AP_{\mathrm{i}}$$

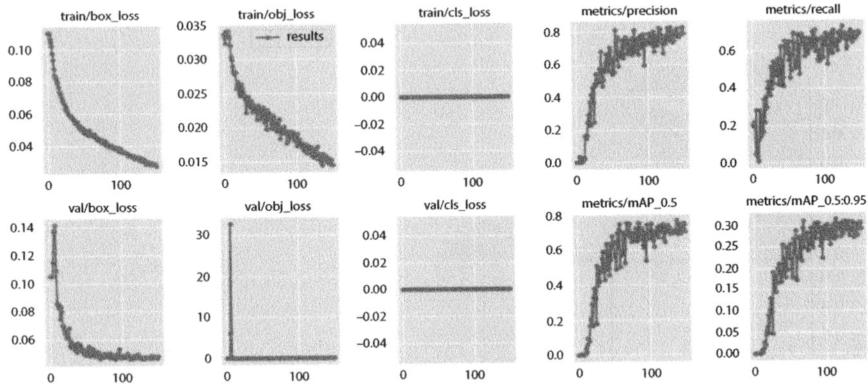

Figure 4.13 Results with fire dataset using YOLOv5x.

Figure 4.14 Visual validation set for fire detection.

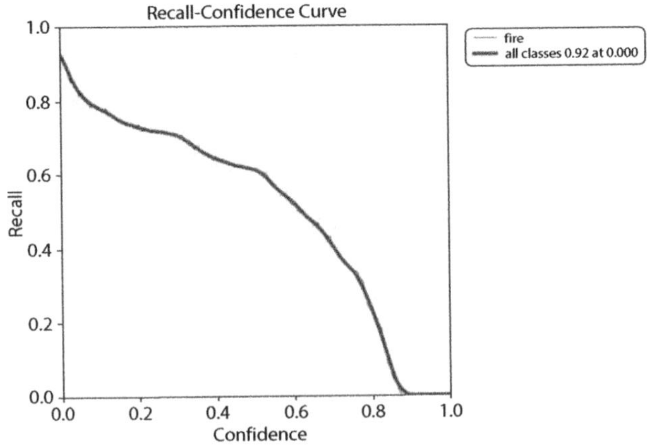

Figure 4.15 Recall-confidence graph for fire detection.

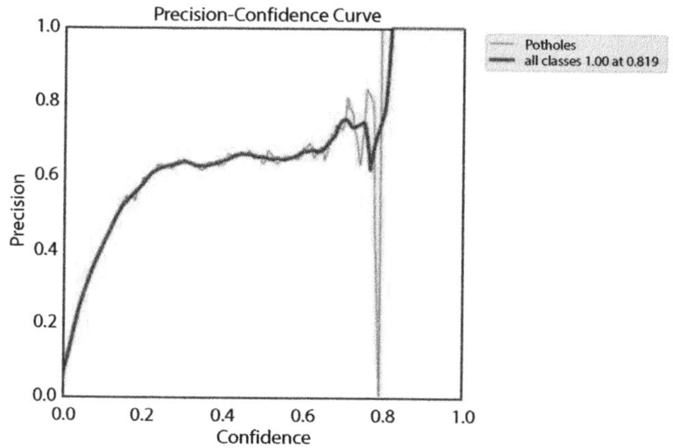

Figure 4.16 Precision-confidence graph for fire detection.

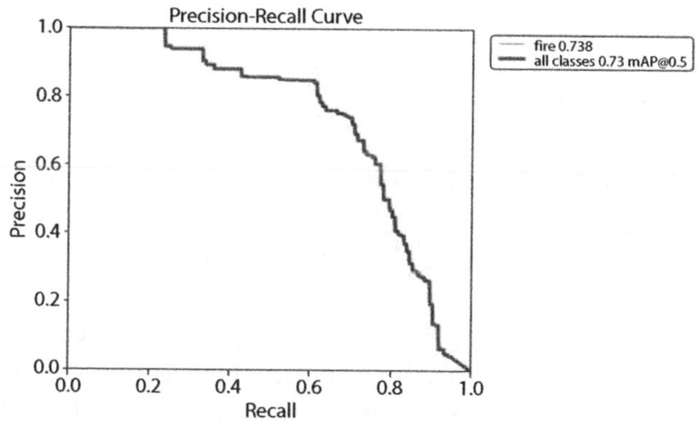

Figure 4.17 Precision-recall curve for fire detection.

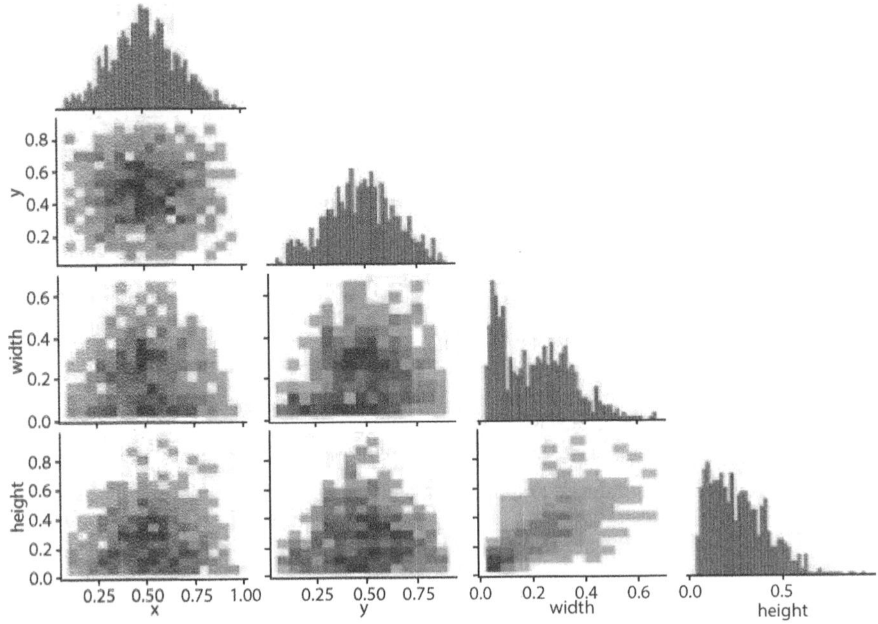

Figure 4.18 Labels correlogram for fire.

4.4 Conclusion

This work introduces a Smart Drone management system that leverages image processing techniques for fire and pothole detection. The system effectively monitors fires and conducts road surveys, achieving 90% accuracy using a single webcam.

The system operates in real-time, capturing frames every two seconds for continuous monitoring. To achieve optimal performance, the detection techniques employ a combination of RGB, HSV, and YCbCr color spaces, each chosen for its specific suitability, efficiency, and properties.

While this initial implementation demonstrates promising results, future research will address various aspects like threshold values and blind spots. These refinements aim to further minimize false alarms and enhance the overall system performance.

The proposed system offers valuable assistance to authorities by enabling swift and efficient actions for infrastructure repairs. Additionally, a more comprehensive approach incorporating GPS and LTE could facilitate precise detection and location of road anomalies and fires.

Furthermore, this work paves the way for future advancements in detecting other pavement issues, city fires, road accidents, and even road quality assessments. Additionally, ongoing research and real-world deployments will be crucial in addressing current accuracy limitations and achieving even better results.

References

1. Zuo, Z., Liu, C., Han, Q.-L., Song, J., Unmanned Aerial Vehicles: Control Methods and Future Challenges. *IEEE/CAA J. Autom. Sin.*, 9, 4, 601–614, April 2022, doi: 10.1109/JAS.2022.105410.
2. Xiang, T.-Z., Xia, G.-S., Zhang, L., Mini-Unmanned Aerial Vehicle-Based Remote Sensing: Techniques, applications, and prospects. *IEEE Geosci. Remote Sens. Mag.*, 7, 3, 29–63, Sept. 2019, doi: 10.1109/MGRS.2019.2918840.
3. Hamza, A., Akram, U., Samad, A., Khosa, S.N., Fatima, R., Mushtaq, M.F., Unmaned Aerial Vehicles Threats and Defence Solutions. *2020 IEEE 23rd International Multitopic Conference (INMIC)*, Bahawalpur, Pakistan, pp. 1–6, 2020, doi: 10.1109/INMIC50486.2020.9318207.
4. Reddy Maddikunta, P.K. *et al.*, Unmanned Aerial Vehicles in Smart Agriculture: Applications, Requirements, and Challenges. *IEEE Sens. J.*, 21, 16, 17608–17619, 15 Aug.15, 2021, doi: 10.1109/JSEN.2021.3049471.
5. Shakhatreh, H. *et al.*, Unmanned Aerial Vehicles (UAVs): A Survey on Civil Applications and Key Research Challenges. *IEEE Access*, 7, 48572–48634, 2019, doi: 10.1109/ACCESS.2019.2909530.
6. Outay, F., Mengash, H.A., Adnan, M., Applications of unmanned aerial vehicle (UAV) in road safety, traffic and highway infrastructure management: Recent advances and challenges. *Transp. Res. Part A Policy Pract.*, 141, 116–129, 2020 Nov, doi: 10.1016/j.tra.2020.09.018, Epub 2020 Oct 1, PMID: 33024357, PMCID: PMC7527789.
7. Yuan, C., Liu, Z., Zhang, Y., Aerial Images-Based Forest Fire Detection for Firefighting Using Optical Remote Sensing Techniques and Unmanned Aerial Vehicles. *J. Intell. Robot. Syst.*, **88**, 635–654, 2017, https://doi.org/10.1007/s10846-016-0464-7.
8. Yuan, C., Liu, Z., Zhang, Y., Aerial Images-Based Forest Fire Detection for Firefighting Using Optical Remote Sensing Techniques and Unmanned Aerial Vehicles. *J. Intell. Robot. Syst.*, **88**, 635–654, 2017, https://doi.org/10.1007/s10846-016-0464-7.
9. Aruna, S., Lahari, P., Suraj, P., Junaid, M.W.F., Sanjeev, V., Secure Communication and Pothole Detection for UAV Platforms, in: *Computational Intelligence and Data Analytics*. Lecture Notes on Data Engineering and Communications Technologies, vol. 142, R. Buyya, S.M. Hernandez,

R.M.R. Kovvur, T.H. Sarma (Eds.), Springer, Singapore, 2023, https://doi.org/10.1007/978-981-19-3391-2_13.

10. Aruna, S., Lahari, P., Suraj, P., Junaid, M.W.F., Sanjeev, V., Secure Communication and Pothole Detection for UAV Platforms, in: *Computational Intelligence and Data Analytics.* Lecture Notes on Data Engineering and Communications Technologies, vol. 142, R. Buyya, S.M. Hernandez, R.M.R. Kovvur, T.H. Sarma (Eds.), Springer, Singapore, 2023, https://doi.org/10.1007/978-981-19-3391-2_13.
11. Pan, Q., Wang, J., Yu, H., Zhang, W., Yue, P., The Application of Image Processing in UAV Reconnaissance Information Mining System, in: *The Proceedings of the International Conference on Sensing and Imaging, 2018. ICSI 2018.* Lecture Notes in Electrical Engineering, vol. 606, E. Quinto, N. Ida, M. Jiang, A. Louis, (Eds.), Springer, Cham, 2019, https://doi.org/10.1007/978-3-030-30825-4_4.
12. Pan, Q., Wang, J., Yu, H., Zhang, W., Yue, P., The Application of Image Processing in UAV Reconnaissance Information Mining System, in: *The Proceedings of the International Conference on Sensing and Imaging, 2018. ICSI 2018.* Lecture Notes in Electrical Engineering, vol. 606, E. Quinto, N. Ida, M. Jiang, A. Louis, (Eds.), Springer, Cham, 2019, https://doi.org/10.1007/978-3-030-30825-4_4.
13. Kattenborn, T., Eichel, J., Fassnacht, F.E., Convolutional Neural Networks enable efficient, accurate and fine-grained segmentation of plant species and communities from high- resolution UAV imagery. *Sci. Rep.*, **9**, 17656, 2019, https://doi.org/10.1038/s41598-019-53797-9.
14. Kattenborn, T., Eichel, J., Fassnacht, F.E., Convolutional Neural Networks enable efficient, accurate and fine-grained segmentation of plant species and communities from high-resolution UAV imagery. *Sci. Rep.*, **9**, 17656, 2019, https://doi.org/10.1038/s41598-019-53797-9.
15. Back, S., Cho, G., Oh, J. *et al.*, Autonomous UAV Trail Navigation with Obstacle Avoidance Using Deep Neural Networks. *J. Intell. Robot. Syst.*, **100**, 1195–1211, 2020, https://doi.org/10.1007/s10846-020-01254-5.

5

A Comprehensive Approach to Cybersecurity and Healthcare Systems Using Artificial Intelligence and Robotics

Harshvardhan P. Ghongade[1]* and Anjali A. Bhadre[2]

[1]*Department of Mechanical Engineering, Brahma Valley College of Engineering and Research Institute, Nashik, India*
[2]*Department of Information Technology, G.H. Raisoni College of Engineering and Management, Pune, India*

Abstract
This study provides a detailed assessment of the intersection between cybersecurity and healthcare systems, specifically focusing on the utilization of artificial intelligence (AI) and robots over the past six years. Cybercriminals perpetually engage in the exploration of novel techniques to infiltrate corporate networks and pilfer important data. Individuals commonly adhere to consistent security protocols on a regular basis. The increased utilization of several devices in the workplace poses challenges for security specialists in managing and updating data. The significance of AI in cybersecurity is growing due to its ability to address the difficulties as mentioned earlier. Furthermore, the healthcare sector has experienced advantageous outcomes as a result of significant advancements in AI and robotics. The use of AI methodologies, including deep learning and machine learning, has enabled the advancement of healthcare systems that possess the ability to independently detect disorders from medical pictures and provide related reports. This research investigates the possessions of AI and robots on enhancing the cybersecurity and healthcare sectors. The scholarly literature suggests that the use of AI in the domains of healthcare and cybersecurity is a relatively nascent and interesting topic that merits more examination. This study has the potential to offer academics significant insights and information that can be utilized in future research attempts.

**Corresponding author*: ghongade@gmail.com

Tanupriya Choudhury, Abhijit Kumar, Ravi Tomar, S. Balamurugan and Ankit Vishnoi (eds.) Cyber-Physical Systems for Innovating and Transforming Society 5.0, (77–120)

Keywords**:** Cybersecurity, AI, robotics, healthcare

5.1 Introduction

Robotics and artificial intelligence (AI) are prominent domains within scientific and engineering investigations. The phrases mentioned earlier are frequently employed interchangeably in characterizing the advancement of technologies that facilitate the augmentation of machine intelligence. Nevertheless, a notable distinction exists between the two. Artificial intelligence is the field of research that empowers robots to exhibit human-like functionality. In contrast, robotics is the discipline concerned with developing and implementing techniques to achieve this objective. Collectively, these technologies demonstrate significant potential for the future.

A topic that in recent years has become familiar to just about everyone, hardly a day goes by without news media reporting on the latest cyberattack, whether it is conducted by criminal or government organizations. The study of strategies we may employ to lessen the possibility of such assaults, wherever they come and for whatever reason, is known as cybersecurity. A paper surveys the field of robot learning from demonstration, which is a key aspect of AI in robotics. In this article, the authors give a general overview of the various methods for teaching robots to learn from examples, such as inverse reinforcement learning, apprenticeship learning, and behavioral cloning. They also talk about the difficulties and potential developments in this area [1].

A paper surveys the field of AI-based intrusion detection systems, which are a key aspect of using AI for cybersecurity. Rule-based systems, signature-based systems, and anomaly-based systems are just a few of the methodologies utilized for AI-based intrusion detection that the authors present an overview of. Additionally, they go into this field's difficulties and potential directions [2]. This research's goal is to provide an overview of AI from the perspective of cybersecurity, including what it is, how we may define it, and how we can use it to try to enhance the security features of both businesses and our own personal life. We may conceive of it as attempting to counteract any threat resulting from our reliance on and usage of information and communication technology. A paper surveys the field of robotic security systems, which is the intersection of robotics and cybersecurity. The authors provide an overview of the different types of robotic security systems, including those used for surveillance, reconnaissance, and search and rescue. The difficulties and prospects for this field are also discussed [3]. If you think about it for a moment, this not only includes using the smartphones tablets, and desktop computers that we use for work, personal, business, or leisure, but all the aspects of everyday life that depend on the use of information technology. Research discusses the challenges and future directions of cybersecurity for industrial control systems, which are a key aspect of the intersection of AI, robotics, and cybersecurity. The authors highlight the unique challenges of securing industrial control systems and the importance of developing new security technologies and standards to address these challenges [4] because information technology is so prevalent, problems with cybersecurity affect all of our systems and gadgets that are connected to the internet. Almost every part of our working life, including the functioning of factories, transit, and offices globally are included in this, as well as cars for private and public transportation, the infrastructure bringing power and water to our houses, and many other areas. Since practically every part of our life now depends on information and communications technology, cybersecurity has evolved into a basic requirement for everyone. At the same time, we are aware of the numerous ways in which modern information processing systems are susceptible to assault. One more research discusses the techniques and challenges of AI-based malware detection, which is another key aspect of using AI for cybersecurity [5]. It is easy to argue that our increasingly linked world is the issue and that we should change how we interact with it. However, in most cases, going back is impossible, and in truth, we almost likely do not want to. Modern information and communication technologies have a significant positive impact on our ability to work from home, increase productivity, and engage in a variety of previously unimagined kinds of communication and social contact. If we accept that information and communications is here to stay, what are we going to do about the major security threats we all face? In this study, we will introduce some of the techniques that can be used to reduce these threats, especially from the AI and robotics perspective. It is important to realize that providing security is not just about more and better technology.

A contemporary healthcare system is made up of several components, each of which gathers and analyzes data. Massive volumes of data are produced by healthcare providers, intermediaries, and government programs like Medicare and Medicaid. Patients can provide information on the care they get, their health state, the results of their treatment, and related expenditures. Nearly all these data are now digitized, and some of them may be used for AI research. In the medical profession, AI has a broad variety of uses, including increasing diagnostic precision, carrying out robotic operations, identifying possible drug candidates, and selecting the most efficient treatments for specific patients. However, much like any technology or breakthrough, AI creates ethical questions that its creators, users, and significant stakeholders like patients may want to take into consideration [26]. We will call attention to the ethical ramifications of some components of the healthcare system that, in our opinion, users and developers of AI systems should consider. Here, we will concentrate on a specific subset of AI applications that are most closely associated with the provision of healthcare services. What are the moral dilemmas, though? There are many. An AI model systematic mistake is particularly detrimental to the healthcare industry, considering that the results of these models may have an impact on crucial and even life-and-death choices [27]. Sometimes these deliberate mistakes can result in discriminatory judgments, especially if they target entire groups of socially disadvantaged individuals, such as women, children, persons of color, or those with poor incomes. With that being said, we will be discussing some points to take care of when it comes to robots in healthcare. The lack of transparency in AI models is one sort of ethical issue that is particularly pertinent to this technology. It is sometimes challenging or impossible to determine how AI derives its judgments [28]. Particularly if the AI makes use of ML techniques, which implies that the models are always evolving depending on the data they are using. Because physicians and healthcare institutions depend on AI developers to produce tools and technologies that are reliable and efficient to employ on their patients, this is a particularly serious issue in the context of healthcare [29]. However, there are currently few guidelines or rules for assessing the efficacy and safety of many AI-based medical solutions. However, doctors and other healthcare workers are responsible ethically and legally for the choices that AI is increasingly guiding. Physicians and healthcare facilities who use AI in ways that may have an impact on healthcare choices must be aware of the limitations of the techniques, data, and models when they are applied to their specific patient populations. In this research, we will concentrate on the ethical problem of competing or conflicting interests. This issue arises particularly in the area of healthcare. Robots are being employed for a variety of minimally invasive surgeries. Many modern hospitals feature robots that function occasionally in lieu of surgeons and others that help doctors. This is where AI, specifically the field of robotics, came in and had a big influence on healthcare. Some of the algorithms that were linked to those robots aided them in doing activities depending on the instructions given and trained to them with very good and high precision.

5.1.1 Hypothesis

1. What are the fundamental issues with cybersecurity?
2. What are the healthcare industry's general issues?
3. What role does AI play in the field of robotics?
4. Describe the various traits of AI.
5. What are the problems with AI in cybersecurity and healthcare, and how may they be solved?
6. What research gaps exist in cybersecurity and healthcare for AI?
7. From the perspectives of cybersecurity and healthcare, what is the future of AI?

We have compiled the research questions listed above, and the information from studies on AI and robotics, Cybersecurity, and Healthcare is used to further answer the questions.

5.1.1.1 What are the General Problems in Cybersecurity?

Cybersecurity is a field that deals with protecting information, communication, and networks from malicious attacks. Attackers use cyberspace to carry out their crimes; thus, it is crucial to secure them. Governments and corporations need to look after their systems and data since anyone can access the internet without permission. However, not all security measures are good when protecting the internet.

The worldwide web has become a haven for cybercrime in recent years. Hackers have found many new ways to exploit systems and data. Many attacks target government systems. This is because our system of government is involved in much of our politics. Other targets are corporations that handle our country's financial wealth. Many cybercrimes are committed by state agencies or other high-profile organizations. They are capable of carrying out dangerous plans in secrecy. Fortunately, there is a lot of work being done to secure cyberspace. A few of the most important general problems include:

1. Increase in cyberattacks: The number of cybercrimes continues to grow annually as criminal organizations try to capitalize on their efforts, such as ransomware and crypto-jacking. However, in 2021, one of the biggest concerns was the rise of this type of crime. The number of cyberattacks in 2021 increased by 50% over the previous year. However, certain regions were hit harder

by the attacks, such as education, healthcare, and research. This might indicate that cyber threat actors are concentrating their efforts in regions where they are most exposed. An attack rate that has risen so quickly bodes ill for 2022. Cyber threat actors' use of automation, deep learning, and automation to improve their techniques will only lead to a rise in the number and intensity of attacks.

2. Ransomware attacks are on the rise: Attacks involving ransomware are increasing. In 2017, the WannaCry epidemic brought ransomware to public attention. Ever since, a sizable number of ransomware businesses have emerged, posing a costly and visible threat to all businesses. In 2021, ransomware organizations have shown their ability and willingness to impact businesses in addition to their immediate targets. The most famous example is the imperial pipeline hack. One of the primary pipelines used by the ransomware gang Dark Side was shut down.
3. Mobile devices bring new risks: The implementation of Bring-Your-Own-Device (BYOD) rules is another result of the transition to remote working. Organizations can increase employee productivity and retention by allowing them to work from their own devices, but this practice also offers important information about security and susceptibility to diseases that might endanger company systems and solutions. You become incapable of responding. Cybercriminals have modified their ways in 2021 to capitalize on the rising use of mobiles. Triada, FlyTrap, and MasterFred malware, among other mobile malware trojans, have all recently surfaced. These mobile trojans approach the target device and request the required rights through lax app store security measures, social media, and other similar strategies.

5.1.1.2 *What are the General Problems in Healthcare?*

1. Concerns about health equity: The health sector has long acknowledged that different demographic groups experience varied levels of healthcare. These discrepancies go beyond only salaries and medical expenses. On the other hand, environmental influences have a significant effect on health and wellbeing. One of these factors, or social determinants of health, is the zip code. Accessibility to employment, housing,

education, transit, and healthful food, as well as ethnic and cultural diversity, clean air and water, and all of these factors are important. In certain areas, enduring racial and social inequality has also put generations' worth of health at risk. All of these factors have an effect on a person's overall health and capacity to get healthcare. Health crises for the underserved sometimes include hospitalization or emergency room visits and incur considerable medical expenses.

2. Opportunities (and pitfalls) of technology: The current health issue has numerous opportunities, but it also has the potential to cause a lot of issues if not properly addressed. Data are being used more and more in health. The difficulty is in managing this ocean of data. According to Frontiers in ICT research, healthcare professionals and health systems were already producing about 80MB of data per patient year before the epidemic. In addition to information from electronic health records, this data also contains information and details such addresses, demographics, claim and insurance information, payment history, and schedules.
3. Expensive medical bills: The exorbitant expense of healthcare is arguably the most serious issue facing our present healthcare system. Over 45% of Americans feel it is difficult to afford medical care, according to a Kaiser Family Foundation poll, and more than 40% say they pay for treatment. Due to rising healthcare expenses, more people are choosing not to see a doctor when they are unwell or forgo routine checkups entirely. One-fourth of Americans miss doses or do not take prescribed drugs because they cannot afford the pills they need. Each of these behaviors can lead to serious health problems and, therefore, increased medical costs.

5.1.1.3 *What is the Significance of AI and the Field of Robotics?*

Robots are becoming increasingly advanced both technologically and structurally. The primary focus of robotics today is on repairing and saving lives. For example, doctors use robot arms in hospitals to perform complicated surgeries without putting their patients at risk. Artificial intelligence is quickly becoming essential in many areas of life including healthcare and cybersecurity. This is due to the fact that it saves lives, reduces costs and makes life easier. However, there are still many unknowns with AI, which is why it is significant to consider the positives and negatives before implementing this technology in both healthcare and cybersecurity. Artificial intelligence has a lot of potential in healthcare; it can perform complex tasks and can help doctors treat patients more effectively. For example, it can assess physicians in diagnosing and treating diseases and assist them in performing triage and radiology procedures. Reinforcement learning programs help medical professionals save lives by performing life-saving surgeries on human beings. In addition, predictive models help medical professionals manage patients' records and identify issues with patient care systems. Additionally, AI helps with patient counseling by assisting with diagnosis and providing psychological support to patients and essentially has the budding to transform our healthcare system.

5.1.1.4 *What are the Challenges of AI in Cybersecurity and Healthcare and How can these be Overcome?*

The progress of computers to accomplish jobs previously reserved for humans is called AI. It has the potential to revolutionize a variety of facets of our life, including the fields of health and education, as well as the military and business. However, it is also a significant cause of worry since it poses responsibility, ethics, and safety issues.

Artificial intelligence is still in its infancy so there are still many challenges to overcome. For instance, AI is not very good at handling controversial or negative data, as it can have a conflictive effect on the system. It is also susceptible to adversarial behavior since hackers can use AI for their own purposes by programming it against the systems they target. Many cybersecurity experts believe that AI will be most beneficial in situations involving classified data, where security measures are necessary but impossible. The cybersecurity industry is getting bigger every year. As more and more people rely on technology in their daily lives, it is important to make sure these devices and computers are safe from hackers. There are some cybersecurity issues that are easy to fix. For instance, many individuals use the same password for both their social media and email accounts for their girlfriends. This makes it easier for hackers to steal passwords and use them to break into those accounts. They can then steal your personal information and use it to commit identity theft. Another problem with cybersecurity is that ordinary people are not fully aware of how to protect themselves. They are also unaware of the dangers of opening emails or attachments that appear to come from people they know. These emails may contain viruses that can harm your device. It could also be a phishing scam that steals your personal information.

The fundamental healthcare issue, however, has a few other remedies, as well. Collaboration between local, state, and federal governments, as well as healthcare professionals, is necessary to find answers to the problem of excessive healthcare expenditures. To address environmental variables and enhance access to healthcare in marginalized neighborhoods, it is possible to employ housing, transportation, and collaborations with churches and non-profit health groups. To satisfy the demands of patients, healthcare managers might put up a several kinds of programs. In many remote areas, for instance, telemedicine may assist patients who lack access to transportation, but internet connection is still a problem. One of the other projects is elder home care, a medical staff that places emphasis on patient care, and interaction with the community.

5.1.1.5 *What is the Current State of Research in AI in Terms of Cybersecurity and Healthcare?*

Artificial intelligence and cybersecurity are two of the most important technologies today. Cybersecurity and healthcare are also two areas that are rapidly developing, expanding, and gaining more relevance in our daily lives. However, AI technologies have many flaws that need to be addressed, which is why more research is needed to make them more useful. Both areas are in a stage of development; therefore, they have many challenges to overcome before they can revolutionize our lives.

Artificial intelligence has a lot of potential in cybersecurity and healthcare since it can help detect and prevent cybercrime when we take the field of cybersecurity. And in healthcare, it can help diagnose a disease from its very early stage and reduce the workload on the doctors, as well.

Currently, cybercrime is mostly detected through human involvement, which is slow and error-prone. Artificial intelligence can also help with the investigation process by analyzing data collected from various sources and identifying potential threads. It can also help with countermeasures by developing mechanisms that stop attacks before they happen. With that being said, AI has the potential to become an invaluable tool for cybersecurity and healthcare when applied practically.

5.1.1.6 *What is the Future of AI from a Cybersecurity and Healthcare Perspective?*

Robotics and AI have many exciting applications that will become clear once they are ready for use by the public. For now, these technologies are primarily used in scientific research or in niche applications by professionals only. However, there is no shortage of interest from amateurs who want to create their own robot companions. It is clear that these technologies have a huge future.

Artificial intelligence has many applications, from natural language processing (NLP) to pattern recognition, and will change our lives in many years when we take a look at how it changes and is changing our daily lives from the perspective of cybersecurity and healthcare. It is obvious that AI has a very large and good future.

5.2 Methodology

Several research papers used in this research were explained in this part. Consequently, we provide and clarify the current surveys in all the areas of this research including AI and robotics, cybersecurity, and healthcare.

5.2.1 Applications of AI in Cybersecurity Defense

The AI model provides highly powerful defensive capabilities for cybersecurity protection that will help defend various systems against cyberattacks and support digital forensic investigations. Having said that, we highlight a few of the uses of AI in cybersecurity defense. Additionally, we encourage the reader of this research to look at these publications for additional information on AI's role in cybersecurity protection.

i. Malware, which is short for "malicious software," is simply defined as "malicious software" and is used by AI for detection and categorization. It is a document containing software or code that is typically distributed through a network [1, 2]. It is designed or intended to utilize a variety of techniques, including ransomware, spyware, viruses, trojans, and adware, to harm the computer systems, mobile devices, and online applications of its intended victims [3, 4].

   Several algorithms and techniques have been used to detect malware [5]. Detection of malware using AI techniques can be done when a model is trained using a dataset that can help in classifying the type of malware [6].

ii. Artificial intelligence for network intrusion detection: Numerous programmers came up with and built various approaches to network intrusion detection. A real-time anomaly detection method was reported by Ding *et al.* [7] who succeeded in reaching high accuracy. Additionally, Alom and Taha [8] achieved a reasonable accuracy of 91.86% after doing K-means clustering. According to Chen *et al.* [9], deep convolutional neural networks (DCNNs) are utilized to identify DDoS assaults. More academics that have studied the same topic include Xia *et al.* [13], Biswas [11], Clements *et al.* [12], and Mirsky *et al.* [10].

iii. Artificial intelligence for traffic identification and classification: At a time, several applications are flowing in any network, and the one and single most important phase in identifying and recognizing multiple classes is the use of network traffic classification. A researcher [14] utilized a deep learning model to distinguish the flowing of traffic in a network after diving it into 25 protocols, he was successfully able to get 100% and 91.74%, depending on the type of protocol. Another research [15] used a convolutional neural network (CNN) model to distinguish the classes of traffic and try to recognize the application category.

iv. AI for spam detection: Spam emails, to put it simply, are any unwelcome or virus-containing emails. In addition to acting as a detector of all those viruses, spam detection systems also work as a preventer of emails by stopping them from introducing viruses into one's inbox. One of the techniques that developers have suggested is an autoencoder that functions and further distinguishes spam mail by Mi *et al.* [16], with a 95% accuracy rate. A different researcher created a machine-learning approach and algorithmic phishing email detection system [17]. The reader of this paper can refer to the following works related to this by Aksu *et al.* [18], Yi *et al.* [19], and Benavides *et al.* [20].

v. Artificial intelligence for insider threat detection: A document that demonstrates and clearly explains how to examine and assess a user's system logs using a DNN or recurrent neural network (RNN) model, as well as how to find abnormalities that might lead to an insider threat incident. Tuor *et al.* [21] described how to do this.

vi. Artificial intelligence for digital forensics: AI technology become most significant in investigations nowadays and also improves the methods and ways of detecting cybercrime. The specialists of forensics found this very useful as it helps them effectively and quickly find the actual source and cause of the problem; on the other hand, the use of AI in digital forensic protects a lot of money and time. Some machine-learning techniques or algorithms have been utilized to classify file fragments. For example, papers are written by Beebe *et al.* [22], Axelsson *et al.* [23], and Calhoun and Coles [24]. Another researcher [25] planned a technique that works based on deep learning for file fragment classification.

5.2.2 Applications of AI in Healthcare

i. Disease Detection systems: One of the most significant tasks in healthcare is the detection of various diseases. It lessens the stress on doctors, because those systems may be replaced to run automatically instead of manually for various other duties. Researchers have suggested a method in 2019 that might assist physicians in identifying and categorizing skin conditions, such as melanoma and eczema [26]. An ML algorithm is used in detecting skin cancer where it differentiates healthy skin from diseased one and high accuracy was achieved [27]. Many systems for brain cancer classification have also been invented by developers, which include an approach by Sha *et al.* [28]; they developed a system using DCNNs to detect brain tumors after magnetic resonance imaging (MRI) generated the high-quality images of the inside of the brain. The reader of this research can also go through these articles for disease detection systems: Ahmad *et al.* [29], Ahmad *et al.* [30], Shabbir *et al.* [31], and Hussain *et al.* [32].
ii. Test Analysis and Diagnosis: Because all those AI-based apps will have a huge influence on interpreting medical scans, including X-rays, MRI pictures, CT scans, and many more, it is getting simpler for physicians to simply comprehend the problem of their patients when there is an AI application. As the effort associated with scanning analysis is lessened, medical physicians feel more at ease [33]. The AI-based approach will assist in realizing and comprehending whether any gene might cause cancer while evaluating biological data such as DNA and

RNA [34]. The AI can help identify any disease risk or existence. The characteristics depend on outside factors [35]. It further helps in alerting people about any disease-infected area [36].

iii. Chatbots: These days, hospitals and other clinics hold a number of websites, mobile applications, and web applications. These websites, mobile applications, and web applications feature chatbots that act to aid patients directly from where they are and try to learn more about their health issues [37]. Every time a patient enters a hospital, the first thing the medical staff does is screen the patient to learn about their beginning circumstances. In this situation, AI chatbots can take the role of these time-consuming procedures [33]. Additionally, chatbots may be used as interacting agents between language processing and speech recognition technology [38]. As a whole, majority of the modern healthcare institutions have these kinds of chatbots which help patients in different ways [39].

iv. Health Monitoring: When it comes to patient prevention through condition monitoring, this is crucial. The monitoring system may occasionally be able to keep a patient in their present state when an illness is caught early by informing the doctors. Algorithms and AI approaches are used to assist it. A smart health monitoring system has been proposed by some researchers [40], the system can keep track of patients' health, and it also contains a feature that enables patients' families to access and check on their patient's health status. Anandh [41] created a system that uses AI algorithms to provide body temperature. Papers written by Soppimath *et al.* [42] and Srinivasan *et al.* [43] can be checked to get more health monitoring systems that were trained based on AI algorithms and techniques.

v. Digital Consultation: The world is getting increasingly digital; thus, this is a fairly broad area. A digital consultation is just a video call between a doctor or other healthcare professional and a patient made possible through a smartphone or online application. Through these tools, the patient and the doctor will communicate. Examples of the evolution of digital healthcare include patients' engagement in the development and higher expectations for patient access to healthcare [44–46]. Most primary care doctors can now operate from home, and in this scenario, digital consultation will undoubtedly occur [47, 48]. This reader can check [49] and [50] to get more ideas about digital consultations and their cost-effectiveness.

5.2.3 Data Source

The literature in this paper is made up of several research publications and articles from different sources. Figure 5.1 shows the pictorial or graphical representation of the data sources used in this research and their respective percentages.

Additionally, we have made a table of the databases and their respective URLs that were all used in this research, which can be seen in Figure 5.2.

5.2.4 Exploration Criteria

This study will concentrate more on the use of AI and robots in cybersecurity and healthcare throughout the last six years, from 2017 to 2022, as noted in the abstract. In light of the foregoing, we gathered all the references and brought out the percentage of the papers used in this research for each and every respective year. The graphic representation of the same is shown in Figure 5.3 where all the percentages are clearly stated.

Cybersecurity is an ever-evolving field, and the systems developed in the past five years have been instrumental in helping protect individuals

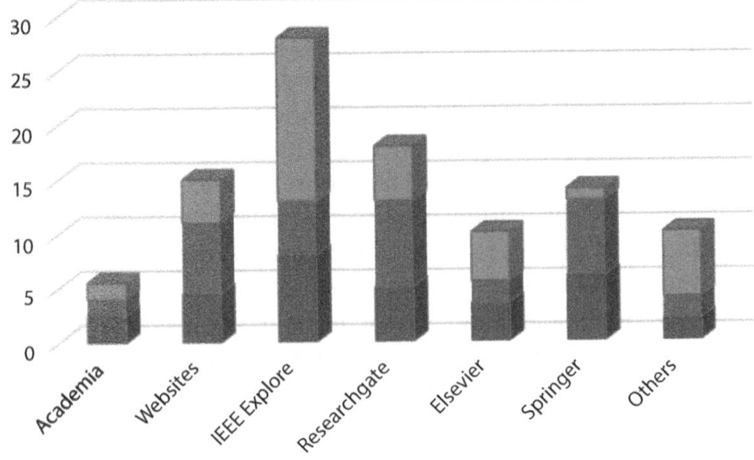

Figure 5.1 Research papers from data sources.

Database Engines	Sources Address
IEEE Xplore	https://www.ieeexplore.ieee.org/
Springer	https://www.springer.com/
Elsevier	https://www.elsevier.com/
Academia	https://www.academia.edu/
ResearchGate	https://www.researchgate.net/

Figure 5.2 Database engines and their URLs.

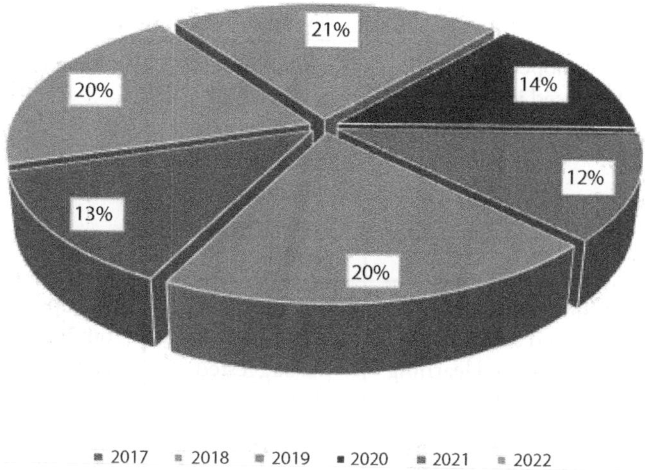

Figure 5.3 Percentage of research papers from 2017 to 2022.

and organizations from cyber threats. In this article, we will take a look at some of the most important cybersecurity systems developed in the past five years in Table 5.1. Let us first examine how AI and ML have evolved in the field of cybersecurity. Systems that can identify and respond to cyber threats in real-time have been developed using AI and ML. These technologies can analyze vast volumes of data to spot trends and abnormalities that can point to an impending attack. Systems that can recognize and react to harmful code have also been created using AI and ML, as well as systems that can detect and respond to phishing attacks. These are just a few of the many cybersecurity systems developed in the past six years. As the field of cybersecurity continues to evolve, new and improved systems will be developed to protect individuals and organizations from cyber threats (Table 5.2).

Table 5.1 Summary of AI-based cybersecurity systems developed in the past six years.

[8]	2017	Cybersecurity network intrusion detection with unsupervised deep learning	Attained a respectable accuracy of 91.86%	Usability issues
[52]	2017	CNNs' ability to identify new assaults is evaluated.	The CNN model obtained an 81.57% of accuracy rate.	High dimensional data
[53]	2017	Developed an RNN-based intrusion detection system	The RNN model has an 83.28% detection rate in the binary classification, according to the results.	Personal Integrity
[54]	2017	A unique fuzziness-based semi-supervised learning strategy that uses unlabeled data with supervised learning algorithm assistance improves the classifier's performance for intrusion detection systems (IDS).	A very high level of accuracy for the suggested algorithm.	The proposed method outperforms J48, Naïve Bayes (NB), NB Tree, Random forests, Random Tree, multi-layer perceptron's, and support vector machine (SVM) algorithms in terms of accuracy.
[56]	2018	A safe malware detection system using encryption	Achieved 98.93%	Efficiency
[57]	2018	An Android malware family categorization has been proposed, along with a representative sample selection.	FalDroid – 94.2%	Usability

(Continued)

Table 5.1 Summary of AI-based cybersecurity systems developed in the past six years. (*Continued*)

[58]	2018	For learning unsupervised features, a non-symmetric deep autoencoder (NDAE) has been suggested.	A 98:81% training time reduction and a 5% increase in accuracy are possible.	Huge amount of complex
[59]	2019	A technique to detect malware based on how often opcodes are used	The suggested method can identify the virus with about 100% accuracy.	Less number of datasets.
[60]	2019	Using data and application programming interfaces (APIs), to identify malware	AUC 99.3%	Privacy
[55]	2019	Examination of extracted characteristics from big-data sources in real time.	Precision, Recall, True Positive Ratio, and F1 > 99%, FPR < 0.1%	Effectiveness
[62]	2019	A variety of file formats, including Microsoft Document File. doc and Portal Document File. pdf, were used to demonstrate how to locate malware payloads.	The accuracy of finding ransomware was 91.7% and 94.1%, respectively.	Limited incremental rate
[63]	2019	Deep learning-based proposed method for virus detection using behavior graphs	Accuracy of 98.60%	Unstructured

(*Continued*)

Table 5.1 Summary of AI-based cybersecurity systems developed in the past six years. (*Continued*)

[65]	2020	proposed a dynamic technique for detecting and predicting Windows malware	Prediction: 0.997% FPR of 0.000 and 0.070% FNR.	Trust
[65]	2020	suggested using a method named Source-Finder to locate malware source code repositories.	The study shows that the proposed technique locates malware repositories with 89% accuracy and 86% recall.	Poor understanding of safety
[67]	2021	They provide a novel approach for automatic hyperparameter optimization based on Bayesian optimization to produce the best possible DNN design.	With accuracy scores of 82.95% for the KDDTest+ dataset and 54.99% for the KDDTest-21 dataset, BO-GP has the greatest accuracy ratings.	Appropriateness
[85]	2022	ML-based malware classification for Android devices using repacked app detection and removal	Detection accuracy of 98.2%	Efficiency
[86]	2022	Malware threads classification	An accuracy of 98% in detecting and classifying the malware threads	Trust
[61]	2022	Approaches in malware detection systems that rely on visualization	The approach achieved 100% accuracy	Poor and little amount of dataset to get high accuracy

Table 5.2 Summary of datasets, samples, and methodology used in the past AI-based cybersecurity systems.

Reference	Title of paper	Methodology	Datasets and samples used
[85]	AndroMalPack: enhancing the ML-based malware classification by detection and removal of repacked apps for Android systems	Algorithm inspired by nature	AndroZoo dataset
[54]	Fuzziness-based, semi-supervised learning approach for intrusion detection system	Random forests, NB Tree, J48, NB, Random Tree, multi-layer perceptrons, and SVM	Unlabeled samples assisted with a supervised learning algorithm.
[53]	Deep learning approach for intrusion detection using RNNs	Binary classification (Normal, Anomaly) and five category classifications using the RNN-IDS model (Normal, DoS, R2L, U2R, and Probe).	NSL–KDD dataset
[86]	Binary and multi-class malware threads classification	NB and Gaussian discriminant analysis	MaleVis Dataset
[59]	Detection of advanced malware by ML techniques	ML techniques	Kaggle Microsoft malware classification challenge dataset
[67]	Bayesian hyperparameter optimization for deep neural network-based network intrusion detection	Deep neural network algorithms	NSL–KDD dataset

(Continued)

Table 5.2 Summary of datasets, samples, and methodology used in the past AI-based cybersecurity systems. (*Continued*)

Reference	Title of paper	Methodology	Datasets and samples used
[56]	A secure encryption-based malware detection system	Privacy–Preserving NB classifier (PP–NBC)	4-Gram API fragment sequence
[66]	Source finder: Finding malware source code from publicly available repositories	ML techniques in detecting the malware	Unidentified
[61]	Disarming visualization-based approaches in malware detection systems	Visualization-based techniques	Malimg dataset
[8]	Network intrusion detection for cybersecurity using unsupervised deep learning approaches	K-means clustering	NSL–KDD dataset
[60]	ASSCA: API sequence and statistics features combined architecture for malware detection	Dynamic behavior	Malicious samples from the viral Share and VirusTotal databases, as well as samples from the system exe files for Windows 7 and Windows XP.
[62]	A novel malware detection system based on ML and binary visualization	Neural network and deep learning are used in the detection of the malware.	Not mentioned
[52]	Intrusion Detection Using CNNs for Representation Learning	In testing the set, 17 extra attack kinds were added, and a new attack was also found.	NSL–KDD dataset

(*Continued*)

Table 5.2 Summary of datasets, samples, and methodology used in the past AI-based cybersecurity systems. (*Continued*)

Reference	Title of paper	Methodology	Datasets and samples used
[65]	A dynamic Windows malware detection and prediction method based contextual understanding of API call sequence	Markov chain sequences are used to show how API functionalities relate to malware and excellent software.	Informatics for intelligence and security sets of data Dataset of Brazilian malware
[63]	Malware detection based on deep learning of behavior graphs	The behavior-based deep learning framework and stacked autoencoders	Malware samples from VX heaven
[57]	Android malware familial classification and representative sample selection via frequent subgraph analysis	FallDroid	Drebin Dataset, FallDroid I and II, Genome Project Dataset
[55]	An investigative study on motifs extracted features on real time big- data signals	Visualization and deep learning techniques were used	There are nine viral families in the viral Share community, and each includes 1000 varieties.
[58]	A deep learning approach to network intrusion detection.	By stacking the NDAEs, a layer-wise unsupervised representation learning method was produced.	Statistics from KDD Cup '99 and NSL-KDD

In the past six years, healthcare systems have undergone a dramatic transformation. Advances in technology, data analytics, and AI have enabled the development of new and improved healthcare systems that are revolutionizing the way healthcare is delivered. These systems are designed

Table 5.3 Significant healthcare systems developed in the past six years.

Reference	Year	Topic addressed	Performance	Limitation
[68]	2017	Human skin cancer detection system	84% predictive value and 75% sensitivity	Unstructured data
[69]	2017	Skin cancer classification using deep learning	High performance achieved	Lack of elaboration
[70]	2017	Review of common AI disease including cancer, cardiology, and neurology	Perfect analysis in the review	Data exchange and safety
[71]	2018	Detection of onychomycosis and normal nails	Sensitivity of 96.7% and a specificity of 96.7%	Too much load of different dataset
[72]	2018	Skin disease identification	88% in detection	Efficiency
[73]	2018	Diagnosis of skin cancer	Detection accuracy of 90%	Less flexible
[74]	2019	Approach on melanoma and other skin cancer types	99% of accuracy in classifying skin cancer	Less amount of data
[64]	2019	Device application for skin cancer detection	They achieved an overall accuracy of 75.2% in detecting the skin cancer using the application	Detection of only two diseases
[75]	2019	Review of AI in applications in India	Detailed review of the topic	Ethical consideration
[76]	2020	Brain tumor/cancer detection	CNN architecture = 86% VGGNet = 97%	Smaller number of the images used
[77]	2020	Skin cancer detection	97.9% Accuracy was achieved	Interoperability

(Continued)

Table 5.3 Significant healthcare systems developed in the past six years. (*Continued*)

Reference	Year	Topic addressed	Performance	Limitation
[78]	2020	Classification of skin cancer	Achieved an accuracy of 94.5%	Poor documentation
[79]	2021	Detection of brain cancer	SVMs = 92.4% Five-layer Custom CNN = 97.2%	Less amount of dataset
[80]	2021	Review of common healthcare applications and projects	Clearly explained about the algorithms and techniques	Poor abstraction
[81]	2021	The model can identify photographs that do not fit into the eight classifications that are often utilized (classified as unknown images)	94.9 Accuracy	Safety
[82]	2022	Detection and classification of brain tumor that are generated by MRI	98.87% overall classification and detection accuracy	Huge amount of complex
[83]	2022	Chatbot system for women's healthcare	96% for prediction of PCOS	Restrictions (only for women)
[84]	2022	Detection of skin cancer using different algorithms	Accuracy of the proposed ensemble is 93.5%	Trust
[51]	2022	Classification of skin lesion	Overall, of 98% accuracy in classifying skin lesion	Privacy

to improve patient outcomes, reduce costs, and provide better access to care.

Table 5.3 presents some of the most significant healthcare systems developed in the past six years. These systems are designed to address a variety of healthcare needs, from patient monitoring and diagnosis to population health management. Each system is designed to provide a unique set of features and benefits to healthcare providers and patients alike. These healthcare systems are just a few of the many that have been developed in the past five years. As technology continues to advance, healthcare providers will continue to develop new and improved systems to improve patient outcomes and reduce costs.

The past six years have seen a dramatic shift in the way healthcare systems are developed and implemented. With the advent of new technologies and the increasing emphasis on patient-centered care, healthcare systems have become more efficient and effective. Table 5.4 highlighted some of the various healthcare systems developed in the past six years, their methodologies, and the datasets & samples used.

5.2.5 Artificial Intelligence and Robotics

The discipline of AI in computer science aims to create smart computers that can think and act like people. Computer systems that can solve complicated issues, see patterns, and pick up new skills are created using AI. Tasks like scheduling, data processing, and decision-making may be automated with AI systems. Artificial intelligence is also used to develop robots that can interact with humans and the environment; it has tenders in various industries, including healthcare, finance, and transportation, and it can be used to improve customer service, automate manufacturing processes, and develop autonomous vehicles. Also used to develop virtual assistants, such as Amazon Alexa and Google Assistant, AI can understand natural language and respond to voice commands. It is an ever-evolving field of research, and its potential applications are limitless.

Artificial intelligence is significantly influencing cybersecurity and healthcare; it is being utilized in cybersecurity to detect threats to the network more rapidly and accurately than ever before. These AI-based systems are able to recognize harmful behavior, identify malicious actors, and respond to threats in real-time. This is helping to reduce the amount of time recognized takes to detect and respond to cyber threats, as well as reducing the cost of responding to them.

In healthcare, AI is being used to diagnose and treat diseases more accurately and quickly than ever before. Using AI-based systems, which can

Table 5.4 An overview of the datasets, samples, and methodologies utilized in earlier AI-based healthcare systems.

Reference	Title of paper	Methodology	Dataset and samples used
[83]	Intelligent Medical Chatbot System for Women's Healthcare	Logistic Regression Algorithm, ML Algorithm, and KNN.	DialogFlow
[82]	A robust approach for brain tumor detection in MRI using Finetuned EfficientNet	DCNN	Brats2015 Brain Tumor Dataset
[75]	Artificial intelligence in healthcare in developing nations: The beginning of a transformative journey	SWOT analysis	Review*
[84]	Skin cancer detection using combined decision of deep learners	SVM, NB, and K-Nearest Neighbor (KNN)	ISIC Public Dataset
[70]	Artificial intelligence in healthcare: Past, present and future	Support Vector/ Neural Networks	Review*
[77]	Region-of-interest based transfer learning assisted framework for skin cancer detection	CNNs	DermIS
[69]	Dermatologist-level classification of skin cancer with deep neural networks	Deep learning algorithms	Not Specified

(*Continued*)

Table 5.4 An overview of the datasets, samples, and methodologies utilized in earlier AI-based healthcare systems. (*Continued*)

Reference	Title of paper	Methodology	Dataset and samples used
[79]	Brain tumor detection using CNN	Algorithms using SVMs, K-NN, multi-layer perceptrons, NB, and random forests	HAM10000
[68]	A ML algorithm for identifying atopic der-mastitis in adults from electronic health records	ML algorithms	ISIC Dataset
[51]	Skin lesion classification system using a K-NN algorithm	KNN and CNN	ISIC Public Dataset
[80]	Unbox the black box for the medical explainable AI via multi-modal and multicenter data fusion: A minireview, two showcases and beyond	Rule-based decision support system	Review*
[71]	Deep neural networks show an equivalent and often superior performance to dermatologists in onychomycosis diagnosis: automatic construction of onychomycosis datasets by region-based convolutional DNN.	CNNs	Not identified

(*Continued*)

Table 5.4 An overview of the datasets, samples, and methodologies utilized in earlier AI-based healthcare systems. (*Continued*)

Reference	Title of paper	Methodology	Dataset and samples used
[76]	Brain tumor detection using deep learning models	VGGNet and CNN	HM1000
[81]	Skin lesions classification into eight classes for ISIC 2019 using DCNN and transfer learning	DCNN in Addition to GoogleNet	ISIC Dataset
[78]	Analysis of basic neural network types for automated skin cancer classification using Firefly optimization method	Neural and Fuzzy Approach	ISIC Dataset
[74]	Integrated design of deep features fusion for localization and classification of skin cancer	VGG-16 Model, Alex, and the Otsu Algorithm	HAM10000
[64]	An on-device inference app for skin cancer detection	CNN using Tensorflow	ISIC Dataset
[72]	Automated skin disease identification using deep learning algorithm	InceptionV2, InceptionV3, MobileNet	ISIC Dataset
[73]	Diagnosis of skin diseases using CNNs	CNNs	ISIC Dataset

analyze massive amounts of data to uncover patterns and trends in patient health, may help doctors make more accurate diagnoses and provide better treatment. Artificial intelligence is increasingly being used to automate administrative tasks like appointment scheduling and insurance claim processing in order to save costs and boost efficiency.

Artificial intelligence appears to have a bright future in both cybersecurity and healthcare. More rapidly and precisely than ever, AI may be used to detect and address cyber threats. Artificial intelligence may also assist healthcare businesses and better secure patient data by identifying possible security flaws. Healthcare practitioners might concentrate on more crucial activities by using AI to automate menial chores. AI may also be used to examine vast volumes of data and find patterns and trends that can be utilized to enhance patient outcomes and treatment. Finally, AI can automate illness diagnosis and treatment, freeing up medical experts to work on more challenging situations.

5.2.5.1 Characteristics of Artificial Intelligence

1. Automation: Artificial intelligence can do things like recognize patterns, make judgements, and solve problems that would typically need human intelligence. Data analysis, NLP, and picture identification are a few examples of complicated jobs and processes that AI can automate.
2. Machine Learning: AI has the capacity to learn from its surroundings and past experiences. Using ML techniques, AI can learn from data and utilize it to enhance its performance. The AI technique known as ML, on the other hand, allows computers to learn without explicit programming. Building computer programs that can access data and use it to learn for themselves is the aim of ML. To find patterns in the information and improve future judgments based on the examples we present, the learning process involves observations or data, such as examples, firsthand experience, or instruction. The main goal is to give computers the ability to learn on their own, without the aid of humans, and change their behavior as a consequence.

   i. Supervised Learning: This kind of ML algorithm makes predictions using labeled data. A labelled dataset with input data and the associated predicted output is used to train the algorithm. After that, the system makes predictions on fresh, unlabeled data using the labelled data.

ii. Unsupervised Learning: This is a kind of ML method that generates predictions from unlabeled data. An unlabeled dataset, which consists of input data without any corresponding predicted output, is used to train the algorithm. Afterward, the program makes predictions on fresh, unlabeled data using the unlabeled data.

Reinforcement Learning: This is an algorithm that uses rewards and punishments to learn. The algorithm is trained in an environment, which contains input data and the corresponding rewards or punishments. The algorithm then uses rewards and punishments to make decisions and take actions in the environment. Figure 5.4 shows that types of machine learning encompasses three main types - supervised, unsupervised, and reinforcement.

1. Natural Language Processing: AI can understand and process natural language, such as spoken words and written text. This allows AI to interact with humans in a more natural way. Similar to this, the aim of the AI branch of NLP is to enable computers to understand, evaluate, and alter human language. To analyze text, NLP algorithms are employed, allowing computers to understand the structure and meaning of the language in order to extract insights from text data. Natural language processing can be used to automate tasks such as sentiment analysis, text classification, and entity extraction.
2. Adaptability: AI can adapt to changing environments and conditions; it can learn from its mistakes and use the data to improve its performance. On the other hand, Adaptability in AI refers to the ability of an AI system to adjust its behavior in reaction to environmental changes or the user's preferences. This allows the AI system to remain effective and efficient over time, even as the environment or user preferences change. This is important for AI systems that are used in dynamic environments, such as self-driving cars, where the environment is constantly changing. Adaptability also allows AI systems to learn from their mistakes and improve their performance over time.
3. Automated Reasoning: AI can reason and draw conclusions from data. This allows AI to make decisions and solve

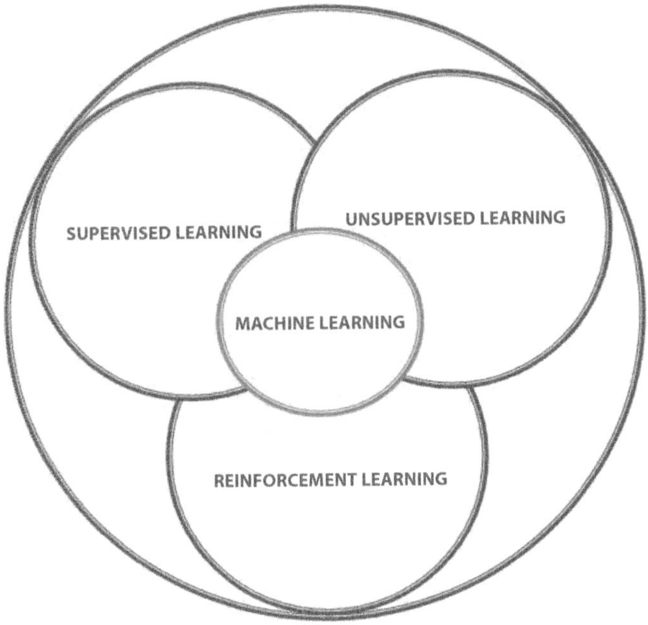

Figure 5.4 Types of ML.

problems without human intervention. On the other hand, automated reasoning is a subfield of AI that focuses on using computers to reason logically about a given problem. Automated reasoning systems use algorithms to analyze a set of facts and rules to draw logical conclusions. Automated reasoning systems can be used to solve problems in many different areas, such as mathematics, law, medicine, engineering, and philosophy. Automated reasoning can also be used to create new knowledge by combining existing facts and rules. Because they may lessen the amount of human labor needed for problem-solving, automated reasoning systems are becoming more and more crucial in the development of AI systems.

4. Autonomous Agents: AI can act independently and autonomously. This allows AI to act without human input or direction. On the other way, autonomous agents in AI are computer programs that can act independently in a given environment. They can perceive their environment, make decisions, and take actions to achieve their goals. Autonomous agents are used in many areas of AI, consisting

of computer vision, NLP, and ML. Autonomous agents can be used to automate tasks, such as scheduling, planning, and decision-making. They can also be used to interact with humans, such as in virtual assistants, chatbots, and autonomous vehicles. Autonomous agents can be used to improve the efficiency of existing systems, as well as to create entirely new systems.

5.2.5.2 The Robotics Field

Robotics is a field of engineering that focuses on the design, construction, and operation of robots. It involves the application of mechanical, electrical, and computer engineering principles to the design, manufacture, and operation of robots. Robotics is used in a variety of applications, including manufacturing, medical, military, and space exploration. Robotics engineering involves the design, construction, and operation of robots. This includes the development of robotic systems, sensors, and actuators, as well as the integration of these components into a functioning robotic system. Robotics engineers must also consider the safety and reliability of the robot, as well as its ability to interact with its environment. Robotics engineers must also consider the application of the robot. This includes the development of algorithms for robot control, navigation, and manipulation. Robotics engineers must also consider the ethical implications of their work, as robots are increasingly being used in a variety of applications, including those involving human interaction. Robotics engineering is a rapidly growing field, and the demand for qualified engineers is increasing. Robotics engineers are in high demand in a variety of industries, including manufacturing, medical, military, and space exploration. As technology continues to advance, the demand for robotics engineers is expected to continue to grow.

Robotics is becoming increasingly important in many areas of our lives. Robotics can be used to automate processes, reduce labor costs, and increase efficiency. Robotics can also be used to improve safety, reduce human error, and increase accuracy. Robotics can also be used to explore new environments, such as space, and to perform dangerous tasks that would otherwise be too risky for humans. Additionally, robotics can be used to improve healthcare, such as through surgical robots and robotic prosthetics. Finally, robotics can be used to improve the quality of life for people with disabilities, by providing them with more independence and mobility.

The future of robotics is an exciting one. Robotics technology is advancing rapidly, and it is expected to continue to do so in the coming years. Robotics will continue to be used in a variety of industries, from manufacturing to healthcare, and even in the home. As robots become more capable and more intelligent, they will be able to take on more complex tasks and interact with humans in more meaningful ways. In the future, robots may be able to perform tasks that are currently too difficult or dangerous for humans to do. They may also be able to provide companionship, help with household chores, and assist the elderly and disabled. As robotics technology continues to evolve, it is likely that robots will become an integral part of our lives.

5.2.5.2.1 Different Types of Robotics

Figure 5.5 show that the current utilization scenario of the robotics filed.

1. Surgical Robotics: These are robotic systems that are used to assist in surgical procedures. They are designed to improve the accuracy and precision of the surgeon, and to reduce the risk of complications and errors. Surgical robots typically consist of a robotic arm attached to a console, which is operated by the surgeon. The robotic arm is equipped with

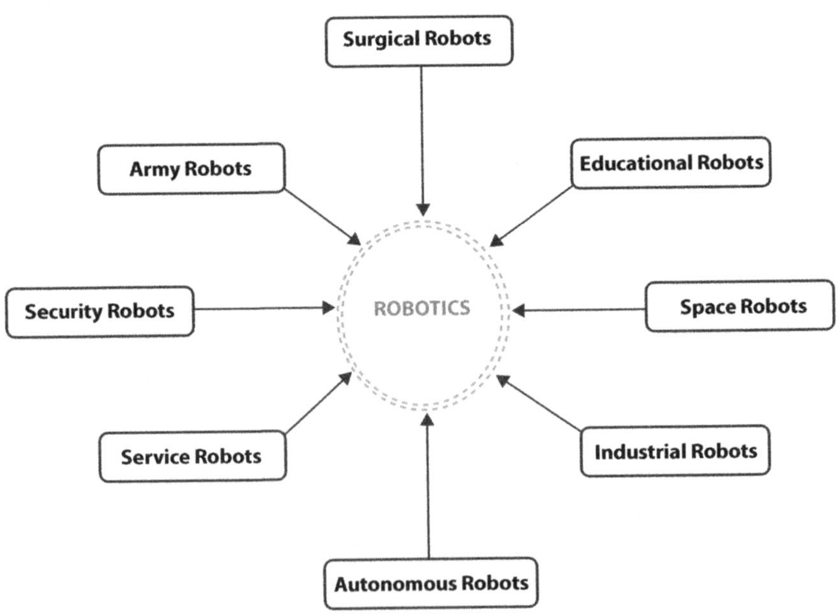

Figure 5.5 A few types of robotics.

various tools and instruments, such as a camera, scalpel, and forceps, which are used to perform the surgery.

2. Army Robotics: This is the use of robots and robotic technology in military applications. This includes the use of unmanned aerial vehicles (UAVs), unmanned ground vehicles, unmanned underwater vehicles, and other robotic systems for reconnaissance, surveillance, target acquisition, and other military missions.
3. Security robotics is the use of robots to provide security services such as surveillance, access control, and perimeter protection. These robots are typically equipped with sensors, cameras, and other technologies to detect and respond to potential threats. They can be used to patrol areas, monitor access points, and detect intrusions. They can also be used to provide real-time information to security personnel, allowing them to quickly respond to any security incidents.
4. Service Robotics: Service robots are designed to interact with humans and assist in a variety of tasks. Examples of service robots include vacuum cleaners, medical robots, and personal assistant robots.
5. Autonomous Robots: Autonomous robots are robots that can make decisions and acting independently without any human input. Examples of autonomous robots include self-driving cars, UAVs, and search and rescue robots.
6. Industrial Robotics: Industrial robots are used in manufacturing and production processes to automate tasks such as welding, painting, assembly, and packaging. These robots are designed to be highly accurate and efficient and are often used in hazardous environments.
7. Space Robotics: Space robots are designed to operate in space and are often used for exploration and research. Examples of space robots include the Mars rovers, space shuttles, and satellites.
8. Educational Robotics: Educational robots are designed to teach students about robotics and programming. These robots are often used in classrooms and can be used to teach students about robotics concepts such as sensors, motors, and programming languages.

When we talk about how robotics will impact the cybersecurity and healthcare sector, we will consider the following;

Robotics is increasingly being used in the field of cybersecurity to help protect networks, systems, and data from malicious attacks. Robotics can be used to automate and streamline many of the tedious, manual tasks associated with cybersecurity, such as vulnerability scanning, malware detection, and patch management. Robotics can also be used to detect and respond to threats in real-time, allowing for faster and more effective responses to cyberattacks.

Robotics can also be used to help identify and mitigate potential threats before they become a problem. By using ML and AI, robotics can analyze data and detect patterns that may indicate a potential threat. This can help organizations identify and address potential threats before they become a major problem. Robotics can also be used to help organizations better understand their security posture. By using robotics to analyze data and identify potential vulnerabilities, organizations may enhance their security posture by having a better understanding of it. In this case, it can be of help to organizations better protect their networks, systems, and data from malicious attacks.

Finally, robotics can be used to help organizations comply with security regulations and best practices. Robotics can help organizations automate the process of ensuring that their networks, systems, and data are compliant with security regulations and best practices. This can help organizations reduce the risk of non-compliance and ensure that their networks, systems, and data are secure.

Similarly, the impact of the robotics in the healthcare sector may include the following;

Robotics in healthcare is a rapidly growing field that has the potential to revolutionize the way healthcare is delivered. Robotics can be used to automate mundane tasks, reduce errors, and improve patient outcomes. Robotics can help in the accuracy improvement and speed of diagnosis and treatment. For example, Robotic systems can evaluate medical photos and find anomalies faster and more precisely than humans. This can help to reduce the time it takes to diagnose and treat patients.

Robotics can also help to reduce the risk of medical errors. Robotic systems can be programmed to follow protocols and procedures more accurately than humans, reducing the risk of mistakes. Robotics can also help to improve the safety of medical procedures. Robotic systems can be used to perform minimally invasive surgeries, reducing the risk of complications and improving patient outcomes.

Robotics can also help to improve the efficiency of healthcare delivery. Robotic systems can be used to automate mundane tasks such as dispensing medications, reducing the amount of time it takes to complete these tasks and freeing up healthcare professionals to focus on more important tasks.

Finally, robotics can help to improve access to healthcare. Robotic systems can be used to provide remote consultations and treatments, allowing patients to access healthcare from anywhere in the world. This can help to reduce the cost of healthcare and make it more accessible to people who may not have access to traditional healthcare services.

5.3 Conclusion

In conclusion, AI and robotics are revolutionizing the way we approach cybersecurity and healthcare systems. Artificial intelligence and robotics are providing us with more efficient and secure solutions for both industries, allowing us to better protect our data and improve healthcare outcomes. Artificial intelligence and robotics are also providing us with new opportunities for automation, which can help reduce costs and increase efficiency. The potential for AI and robotics to revolutionize cybersecurity and healthcare systems is immense, and it is important to continue to explore and develop these technologies in order to maximize their potential. The integration of AI and robotics in cybersecurity and healthcare systems is a promising development that could revolutionize the way we protect our data and provide medical care. Artificial intelligence and robotics have already been used to detect and respond to cyber threats, automate medical diagnosis, and assist with surgical procedures. As technology continues to evolve, it is likely that AI and robotics will become even more prevalent in the healthcare and cybersecurity industries. This could lead to improved security, increased efficiency, and better patient outcomes. Ultimately, the use of AI and robotics in healthcare and cybersecurity systems could have a positive impact on society.

5.4 Future Direction

Artificial intelligence in cybersecurity and healthcare is expected to continue to grow in the future. AI-based systems can be used to detect and respond to cyber threats, as well as to detect and prevent healthcare fraud. Artificial intelligence may be employed to automatically analyze massive volumes of data to find patterns and anomalies that may indicate a security breach or healthcare fraud. It can also be used to create more secure and efficient healthcare systems, such as by automating the process of scheduling appointments and managing patient records. In addition, AI can increase the precision and efficiency of medical diagnosis and therapy, as well as to provide personalized healthcare services. Finally, AI can be used to create more secure and efficient healthcare systems, such as by automating the process of scheduling appointments and managing patient records.

References

1. Ahmad, M., Malware in computer systems: Problems and solutions. *IJID (Int. J. Inform. Dev.)*, 9, 1, 04 2020.
2. Milosevic, N., History of malware, in: *Digital forensics magazine*, vol. 1, pp. 58–66, Aug. 2013.
3. Gupta, S., Types of malware and its analysis. *Int. J. Sci. Eng. Res.*, 4, 2013, [Online]. Available: https://www.ijser.org/researchpaper/Types-of-Malware-andits-Analysis.pdf.
4. Statista, A number of worldwide internet hosts in the domain name system (dns) from 1993 to 2019, [Online]. Available: https://www.statista.com/statistics/264473/number- ofinternet-hosts-in-the-domain-name-system/.
5. Kamoun, F., Iqbal, F., Esseghir, M. A. and Baker, T., AI and machine learning: A mixed blessing for cybersecurity, *2020 International Symposium on Networks, Computers and Communications (ISNCC)*, Montreal, QC, Canada, pp. 1-7, 2020. doi: 10.1109/ISNCC49221.2020.9297323.
6. Anderson, H.S., Kharkar, A., Filar, B., Roth, B., Evading machine learning malware detection, in: *Black Hat USA 2017*, July 22-27, 2017, https://www.blackhat.com/docs/us-17/thursday/us-17-Anderson-Bot-VsBot-Evading-Machine-Learning-Malware-Detection-wp.pdf, accessed November 6, 2018.
7. Ding, N., Ma, H., Gao, H., Ma, Y., Tan, G., Real-time anomaly detection based on long short-term memory and Gaussian Mixture Model, in: *Computers & Electrical Engineering*, vol. 79, pp. 1–11, 2019.
8. Alom, M.Z. and Taha, T.M., Network intrusion detection for cybersecurity using unsupervised deep learning approaches, in: *Proceedings of the 2017 IEEE National Aerospace and Electronics Conference (NAECON)*, Dayton, OH, USA, pp. 63–69, 2017.
9. Chen, J., Yang, Y., Hu, K., Zheng, H., Wang, Z., DAD- MCNN: DDoS attack detection via multi-channel CNN, in: *Proceedings of the 11th International Conference on Machine Learning and Computing: ICMLC '19*, pp. 484–488, 2019.
10. Mirsky, Y., Doitshman, T., Elovici, Y., Shabtai, A., Kitsune, A., An ensemble of autoencoders for online network intrusion detection," arXiv preprint arXiv:1802.09089, pp. 1–15, 2018.

11. Biswas, S.K. and S. K, Intrusion detection using machine learning: A comparison study, in: *International Journal of Pure and Applied Mathematics*, vol. 118, pp. 101–114, 2018.
12. Clements, J., Yangy, Y., Sharma, A.A., Huy, H., Lao, Y., Rallying adversarial techniques against deep learning for network security, arXiv preprint arXiv:1903.11688v1, pp. 1–8, 2019.
13. Xia, S., Qiu, M., Liu, M., Zhong, M., Zhao, H. AI Enhanced Automatic Response System for Resisting Network Threats, in: *Smart Computing and Communication. SmartCom 2019*, Qiu, M. (eds), Lecture Notes in Computer Science, vol 11910, pp. 221–230, Springer, Cham, 2019. https://doi.org/10.1007/978-3-030-34139-8_22.
14. Wang, Z., The Applications of Deep Learning on Traffic Identification, in: *BlackHat*, 2015, https://www.blackhat.com/docs/us15/materials/us-15-Wang-The-Applications-Of-Deep-Learning-OnTraffic-Identification-wp.pdf, accessed March 23, 2019.
15. Lotfollahi, M., Shirali, R., Siavoshani, M.J., Saberian, M., Deep packet: A novel approach for encrypted traffic classification using deep learning," arXiv preprint arXiv:1709.02656, pp. 1–13, 2017.
16. Mi, G., Gao, Y., Tan, Y., Apply stacked auto-encoder to spam detection, in: *Proceedings of the International Conference in Swarm Intelligence*, Beijing, China, pp. 3–15, 2015.
17. Alauthman, M., Almomani, M., Alweshah, M., Omoush, W., Alieyan, K., , Machine learning for phishing detection and mitigation, in: *Machine Learning for Computer and Cyber Security*, B. Gupta and Q.Z. Sheng (Eds.), pp. 1–27, Taylor & Francis, 2019. http://dx.doi.org/10.1007/978-3-030-34139-8_22
18. Aksu, D., Turgut, Z., Üstebay, S., Aydin, M.A., *Phishing analysis of websites using classification techniques*, pp. 251–258, Springer, Singapore, 2019.
19. Yi, Ping, Guan, Yuxiang, Zou, Futai, Yao, Yao, Wang, Wei, Zhu, Ting, Web Phishing Detection Using a Deep Learning Framework, *Wireless Communications and Mobile Computing*, 2018, 4678746, 9 pages, 2018. https://doi.org/10.1155/2018/4678746
20. Benavides, E., Fuertes, W., Sanchez, S., Sanchez, M., Classification of phishing attack solutions by employing deep learning techniques: A systematic literature review, in: *Developments and Advances in Defense and Security*, vol. 152, A. Rocha and R.P. Pereira (Eds.), pp. 51–64, Smart Innovation, Systems and Technologies, 2020. http://dx.doi.org/10.1007/978-981-13-9155-2_5
21. Tuor, A., Kaplan, S., Hutchinson, B., Nicholsand, N., Robinson, S., Deep learning for unsupervised insider threat detection in structured cybersecurity data streams," arXiv preprint arXiv:1710.00811, pp. 1–9, 2017.
22. Beebe, N.L., Maddox, L.A., Liu, L., Sun, M., Sceadan: Using concatenated n-gram vectors for improved file and data type classification. *IEEE Trans. Inf. Forensics Secur.*, 8, 9, 1519–1530, 2013.
23. Axelsson, S., The normalised compression distance as a file fragment classifier. *Digital Invest.*, 7, 8, S24–S31, 2010.

24. Calhoun, W.C. and Coles, D., Predicting the types of file fragments. *Digital Invest.*, 5, S14–S20, 2008.
25. Chen, Q., Liao, Q., Jiang, Z., Fang, J., Yiu, S., Xi, G. *et al.*, File fragment classification using grayscale image conversion and deep learning " In. *Proceedings of the IEEE Symposium on Security and Privacy Workshops*, pp. 140–147, 2018.
26. Soliman, N. and ALEnezi, A., A Method of Skin Disease Detection Using Image Processing and Machine Learning. *Procedia Comput. Sci.*, 163, 85– 92, 2019.
27. Kritika Sujay, R., Pooja Suresh, Y., Omkar Narayan, P., Dr. Swapna, B., Skin disease detection using machine learning. *IJERT*, 9, 2021.
28. Shah, H.A., Saeed, F., Yun, S., Park, J.-H., Paul, A., Kang, J.-M., A Robust Approach for Brain Tumor Detection in Magnetic Resonance Images Using Finetuned EfficientNet. *IEEE Access*, 10, 65426– 65438, 2022, doi: 10.1109/ACCESS.2022.3184113.
29. A. H. Abdel-Gawad, L. A. Said and A. G. Radwan, "Optimized Edge Detection Technique for Brain Tumor Detection in MR Images," in IEEE Access, vol. 8, pp. 136243-136259, 2020, doi: 10.1109/ACCESS.2020.3009898. keywords: {Image edge detection;Genetic algorithms;Tumors;Detectors;Sociology;Statistics;Edge detection;optimization;genetic algorithm;image processing;-medical imaging;tumor detection},
30. Musallam, A.S., Sherif, A.S., Hussein, M.K., A New Convolutional Neural Network Architecture for Automatic Detection of Brain Tumors in Magnetic Resonance Imaging Images. *IEEE Access*, 10, 2775–2782, 2022, doi: 10.1109/ACCESS.2022.3140289.
31. Rizwan, M., Shabbir, A., Javed, A.R., Shabbir, M., Baker, T., Al-Jumeily Obe, D., Brain Tumor and Glioma Grade Classification Using Gaussian Convolutional Neural Network. *IEEE Access*, 10, 29731–29740, 2022, doi: 10.1109/ACCESS.2022.3153108.
32. Hussain, M., J. Bird, J., R. Faria, D., A Study on CNN Transfer Learning for Image Classification, in: *18th UK Workshop on Computational Intelligence*, Nottingham, UK, September 5-7, 2018, January 2019, DOI: 10.1007/978-3-319-97982-3_1.
33. Kumar, A. and Joshi, S., Applications of AI in Healthcare Sector for Enhancement of Medical Decision Making and Quality of Services, in: *2022 International Conference on Decision Aid Sciences and Applications (DASA)*, IEEE, 2022, 978-1-6654-9501-1/22/$31.00, DOI: 10.1109/ DASA54658.2022.9765041.
34. *Understanding Cancer using Machine Learning | by Pier Paolo Ippolito | Towards Data Science*, https://towardsdatascience.com/understanding- cancerusing-machine-learning-84087258ee18 (accessed Aug. 14, 2021).
35. Maharana, A. and Nsoesie, E.O., Correlating the Built Environment with Mental Health through Deep Learning, *JAMA Netw. Open*, 1, 4, e181535–e181535, Aug. 2018, doi: 10.1001/JAMANETWORKOPEN.2018.1535.

36. Kostkova, P., *"A roadmap to integrated digital public health surveillance,". Proc. 22nd Int. Conf. World Wide Web - WWW '13 Companion*, pp. 687–694, 2013, doi: 10.1145/2487788.2488024.
37. Bryant, M., Hospitals turn to chatbots, AI for care | Healthcare Dive, in: *Healtcare Dive*, 2018, https://www.healthcaredive.com/news/chatbots-aihealthcare/516047/ (accessed Aug. 14, 2021).\
38. Jouman Hajjar, A., 6 Chatbot Applications / Use Cases in Healthcare in 2021, in: *AI Multiple*, 2021, https://research.aimultiple.com/chatbot-healthcare/ (accessed Aug. 14, 2021).
39. Kalinin, K., Medical Chatbots: The Future of the Healthcare Industry Konstantin Kalinin, *Healthcare Chatbots: Role of AI, Benefits, Future, Use Cases, Development*, https://topflightapps.com/ideas/chatbots-in-healthcare/ (accessed Feb. 16, 2022).
40. Mihat, A., Mohd Saad, N., Shair, E., Aslam, A., Abdul Rahim, R., Smart health monitoring system utilizing internet of things (IoT) and arduino. *Asian J. Med. Technol.*, 2, 35–48, 2022, Available: 10.32896/ajmedtech.v2n1.35-48.
41. Anandh, R. and Indirani, G., Real Time Health Monitoring System Using Arduino with Cloud Technology. *Asian J. Comput. Sci. Technol.* 7, 29–32, 2018, Available: 10.51983/ajcst-2018.7.s1.1810.
42. Soppimath, V., Jogul, A., Kolachal, S., Baligar, P., Human Health Monitoring System Using IoT and Cloud Technology - Review. *Int. J. Adv. Sci. Eng.*, 5, 924, 2018, Available: 10.29294/ijase.5.2.2018.924-930.
43. Srinivasan, C., Charan, G., Sai Babu, P., An IoT based SMART patient health monitoring system. Indones. *J. Electr. Eng. Comput. Sci.*, 18, 1657, 2020, Available: 10.11591/ijeecs.v18.i3.pp1657-1664.
44. Regeringskansliet, *Vision e-hälsa 2025– gemensamma utgånspunkter för digitalisering i socialtjänst och hälso – och sjukvård*, Socialdepartementet och SKL, 2016, https://www.regeringen.se/499354/contentassets/79df147f5b194554bf401dd88e89b791/vision-e-halsa-2025-overenskommelse.pdf Accessed 12 June 2020. DOI: 10.1186/s12875-020-01321-8.
45. Baird, B., Charles, A., Honeyman, M., Maguire, D., Das, P., *Understanding pressures in general practice*, King's Fund, London, 2016.
46. Greenhalgh, T., Shaw, S., Wherton, J., Vijayaraghavan, S., Morris, J., Bhattacharya, S. *et al.*, Real-world implementation of video outpatient consultations at macro, meso, and micro levels: mixed-method study. *J. Med Internet Res.*, 20, e150, 2018.
47. Chen, J., Lan, Y.C., Chang, Y.W., Chang, P.Y., Exploring doctors' willingness to provide online counseling services: the roles of motivations and costs. *Int. J. Environ. Res. Public Health*, 17, 110, 2019.
48. Allen, T.D., Golden, T.D., Shockley, K.M., How effective is telecommuting? Assessing the status of our scientific findings. *Psychol. Sci. Public Interest*, 16, 40–68, 2015.

49. SKR, *Statistik om hälso – och sjukvård samt regional utveckling 2018*, 2018, https://skr.se/ekonomijuridikstatistik/statistik/ekonomiochverksamhetsstatistik.1342.html Accessed 12 June 2020.
50. Ekman, B., Cost analysis of a digital health care model in Sweden. *PharmacoEcon. Open*, 2, 347–54, 2018.
51. Hatem, M.Q., Skin Lesion Classification System Using a K-Nearest Neighbour Algorithm, in: *Hatem Visual Computing for Industry, Biomedicine, and Art*, 2022, https://doi.org/10.1186/s42492-022-00103-6.
52. Li, Z. *et al.*, Intrusion Detection Using Convolutional Neural Networks for Representation Learning, in: *International Conference on Neural Information Processing*, Springer, Cham, pp. 858–866, November 2017.
53. Yin, C. *et al.*, Deep Learning Approach for Intrusion Detection Using Recurrent Neural Networks. *IEEE Access*, 5, 21954–21961, 2017.
54. Ashfaq, R. *et al.*, Fuzziness based semi-supervised learning approach for intrusion detection system. Fuzziness based semi-supervised learning approach for intrusion detection system. *Inf. Sci.*, 378, 484–497, 2017.
55. Ahmed, S.T. and Patil, K.K., An Investigative study on motifs extracted features opn real-time big-data signals, in: *Proceedings of the 2016 International Conference on Emerging Technological Trends (ICETT)*, Kollam, India, IEEE, pp. 1–4, 2016, Doi: 10.1109/ICETT.2016.7873721.
56. Lin, Z., Fei, X., Yi, S., Yan, M., Cong-Cong, X., Jun, H., A secure encryption-based malware detection system, in: *KSII Transaction on Internet and Information Systems (TIIS)*, vol. 12, April 2018, 1799-1818, doi: 10.3837/tiis.2018.04.022.
57. Fan, M., Liu, J., Luo, X., Chen, K., Tian, Z., Zheng, Q., Liu, T., Android malware familial classification and representative sample selection via frequent analysis. *IEEE Trans. Inf. Forensics Secur.*, 13, 8, 1890–1905, August 2018, doi: 10.1109/TIFS.2018.2806891.
58. Shone, N. *et al.*, A deep learning approach to network intrusion detection. *IEEE Trans. Emerging Top. Comput. Intell.*, 2, 1, 41–50, 2018.
59. Sharma, S., Challa, R., Sahay, S., Detection of Advanced Malware by Machine Learning Techniques, in: *Proceedings of SoCTA 2017*, vol. 01, pp. 333–342, 2019.
60. L. XiaofengFangshuo, J., Xiao, Z., Shengwei, Y., Jing, S., Lio, P., ASSCA: API sequence and statistics features combined architecture for malware detection. *Comput. Netw.*, 157, 99–111, July 2019, doi: 10.1016/j.comnet.2019.04.007.
61. Fasci, L.S., Fisichelle, M., Lax, G., Qian, C., Disarming Visualization-based Approaches in Malware Detection Systems, in: *Computers & Security*, December 2022, doi: 10.1016/j.cose.2022.103062.
62. Baptista, I., Shiaeles, S. and Kolokotronis, N., A Novel Malware Detection System Based on Machine Learning and Binary Visualization, *2019 IEEE International Conference on Communications Workshops (ICC Workshops)*, Shanghai, China, pp. 1-6, 2019, doi: 10.1109/ICCW.2019.8757060.

63. Xiao, F., Lin, Z., Sun, Y., Ma, Y., Malware detection based on deep learning of behaviour graphs. *Math. Probl. Eng.*, 2019, 1–10, February 2019, doi: 10.1155/2019/8195395.
64. Dai, X.F., Spasić, I., Meyer, B., Chapman, S., Andres, F., Machine learning on mobile: An on-device inference app for skin cancer detection, in: *Abstracts of the 4th international conference on fog and mobile edge computing*, IEEE, Rome, 10-13 June 2019, 2019, https://doi.org/10.1109/FMEC.2019.8795362.
65. Amer, E. and Zelinka, I., A dynamic windows malware detection and prediction method based on contextual understanding of API call sequence. *Comp. Secur.*, 92, 1–5, February 2020, doi: 10.1016/j.cose.2020.101760.
66. Rokon, M.O.F., Islam, R., Darki, A., Papalexakis, E., Faloutsos, M., Sourcefinder: Finding malware source-code from publicly available repositories. *RAID*, 1, 1.14311, 2020.
67. Mohammad, M., Hossain, S., Hisham, H., Md Jobair, H.F., Maria, V., Md Abdullah, K., Mohammad, A.R., Muhaiminul I., A., Alfredo, C., Fan, W., Bayesian hyperparameter optimization for deep neural network-based network intrusion detection, in: *IEEE International Conference on Big Data*, 2021.
68. Gustafson, E., Pacheco, J., Wehbe, F., Silverberg, J., Thompson, W., A machine learning algorithm for identifying atopic dermatitis in adults from electronic health records, in: *2017 IEEE International Conference on Healthcare Informatics (ICHI)*, vol. 2017, pp. 83–90, 2017.
69. Esteva, A., Kuprel, B., Novoa, R.A., Ko, J., Swetter, S.M., Blau, H.M. *et al.*, Dermatologist-level classification of skin cancer with deep neural networks. *Nature*, 5427639, 115–8, 2017.
70. Jiang, F., Jiang, Y., Zhi, H., Dong, Y., Li, H., Ma, S., Wang, Y., Dong, Q., Wang, Y., Artificial intelligence in healthcare: Past, present and future. *Stroke Vasc. Neurol.*, 2, 4, 230–243, 2017, doi: 10.1136/svn-2017-000101.
71. Han, S.S., Park, G.H., Lim, W., Kim, M.S., Na, J.I., Park, I. *et al.*, Deep neural networks show an equivalent and often superior performance to dermatologists in onychomycosis diagnosis: automatic construction of onychomycosis datasets by region-based convolutional deep neural network. *PLoS One*, 13, e0191493, 2018.
72. Patnaik, S.K., Sidhu, M.S., Gehlot, Y., Sharma, B., Muthu, Automated skin disease identification using deep learning algorithm. *Biomed. Pharmacol. J.*, 11, 3, 1429–1436, 2018, https://doi.org/10.13005/bpj/1507.
73. Rathod, J., Waghmode, V., Sodha, A., Bhavathankar, P., Diagnosis of Skin diseases using convolutional neural networks, in: *Abstracts of the 2nd International conference on electronics, communication and aerospace technology*, Coimbatore: IEEE, 2018, https://doi.org/10.1109/ICECA.2018.8474593.
74. Amin, J., Sharif, A., Gul, N., Anjum, M.A., Nisar, M.W., Azam, F. *et al.*, Integrated design of deep features fusion for localization and classification of skin cancer. *Pattern Recogn. Lett.*, 131, 63–70, 2020, https://doi.org/10.1016/j.pa trec.2019.11.042.

75. Mahajan, A., Vaidya, T., Gupta, A., Rane, S., Gupta, S., Artificial intelligence in healthcare in developing nations: The beginning of a transformative journey. *Cancer Res., Statist., Treat.*, 2, 2, 182, 2019, doi: 10.4103/crst.crst_50_19.
76. Grampurohit, S., Shalavadi, V., Dhotargavi, V.R., Kudari, M., Jolad, S., Brain tumor detection using deep learning models, in: *Proc. IEEE India Council Int. Subsections Conf. (INDISCON)*, pp. 129–134, Oct. 2020.
77. Ashraf, R., Afzal, S., Rehman, A., Gul, S., Baber, J., Bakhtyar, M., Mehmood, I., Song, O., Maqsood, M., Region-of-Interest Based Transfer Learning Assisted Framework for Skin Cancer Detection. *IEEE Access*, 9160933, 8, 9160933, 147858–147871, 2020, Digital Object Identifier 10.1109/ACCESS.2020.3014701.
78. Balaji, M.S.P., Saravanan, S., Chandrasekar, M., Rajkumar, G., Kamalraj, S., Analysis of basic neural network types for automated skin cancer classification using Firefly optimization method. *J. Ambient Intell. Hum. Comput.*, 12, 7, 7181–7194, 2021, https://doi.org/10.1007/s12652-020-02394-0.
79. Abdusalomov, A.B., Mukhiddinov, M., Whangbo, T.K.. Brain Tumor Detection Based on Deep Learning Approaches and Magnetic Resonance Imaging. *Cancers (Basel)*, 15, 16, 4172, 2023. doi: 10.3390/cancers15164172.
80. Mosa, A.S.M., Yoo, I., Sheets, L., A Systematic Review of Healthcare Applications for Smartphones. *BMC Med. Inform. Decis. Mak.*, 12, 67, 2012, https://doi.org/10.1186/1472-6947-12-67.
81. Kassem, M.A., Hosny, K.M., Fouad, M.M., Fouad, Skin Lesions Classification Into Eight Classes for ISIC 2019 Using Deep Convolutional Neural Network and Transfer Learning. *IEEE Access*, 8, 114822–114832, 2020, doi: 10.1109/ACCESS.2020.3003890.
82. Arif, M., Ajesh, F., Shamsudheen, S., Geman, O., Izdrui, D., Vicoveanu, D., [Retracted] Brain Tumor Detection and Classification by MRI Using Biologically Inspired Orthogonal Wavelet Transform and Deep Learning Techniques. *J. Healthc. Eng.* 2022, 2693621, 18 pages, 2022, https://doi.org/10.1155/2022/2693621.
83. Noble, J.M., Zamani, A., Gharaat, M., Merrick, D., Maeda, N., Lambe Foster, A., Nikolaidis, I., Goud, R., Stroulia, E., Agyapong, V.I.O., Greenshaw, A.J., Lambert, S., Gallson, D., Porter, K., Turner, D., Zaiane, O., Developing, Implementing, and Evaluating an Artificial Intelligence-Guided Mental Health Resource Navigation Chatbot for Health Care Workers and Their Families During and Following the COVID-19 Pandemic: Protocol for a Cross-sectional Study. *JMIR Res. Protoc.*, 11, 7, e33717, 2022. doi: 10.2196/33717.
84. Imran, A., Nasir, A., Bilal, M., Sun, G., Alzahrani, A., Almuhameed, A., Skin Cancer Detection Using Combined Decision of Deep Learners. *IEEE Access*, 10, 118198, Digital Object Identifier 10.1109/ACCESS.2022.3220329.
85. Rafiq, H., Aslam, N., Aleem, M., Issac, B., Randhawa, R.H., AndroMalPack: enhancing the ML-based malware classification by detection and removal of

repacked apps for Android systems. *Sci. Rep.*, 12, 19534, 2022, https://doi.org/10.1038/s41598- 022-23766-w.
86. Ahmed, I.T., Jamil, N., Din, M.M., Hammad, B.T., Binary and Multi-Class Malware Threads Classification. *Appl. Sci.*, 12, 12528, 2022, https://doi.org/10.3390/app122412528.

6

Nonlinear Power Law Modeling for Test Vehicle Structural Response

Harshvardhan P. Ghongade[1]* and Anjali A. Bhadre[2]

[1]*Department of Mechanical Engineering, Brahma Valley College of Engineering and Research Institute, Nashik, India*
[2]*Department of Information Technology, G.H. Raisoni College of Engineering and Management, Pune, India*

Abstract

The complete width engagement impact between the front of a test vehicle and a fixed, rigid, massive barrier represents a common, if not the most common, collision configuration within the context of controlled testing conducted for safety standard compliance or assessment purposes. In cases of the instrumentation of the barrier, specifically that including a load cell array comprised of a sufficient number of individual load cells aligned along the principle test direction, the structural response of the test vehicle during the impact can be characterized within the context of a single degree of freedom, a ubiquitously collinear modeling approach without reliance upon any test vehicle affixed instrumentation. This characterization, based upon the time-parametric force-deflection response, is generally nonlinear aimed at both the closure and separation phases of the collision. Investigated in the subject work, for the totality of each phase, is the use of nonlinear power law formulations for modeling the force-deflection response. A criterion is developed based upon the highest deflection, peak collision force, and internal work absorbed regarding a set of closure phase responses for which such a modeling approach is appropriate. Three distinct power law models are developed and presented for modeling separation phase responses. These models are compared to extant, linear, phasic response models.

***Keywords*:** Nonlinear modeling, collision testing, power law models, structural response

**Corresponding author*: ghongade@gmail.com

Tanupriya Choudhury, Abhijit Kumar, Ravi Tomar, S. Balamurugan and Ankit Vishnoi (eds.) Cyber-Physical Systems for Innovating and Transforming Society 5.0, (121–160) © 2025 Scrivener Publishing LLC

6.1 Introduction

One may define a collision as the physical phenomenon that occurs when two or more distinct objects (or two or more distinct aspects of the same object) attempt to simultaneously occupy the same region of physical space. The kinematic and kinetic responses that arise from the physical phenomenon in question define a set of metrics that are the most objective when it comes to representing the severity of the event. The accurate quantification of these metrics is a typical and common component of the engineering endeavor of vehicular collision reconstruction. The phrase vehicular collision reconstruction, rather than accident reconstruction, is used herein due to the basic fact that that the physical phenomenon in question and the framework utilized for understanding and modeling the physical phenomenon in question (i.e. the episteme) is entirely intransient to legal precepts of human intention.

Within the context of vehicular collision reconstruction, advances in the composite field of vehicle electronics coupled with their broad adaptation has resulted in the establishment of a new paradigm. This paradigm is one of quantifying certain collision severity metrics based upon retrieval of data, from the vehicular collision partner itself, which in turn was generated during the collision and subsequently stored. Certain situations, including, but not limited to, cases involving collision partners for which such system(s) were not included at the time of manufacture, the lack of coverage for data extraction using aftermarket, commercially available hardware and software systems, data loss, lack of vehicle availability or any combination of the aforementioned results in the necessity for relying upon other methods for estimating the salient quantifiable collision severity metrics. One class of such methods involves the analysis of evidence generated during a collision event, the relatively immediate temporal period surrounding a collision event or both. An example is the deposition of tire mark evidence, on a roadway, secondary to vehicle operator mediated braking, steering or both. Cases in which such evidence is present, an antecedent to a collision event, specifically due to operator mediated brake application, however, has become an increasing rarity secondary to the near ubiquitous inclusion of anti-lock brakes as a standard vehicle feature. In most cases, the salient evidence generated is that which occurred during a collision and consists of the residual damage present to the vehicular collision partners.

The importance of residual damage analysis-based methods for quantifying collision severity metrics cannot be understated. In the United States, the National Center for Statistics and Analysis (NCSA), of the National

Highway Traffic Safety Administration (NHTSA), has been involved in the collection of motor vehicle traffic collision data through the National Automotive Sampling System/Crashworthiness Data System (NASS/CDS) for over forty years. For any given traffic collision subject to such an investigation, inclusion within the NASS/CDS requires the determination and coding of the collision phase velocity change for the salient vehicular collision partners. In this regard, the collision phase velocity change ($\Delta\mathbf{v}$) is the metric by which collision severity is quantified and with such determinations predicated upon reconstruction of the collision event. As of 2007, the vast majority of coded velocity changes within the NASS/CDS were based upon residual damage analysis [1]. The phrase, residual damage, which was used in the two preceding paragraphs, requires a working definition. As used in this work, the phrase refers to the quantifiable dimensions of the permanent deformation present to a vehicular collision partner and with such deformation arising from a collision event. The reasoning behind using residual damage as the starting point in quantifying collision severity, is elementary. As the collective independent variable, in a reconstructive analysis, residual damage does not require any measurements during the collision itself. Furthermore, the dimensions of a vehicular collision partner, in the post-collision configuration, can readily be ascertained, even well after the incipient collision event, and through a number of different means. Dimensional data regarding an undeformed reference configuration is readily available for virtually every single production vehicle. The dimensional differences between the reference and post collision configurations define the residual damage profile.

The process of using a given residual damage profile, for a given vehicular collision partner, to quantify the severity of the collision that produced the residual damage profile, clearly requires mathematical modeling. In a general sense, a mathematical model converts a set of inputs (the independent variables) into a set of desired outputs (the dependent variables) by means of its form and generally with the use of model specific parameters. Furthermore, these parameters generally require a priori quantification prior to model utilization for a given case of interest. Advancing from this general statement to one of specificity in regard to the residual damage analysis for vehicular collision reconstruction, there are two empirically based and interrelated mathematical models that have enjoyed long-standing utilization. Both models are intrinsically uniaxial and not time parametric. Based upon controlled collision testing, in a collinear configuration, in which a fixed, rigid, massive barrier (FRMB) was impacted, in each test, by the front of a test vehicle, in a full-frontal width engagement impact, Campbell [2, 3] postulated a linear relationship between the speed of impact and the uniaxial depth of residual deformation (i.e. crush) present to the test vehicle. Campbell generalized this finding by defining the equivalent barrier speed (EBS) as 'a vehicle velocity at which the kinetic energy of the vehicle would equal the energy absorbed in plastic deformation' and by indicating that the EBS was a linear function of the uniaxial residual damage depth.

$$\mathrm{EBS} = \mathrm{b}_0 + \mathrm{b}_1\mathrm{c} \tag{6.1}$$

In Equation 6.1, the model parameters b_0 and b_1 are typically referred to as the Campbell model coefficients. The term b_0 represents the maximum EBS that results in a zero valued residual damage depth (c) and the term b_1 is the slope of the linear relationship. The second empirical relationship, postulated by Campbell [3] but most commonly associated with McHenry [4] was of a linear response in the collision force magnitude, normalized per unit length of direct contact damage, and the uniaxial depth of residual damage.

$$\frac{|F|}{L} = A + Bc \tag{6.2}$$

In Equation 6.2, $|\mathrm{F}|$ is the magnitude of the collision force, L is the length of direct contact damage, A is the maximum normalized collision force that results in a zero valued residual damage depth, and B is the slope of the linear relationship. The length of direct contact damage is taken as being time invariant with respect to the collision (i.e., the value for L is taken as being the same in the reference and residual damage configurations). The model parameters A and B are commonly referred to as the CRASH3 (the acronym deriving from the third iteration of the Calspan Reconstruction of Accident Speeds on the Highway model) coefficients. The parameters from both models are collectively referred to as stiffness coefficients.

It is relevant, at this point in the presentation, to note the fact that collisions are not instantaneous events (this does not preclude the ability to accurately model collisions as such). For the vast majority of collisions of the type of interest, excluding certain sideswipe type collisions, the finite collision duration can be divided into two phases. The closure phase initiates at the first point in time that the collision partners seek to occupy the same region of physical space and terminates at the point in time in which the collision partners achieve a common velocity. The second phase, the separation phase, initiates contemporaneously with the terminus of the closure phase and terminates at the first point in time at which the collision force magnitude reaches zero. The collision force is internal to the collision partner system. During closure, the work done by the collision force is internal work absorbed (IWA) and during separation, the work done by the collision force is internal work recovered (IWR). The difference between the IWA and the IWR is the internal work dissipated (IWD).

These definitions are of importance to the subject work. Equations 6.1 and 6.2 both relate an independent variable that is a terminus of separation variable to a dependent variable that is a terminus of closure variable (one may write the second relationship on an average basis, however, such would not be correct in regard to the work-energy relationship discussed subsequently). The CRASH3 model was explicitly developed for the closure phase. The lack of inclusion of a separation phase is functionally equivalent to treating the IWR, the coefficient of restitution (the ratio of the separation velocity to the closing velocity) and the separation velocity as being zero valued. The kinetic energy associated with the EBS from Equation 6.1 can be obtained simply as:

$$\frac{1}{2}\mathrm{mEBS}^2 = (\mathrm{b}_0 + \mathrm{b}_1\mathrm{c})^2 \tag{6.3}$$

Equation 6.2 has been traditionally treated as if it were a time parametric force-deflection response. Double integration of this equation over L and c has been taken as producing an energy that is equal to that of equation (3). The integrated result is a quadratic in c, which means that the equality holds when the polynomial coefficients for each order of c (i.e., $\mathrm{c}^0, \mathrm{c}^1$ and c^2) are equal. This approach allows for a set of equations that relate the parameters of the two models and for which one need only estimate a value for b_0, for a given value of c, L and EBS, in order to quantify the remaining three parameters.

The modeling of collisions in which the collision partners 'stick together' with no recovery of the IWA may be appropriate for certain impact situations. However, even for the FRMB impact case described previously, the case of a test vehicle coming to rest against the barrier face is not one that is seen empirically. From the mathematical modeling perspective, for the closure phase of a collinear impact, the modeling of each deformable collision partner as a single degree of freedom (SDOF) model comprised of a single lumped mass coupled to a single, linear, relative displacement element (i.e. linear spring) can readily be found in the early literature [5] and as part of the formative basis of the CRASH3 damage analysis algorithm [4].

The question of whether a dynamic model containing both the closure and separation phases could be developed that (a) could account for the ordinate offsets of the empirical models and (b) maintain the linearity of the empirical models for collisions resulting in non-zero valued residual damage depths was previously addressed by the subject author [6]. Three findings from the cited work, for an affirmative response, are salient. The first finding was that the closure phase force-deflection response had to be uniformly and ubiquitously linear. The second finding was that an elastic limit, defined as a specific value of $|F|$, EBS or IWA was needed. Collisions at a severity up to and including the elastic limit values resulted in a non-linear separation phase response that terminated at the origin of the force deflection curve. For such collisions, the separation phase response could not be linear as the only linear path was a reverse traversal of the linear closure phase response, thereby producing full recovery of the IWA (equivalently, a separation velocity magnitude being equal to the closing velocity magnitude and a unity valued coefficient of restitution). The non-linear response allowed for both a zero valued residual damage depth and a coefficient of restitution with less than unity valuation. The third finding was that for collisions exceeding the elastic limit, the separation phase had to be uniformly and ubiquitously linear with a force-deflection response slope of greater magnitude than the closure phase response. Any nonlinearity or multilinearity in the response for collisions exceeding the elastic limit were patently manifest in the relationship between any terminus of closure phase parameters and the depth of residual damage.

The linear model for the separation phase, as described above, however, tends to be problematic when it comes to the FRMB impact case under consideration due to the fact that it results in an overestimation of the IWR. One approach to deal with this issue, as found in the literature, has been to interpose a modeled path, for the force-deflection response, from the start of the separation phase, having infinite slope, and terminating at a normalized force value such that the subsequent finite slope response produces an IWR that matches the value determined from testing [7–10]. In view of the subject author, this approach is unjustified, even as a modeled response. While it produces linearity in regard to the residual damage relationships and matches the IWR, the modeling approach requires a time parametric drop in force magnitude, from peak value, while the time parametric deflection remains at peak value. There is no physical phenomenon that would serve as a basis for this requirement.

Returning to the scope of residual damage-based models, it should be noted that other models have been proposed. Other, linear, models include a constant force model [7], a saturation force model (finite linear slope followed by zero slope region) [7] and a bilinear model [7, 11]. A non-linear power law model has also been proposed [12]. It is important to note that these models retain the non-time parametric nature of the original residual damage-based models.

The non-linear power law model, as a dynamic model, has been explored previously, by the author, for modeling the closure phase [13], as well as the separation phase [14], for the FRMB impacts of interest. The objective of the subject work is the further exploration of this modeling approach within the FRMB impact context. Two points regarding the choice of this context are worthy of note. The first, being rather obvious, is that controlled collision testing provides one of the most comprehensive sources of data when it comes to quantifying model parameters. Secondly, the subject FRMB impact context is one that is incumbent in testing conducted for United States (US) Federal Motor Vehicle Safety Standard (FMVSS) 208D frontal impact compliance requirements, US high-speed frontal impact New Car Assessment Program (NCAP) testing and for testing conducted for research purposes. Collectively, testing of this type represents a significant component of all testing conducted by various contracted groups, on behalf of NHTSA.

6.2 Theory

Within the context of understanding a given physical phenomenon of interest, it can readily be stated that the purpose of employing mathematical modeling is to engender tractability. This, in turn, consists of (a) defining a set of variables that serve as inputs, (b) defining a set of variables that serve as outputs and (c) defining the operative relationships between these variables. There is generally a correlation between increasing levels of model complexity and the ability for modeling more aspects of the phenomenon, modeling a given aspect to a greater level of detail or both. The downside is that more complex models typically involve additional parameters and require additional data when compared to simpler models. Finally, it should also be noted that great care must be taken in employing models for situations that are beyond the strictures of the model.

With this caveat established, we can consider the graphical depiction of a collinear collision between two collision partners as shown in Figure 6.1. Because the problem is formulated as a collinear impact in R^1

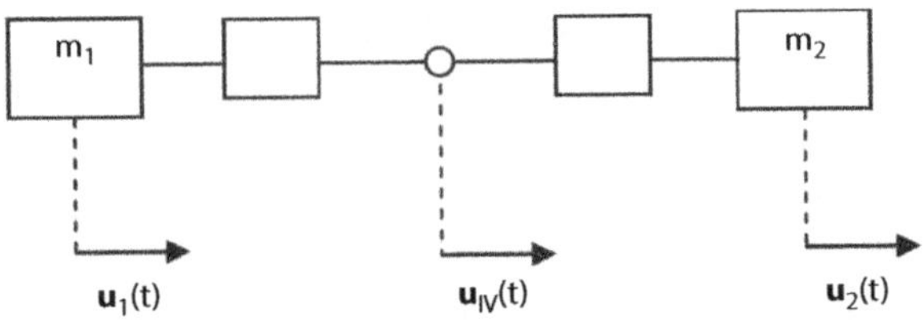

Figure 6.1 Introductory collision model.

for the entirety of the collision event, the single axis of the inertial frame of reference, $\mathbf{X}$, is aligned with the single axis, $\mathbf{x}_1$ and $\mathbf{x}_2$, of each collision partner for all times of interest. This formulation, in and of itself, properly references vectors in each body frame to the inertial frame of reference. Equivalently, this can also be stated as the direction cosine matrix (DCM) that transforms vector components from each body frame to the inertial frame of reference is time invariant as the identity matrix (this also holds for the inverse transform).

$$^{G}R_{B_1}(t) = I^{G}R_{B_2}(t) = I_3 \ \forall t \tag{6.4}$$

This does not hold for the case of general planar motion or general spatial motion.

Each collision partner is modeled as a single lumped mass coupled to a massless force carrying member. The latter represents the modeled structural properties, for the impacted region, for each collision partner. Because the spatial dimension of the problem is one, each collision partner has a SDOF, which is translational along the $\mathbf{X}$-axis. This SDOF is parameterized by translational displacement and is denoted as $\mathbf{u}_1(t)$ for the first collision partner and $\mathbf{u}_2(t)$ for the second collision partner. We seek to define the modeled structural response characteristics of each collision partner independently rather than effectively. This results in use of a massless node, representing the common collision interface, with displacement $\mathbf{u}_{IV}(t)$.

We define the deflection for each collision partner as the relative displacement between the center of mass of the same and the common collision interface. This is a direct measure of the dimensional change experienced by the massless element for each collision partner.

$$\delta_1(t) = u_1(t) - u_{IV}(t)$$
$$\delta_2(t) = u_{IV}(t) - u_2(t) \tag{6.5}$$

This rather simple model may be reduced even further due to the modeled nature of the FRMB. Because the FRMB is fixed, it experiences no displacement during the collision event. Because the FRMB is rigid, it experiences no deflection during the collision event. Finally, because the barrier face is the common collision interface, the displacement of the same is zero. The two equations under Equation 6.5 reduce to one singular operative equation for this case.

$$\delta_1(\mathrm{t}) = \mathbf{u}_1(\mathrm{t}) \tag{6.6}$$

For this case, the displacement experienced by the vehicle's center of mass, during the collision, equals the structural deflection experienced by the vehicle. This does not hold if the opposing collision partner is deformable. References in the literature and elsewhere to phrases such as 'force displacement response,' when referencing the force deflection response, are only correct when Equation 6.6 holds.

There are a number of statements that can readily be made without crystallizing the form of the force-deflection model. The application of Newton's second law of motion to the vehicle yields the general form of the equation of motion for the test vehicle.

$$\mathrm{m}_1\ddot{\mathbf{u}}_1(\mathrm{t}) = -\mathbf{F}(\mathrm{t}) \tag{6.7}$$

Where m_1 is the mass of the test vehicle, $\mathbf{F}(t)$ is the time varying collision force (the sole force considered during the collision and internal to the two-collision partner system) and the standard overdot notation is employed for representing simple time derivatives. When the FRMB is a load-cell barrier in which each load cell measures force axially, the collision force can be directly obtained by summing, at each point in time, the force measured by each load cell. This holds for the model because of the time invariant orientation noted previously and the treatment of the barrier as being rigid. The time varying force on the test vehicle is equal in magnitude but opposite in direction by Newton's third law. The second statement is that the equations for the IWA and the IWR for the two-collision partner system [15] reduce by considering the mass of the FRMB in the limit.

$$\text{IWA} = \frac{1}{2}\frac{m_1 m_2}{m_1 + m_2} v_c{}_c^2 \underset{m_2 \to \infty}{\rightarrow} \text{IWA} = \frac{1}{2} m_1 v_c^2 \tag{6.8}$$

$$\text{IWR} = \frac{1}{2}\frac{\mathrm{m_1 m_2}}{\mathrm{m_1 + m_2}} \mathbf{v}_s{}^2 \underset{\mathrm{m_2} \to \infty}{\rightarrow} \text{IWR} = \frac{1}{2} \mathrm{m_1 v_s}^2 \tag{6.9}$$

Where $\mathbf{v}_c$ is the closing velocity and $\mathbf{v}_s$ is the separation velocity, which are defined as:

$$\mathbf{v}_c = \dot{\mathbf{u}}_1(\mathrm{t_o}) - \dot{\mathbf{u}}_2(\mathrm{t_o}) = \dot{\mathbf{u}}_1(\mathrm{t_o}) - 0 = \dot{\mathbf{u}}_1(\mathrm{t_o}) \tag{6.10}$$

$$\mathbf{v}_s = \dot{\mathbf{u}}_1(\mathrm{t_s}) - \dot{\mathbf{u}}_2(\mathrm{t_s}) = \dot{\mathbf{u}}_1(\mathrm{t_s}) - 0 = \dot{\mathbf{u}}_1(\mathrm{t_s}) \tag{6.11}$$

In Equation 6.10, the time value $t = t_0$ denotes the time at which the closure phase initiates. The closure phase terminates at $t = t_c$. For this collision configuration, *a* common velocity is reached, for the collision partners, at the terminus of closure. Clearly, this common velocity, $\mathbf{v}_{com}$, is equal to zero due to the modeled properties of the FRMB. In Equation 6.11, the time value $t = t_s$ denotes the time at which the separation phase terminates. In both equations, the velocity of the FRMB is zero, thereby leading to the reduction shown to the right of the last equality in each equation. The relationships shown in Equations 6.7 to 6.11 are derived without any presumption regarding the nature or form of the force-deflection response of the test vehicle and hold regardless of the nature or form of the forcedeflection response of the test vehicle.

We now proceed with the consideration of specific force-deflection models. The linear model, serving as comparison, for the subject nonlinear power law model, requires review.

6.2.1 Linear Closure Phase Force-Deflection Model

The linear model derives its name as a result of the collision force being modelled as a linear function of the deflection.

$$\mathbf{F}(\mathrm{t}) = \mathrm{k}\delta_1(\mathrm{t}) = \mathrm{k}\mathbf{u}_1(\mathrm{t}) \tag{6.12}$$

The form to the right of the final equality in this equation is based upon Equation 6.6. Substitution of Equation 6.12 into Equation 6.7 followed by algebraic rearrangement leads to the operative second order linear differential equation of motion for the linear closure phase model.

$$\mathrm{m}_1\ddot{\mathbf{u}}_1(\mathrm{t})+\mathrm{k}\mathbf{u}_1(\mathrm{t})=0 \tag{6.13}$$

For this model, the length of the massless element, at $t_0=0$ is taken as being equal to the reference length of the element (i.e. the length at which the element carries zero force). This allows for an initial condition of $\mathbf{u}_1(0)=\mathbf{u}_{10}=0$. The other initial condition is of a finite, non-zero, initial velocity, $\mathbf{v}_1(0)=\mathbf{v}_{10}$, for the test vehicle. The time domain kinematic solutions for the closure phase, for this model, are [14]:

$$\mathbf{u}_1(\mathrm{t})=\mathbf{v}_{10}\omega^{-1}\sin(\omega\mathrm{t}) \tag{6.14}$$

$$\dot{\mathbf{u}}_1(\mathrm{t})=\mathbf{v}_{10}\cos(\omega\mathrm{t}) \tag{6.15}$$

$$\dot{\mathbf{u}}_1(\mathrm{t})=\mathbf{v}_{10}\cos(\omega\mathrm{t}) \tag{6.16}$$

Where the closure phase circular frequency, ω, is equal to the real root of $(\mathrm{k}/\mathrm{m}_1)^{0.5}$. The time at which closure terminates is determinable from Equation 6.15 and by knowing that the velocity of the test vehicle, at that point, is the common velocity, which is zero. Because the initial velocity is known to be non-zero valued, the equation holds when the cosine term is zero-valued. Because the cosine function is periodic, it is the first solution that is used. This leads to a solution of $t_c=\pi/(2\omega)$. Substitution of this result into Equation 6.14 leads to a terminus of closure displacement and deflection of $\mathbf{u}_1(\mathrm{t_c})=\mathbf{u}_{1\mathrm{c}}=\delta_1(\mathrm{t_c})=\delta_{1\mathrm{c}}=\mathbf{v}_{10}\omega^{-1}$. Similarly, the terminus of closure acceleration is determinable as $-\mathbf{v}_{10}\omega$. We may also show that the model is linear by multiplying the acceleration by the mass of the test vehicle and dividing it by the deflection.

$$\frac{-F(t)}{\delta_1(t)}=\frac{m_1v_{10}\omega\sin(\omega t)}{v_{10}\omega^{-1}\sin(\omega t)}=m_1\omega^2=m_1\frac{k}{m_1}=k \tag{6.17}$$

The modeled IWA during closure can be determined by integrating the dot product of the collision force and the differential of the deflection.

$$\text{IWA} = \int_0^{\delta_{1c}} F(\delta_1(t)) \cdot d\delta_1(t) = \frac{1}{2} k\delta_{1c}^2 \tag{6.18}$$

For any given collision test, the terms $m_1, \mathbf{v}_{10}$ and the IWA, as per Equation 6.8 are known. The value of t_c can be determined from Equation 6.7 by using the total barrier force to first solve for the discrete acceleration-time history, followed by numerical integration to determine the discrete velocity-time history and then determining the time at which zero velocity is reached. The discrete displacement-time history can be determined by numerical integration of the discrete velocity-time history. The terminus of closure displacement (here equal to deflection), acceleration, and force values can then be determined by simply the noting the value at $t = t_c$. Thus far, none of the values noted rely upon a model for the force deflection response. When we consider the linear closure phase model, we can readily note that the system is overdetermined once the previously listed terms are known. There are a number of solution approaches that can be employed.

1. Use the measured value of δ_{1c} and solve for ω using $\omega = \mathbf{v}_{10} / \delta_{1c}$. Then solve for k using $\mathrm{k} = \mathrm{m}_1 / \omega^2$. Solve for the modeled value of $\mathbf{F}_c$ using $\mathbf{F}_c = \mathrm{k}\delta_{1c}$. Solve for the modeled value of t_c using $t_c = \pi / (2\omega)$.
2. Use the measured value of the force $\mathbf{F}_c$ to solve for the acceleration at the terminus of closure. Solve for the circular frequency by dividing the terminus of closure acceleration by $-\mathbf{v}_{10}$. Solve for $k \text{using} \mathrm{k} = \mathrm{m}_1 / \omega^2$. Solve for the modeled value of t_c using $t_c = \pi / \left(2\omega\right)$.
3. Use the measured data point $\left\{\delta_{1c}, \mathbf{F}_c\right\}$ to solve for $k$$u$ sing $\mathrm{k} = (\mathbf{F}_c - \mathbf{F}_o) / (\cdot_{1c} - \cdot_{1o}) = \mathbf{F}_c / \cdot_{1c}$. Solve for ω as above and solve for the modeled value of t_c as above.
4. Use the measured value of t_c to solve for ω using $\omega = \pi / (2t_c)$. Solve for k using $k = m_1 / \omega^2$. Solve for the modeled values of δ_{1c} as $\mathbf{v}_{10}\omega^{-1}$, the terminus of closure acceleration as $-\mathbf{v}_{10}\omega$ and the terminus of closure force as $-\mathrm{m}_1\mathrm{v}_{10}\omega$.

6.2.2 Power Law Closure Phase Force-Deflection Model

The power law models for both phases are expressed as force as a function of deflection. Both the force and the deflection are time parametric.

This time parametric nature, denoted as (t), is not shown, in certain situations, in the following derivation, simply for the purposes of clarity. It should not be forgotten that this time dependence is patent. With this noted, the closure phase power law model is:

$$\mathbf{F} = \mathrm{a}_0 \delta_1^{\mathrm{a}_1} = \mathrm{a}_0 \mathbf{u}_1^{\mathrm{a}_1} \tag{6.19}$$

The form to the right of the last equality again derives from Equation 6.6. Equation 6.19 correctly produces an initial zero valued force at an initial zero deflection (at an initial zero displacement). It should also be apparent that this equation is log-linear. For two operands x and y, a power p, and a logarithm of base *b*, the following product, quotient, power and root identities hold.

$$\log_b(xy) = \log_b(x) + \log_b(y) \tag{6.20}$$

$$\log_b(xy^{-1}) = \log_b(x) - \log_b(y) \tag{6.21}$$

$$\log_b(x^p) = \mathrm{p}\log_b(x) \tag{6.22}$$

$$\log_b \sqrt[p]{x} = p^{-1}\log_b(x) \tag{6.23}$$

The logarithm and exponentiation are related by the following, where b is a positive, real number:

$$\log_b(b^y) = y \tag{6.24}$$

For the subject work, the base, *b*, for all evaluations is set to Euler's number, e, and the logarithms are noted as the natural logarithm. This choice is made due to common usage and does not reduce the generality of the derivation secondary to the fact that one may readily convert a logarithm from one basis to another using the following:

$$\log_b(x) = \frac{\log_c(x)}{\log_c(b)} \tag{6.25}$$

With these preliminaries established, taking the natural log of Equation 6.19 leads to the following:

$$\ln(\mathbf{F}) = \ln\left(a_0\delta_1^{a_1}\right) = \ln(a_0) + a_1\ln(\delta_1) \tag{6.26}$$

The slope-intercept appearance of this equation is patent. A point of importance to note is the fact that $\ln(0)$ is equal to negative infinity. Now, if Equation 6.19 is substituted into Equation 6.7, it can readily be seen that the resultant equation of motion is non-linear.

$$m\ddot{\mathbf{u}}_1(t) + a_0\left(\mathbf{u}_1(t)\right)^{a_1} = \mathbf{0} \tag{6.27}$$

A closed form solution for Equation 6.27 is not determinable using the methods that are appropriate for solving linear differential equations. We further note that the closure phase model has two parameters (a_0 and a_1), unlike the linear model, which has a single parameter, and thus requires two equations in order to solve for both parameters. One approach would be to write Equation 6.19 at the terminus and at the start of the closure phase. This, however, is insufficient, due to the fact that the latter reduces to $0 = 0$. A second approach would be to write this equation at any two points, $t = t_a$ and $t = t_b$, for which the deflection and force are not zero-valued. One could then solve for the model parameters as:

$$\begin{aligned} a_1 &= \ln\left(\frac{\mathbf{F}_a}{\mathbf{F}_b}\right)\left(\ln\left(\frac{\delta_{1a}}{\delta_{1a}}\right)\right)^{-1} \\ a_0 &= \mathbf{F}_a\delta_{1a}{}^{-a_1} = \mathbf{F}_b\delta_{1b}{}^{-a_1} \end{aligned} \tag{6.28}$$

Finally, one may use the modeled IWA to determine a second equation. For this model and case, the IWA is:

$$\text{IWA} = \int_0^{\delta_{1c}} \mathbf{F}\cdot d\delta_1 = \int_0^{\delta_{1c}} a_0\delta_1^{a_1}\cdot d\delta_1 = \frac{a_0}{a_1+1}\delta_{1c}{}^{a_1+1} \tag{6.29}$$

We may rewrite the form on the right of the last equality by separating the exponentiated term.

$$\mathrm{IWA} = \frac{a_0\delta_{1c}^{a_1}}{a_1+1}\delta_{1c} = \frac{F_c}{a_1+1}\delta_{1c} \rightarrow a_1 = \frac{F_c\delta_{1c}}{\mathrm{IWA}} - 1 \tag{6.30}$$

Equation 6.30 is the preferred initiating power law modeling equation for the closure phase. The IWA is known as per Equation 6.8 and δ_{1c} and F_{1c} are determinable from the data. Furthermore, the equation has only one unknown, the power, a_1. Clearly, $a_1 \geq 0$ in order to avoid a singularity at $\delta = 0$. We further note that $a_1 > 0$ is more apt secondary to the fact that the deflection raised to a zero power produces a solution of unity for all relevant deflection values. This constraint, in turn, as per Equation 6.30, requires that $F_c\delta_{1c}/\mathrm{IWA} > 1$. When this holds and when the power is known, the coefficient, a_0, can be solved for by writing Equation 6.19 at the terminus of closure and solving directly.

Finally, if one considers two points during the closure response $\{\delta_1, F_1\}$ and $\{\delta_2, F_2\}$, where neither the deflection nor the force is zero-valued, the corresponding IWA is:

$$\begin{aligned}\mathrm{IWA} &= \int_{\delta_1}^{\delta_2} a_0\delta^{a_1} \\ &= \frac{a_0}{a_1+1}\left(\delta_2^{\,a_1+1} - \delta_1^{\,a_1+1}\right) \\ &= \frac{1}{a_1+1}\left(a_0\delta_2^{a_1}\delta_2 - a_0\delta_1^{a_1}\delta_1\right) \\ &= \frac{1}{a_1+1}(F_2\delta_2 - F_1\delta_1)\end{aligned} \tag{6.31}$$

6.2.3 Linear Separation Phase Force-Deflection Model

The separation phase terminates at the first point in time, after the terminus of the closure phase, at which the collision force returns to zero. Since the total barrier force is known, the value of t_s can be directly determined from the data. The terminus of separation acceleration, velocity, and displacement can then be determined in the same manner as was discussed for the terminus of closure. With the terminus of separation velocity known, the IWR can be determined using Equation 6.9. Again, no force-deflection model is needed to make these determinations.

For the linear model for the separation phase, a model for which closed form analytic solutions for the kinematic responses are determinable, the solution process is aided by implementing a new temporal variable, τ, where $\tau = t - t_c$. As a result, $\tau_0 = t_c - t_c = 0$ and $\tau_s = t_s - t_c$. One may wish to use Equation 6.13 with a replacement of t by τ and using the terminus of closure displacement and velocity as the initial conditions. Such an approach, however, does not result in a correct, complete set of kinematic equations. Instead, the correct equation of motion is [14]:

$$\mathrm{m}_1\ddot{\mathbf{u}}_1(\tau) + \bar{\mathrm{k}}\mathbf{u}_1(\tau) = \mathrm{m}_1\ddot{\mathbf{u}}_{1c} + \bar{\mathrm{k}}\mathbf{u}_{1c} \tag{6.32}$$

In this equation, the terms on the right side are evaluated at $\tau_0 = 0$ (i.e. they are the terminus of closure acceleration and displacement). Model parameters with an overbar specifically denote separation phase model parameters. The kinematic solutions are readily determinable as [14]:

$$\mathbf{u}_1(\tau) = \mathbf{u}_{1c} + \ddot{\mathbf{u}}_{1c}\bar{\omega}^{-2}\left(1 - \cos(\bar{\omega}\tau)\right) \tag{6.33}$$

$$\dot{\mathbf{u}}_1(\tau) = \ddot{\mathbf{u}}_{1c}\bar{\omega}^{-1}\sin(\bar{\omega}\tau) \tag{6.34}$$

$$\ddot{\mathbf{u}}_1(\tau) = \ddot{\mathbf{u}}_{1c}\cos(\bar{\omega}\tau) \tag{6.35}$$

In these equations, the separation phase circular frequency is the positive real root of the following:

$$\bar{\omega} = \left(\bar{\mathrm{k}}\mathrm{m}^{-1}\right)^{0.5} \tag{6.36}$$

The modeled value for τ_s is based upon the acceleration response. Because the terminus of closure acceleration is not zero-valued, the cosine term must be zero-valued for the acceleration to be zero at the terminus of separation. This occurs at:

$$\tau_s = \pi(2\bar{\omega})^{-1} \tag{6.37}$$

The modeled terminus of separation displacement and velocity are obtained by substitution of this solution into Equations 6.33 and 6.34, respectively.

$$\mathbf{u}_{1s} = \mathbf{u}_{1c} + \ddot{\mathbf{u}}_{1c}\bar{\omega}^{-2}\ \dot{\mathbf{u}}_{1s} = \ddot{\mathbf{u}}_{1c}\bar{\omega}^{-1} \quad (6.38)$$

For the force-deflection response, we first consider a linear function $y = f(x)$ that has a value $y_a = f(x_a)$ and where $x \geq x_a$. The definition of the slope of the linear function allows the equation to be written in the following manner:

$$\text{slope} = \frac{y - y_a}{x - x_a} \rightarrow y = y_a + \text{slope}(x - x_a) \quad (6.39)$$

One may take a similar approach for the case where $y_b = f(x_b)$ and where $\mathrm{x_b} \geq \mathrm{x}$.

$$\text{slope} = \frac{\mathrm{y_b} - \mathrm{y}}{\mathrm{x_b} - \mathrm{x}} \rightarrow \mathrm{y} = \mathrm{y_b} + \text{slope}(\mathrm{x} - \mathrm{x_b}) \quad (6.40)$$

The boundary points for the linearly modeled force deflection response are $(\delta_{1c}, \mathbf{F}_c)$ at $\tau = 0$ and $(\delta_{1s}, 0)$ at $\tau = \tau_s$. In looking at the two previous equations, we note that y is analogous to $F(\delta(\tau))$, x is analogous to $\delta(\tau)$, the values with the subscript of a are analogous to the values at $\tau = 0$ and the values with the subscript of b are analogous to the values at $\tau = \tau_s$. As a result:

$$\mathbf{F} = \mathbf{F}_c + \bar{\mathrm{k}}(\delta_1 - \delta_{1c}) \quad (6.41)$$

$$\mathbf{F} = \mathbf{F}_s + \bar{\mathrm{k}}(\delta_1 - \delta_{1s}) = \bar{\mathrm{k}}(\delta_1 - \delta_{1s}) \quad (6.42)$$

The modeled IWR can be obtained by multiplying the collision force by the differential of the deflection and integrating over the domain.

$$
\begin{aligned}
\text{IWR} &= -\int_{\delta_{1c}}^{\delta_{1s}} \mathbf{F} d\delta_1 \\
&= \frac{1}{2}(\delta_{1c} - \delta_{1s})\left(2\mathrm{F}_c + \bar{\mathrm{k}}(\delta_{1s} - \delta_{1c})\right) \\
&= \frac{1}{2}(\delta_{1c} - \delta_{1s})\left(2\mathrm{F}_c + \frac{0 - \mathrm{F}_c}{\delta_{1s} - \delta_{1c}}(\delta_{1s} - \delta_{1c})\right) \\
&= \frac{1}{2}\mathrm{F}_c(\delta_{1c} - \delta_{1s})
\end{aligned}
\tag{6.43}
$$

The linear separation phase model is defined by a single parameter. Just as with the linear closure phase, the problem is overdetermined. A number of approaches may again be utilized. For all approaches, it is taken as a given that the terminus of closure values are known, irrespective of how they were determined.

1. Determine $\delta_{1s} = \mathbf{u}_{1s}$ from the data (at_s) and calculate the modeled separation phase stiffness, circular frequency, time of separation and IWR.
2. Use the known IWR to calculate the modeled value of δ_{1s} from Equation 6.43 followed by calculation of the modeled separation phase stiffness, circular frequency and time of separation.
3. Use the data to determine τ_s, calculate the separation phase modeled circular frequency, stiffness, terminus deflection (residual) and IWR.

With the linear model for the separation phase covered, we proceed with considering the power law model for the separation phase.

6.2.4 Power Separation Phase Force-Deflection Model

For the power law model for the separation phase, we first note that the form of the relationship shown by Equation 6.19 is inadequate. As a first option, we consider the form of Equation 6.39 and replace the terms with the corresponding terms from the power law formulation.

$$
\ln(\mathbf{F}) = \ln(\mathbf{F}_c) + \bar{\mathrm{a}}_1\left(\ln(\delta_1) - \ln(\delta_{1c})\right) \tag{6.44}
$$

Rearranging this equation using Equations 6.21 and 6.22 leads to the following result.

$$\ln\left(\frac{\mathbf{F}}{\mathbf{F}_c}\right)=\ln\left(\left(\frac{\delta_1}{\delta_{1c}}\right)^{\bar{a}_1}\right) \tag{6.45}$$

Exponentiating both sides of equality leads to the following result.

$$\frac{\mathbf{F}}{\mathbf{F}_c}=\left(\frac{\delta_1}{\delta_{1c}}\right)^{\bar{a}_1} \tag{6.46}$$

The form shown in Equation 6.46, rather than that shown in Equation 6.44, may aid in showing the problem with this formulation when $\delta_1=\delta_{1s}$. The corresponding force value is $\mathbf{F}_s=0$. This value, when used in Equation 6.44, results in the term on the left of the equality becoming negative infinity. When used in Equation 6.46, the term on the left of the equality reduces to zero. However, neither the residual deflection nor the peak deflection is zero-valued, thereby making the equation incorrect. Setting this issue aside for the moment, if one were to use Equation 6.46 to determine the IWR:

$$\begin{aligned}\text{IWR}&=-\int_{\delta_{1c}}^{\delta_{1s}}\mathbf{F}\cdot d\delta_1=-\int_{\delta_{1c}}^{\delta_{1s}}\mathbf{F}_c\left(\frac{\delta_1}{\delta_{1c}}\right)^{\bar{a}_1}\cdot d\delta_1\\&=\frac{\mathbf{F}_c}{\delta_{1c}^{\bar{a}_1}\left(\bar{a}_1+1\right)}\left(\delta_{1c}{}^{\bar{a}_1+1}-\delta_{1s}\bar{a}_1+1\right)\end{aligned} \tag{6.47}$$

For this model, when the IWR, $\mathbf{F}_c$, δ_{1c} and δ_{1s} are known, the solution for the separation phase power must be determined numerically.

A second option for the form of a power law separation phase model is a horizontally shifted model:

$$\mathbf{F}=\bar{a}_0\left(\delta_1-\delta_{1s}\right)^{\bar{a}_1} \tag{6.48}$$

This form correctly predicts a value of force of $\mathbf{F_s = 0}$ when $\delta_1 = \delta_{1s}$. When $\delta_1 = \delta_{1c}, \mathbf{F} = \mathbf{F_c}$, which allows for the following solution:

$$\bar{a}_0 = \frac{\mathbf{F_c}}{(\delta_{1c} - \delta_{1s})^{\bar{a}_1}} \tag{6.49}$$

Substitution of this result into Equation 6.48 leads to the following result:

$$\mathbf{F} = \frac{\mathbf{F_c}}{(\delta_{1c} - \delta_{1s})^{\bar{a}_1}} (\delta_1 - \delta_{1s})^{\bar{a}_1} \tag{6.50}$$

The IWR, based upon this formulation, is:

$$\begin{aligned} \mathrm{IWR} &= -\int_{\delta_{1c}}^{\delta_{1s}} \mathbf{F} \cdot d\delta_1 \\ &= -\int_{\delta_{1c}}^{\delta_{1s}} \left(\frac{\mathbf{F_c}}{(\delta_{1c} - \delta_{1s})^{\bar{a}_1}} (\delta_1 - \delta_{1s})^{\bar{a}_1} \right) \cdot d\delta_1 \\ &= \frac{\mathbf{F_c}}{(\delta_{1c} - \delta_{1s})^{\bar{a}_1}} \left(\frac{(\delta_{1c} - \delta_{1s})^{\bar{a}_1 + 1}}{\bar{a}_1 + 1} \right) \\ &= \frac{\mathbf{F_c}}{\bar{a}_1 + 1} (\delta_{1c} - \delta_{1s}) \end{aligned} \tag{6.51}$$

For this model, when the IWR, $\mathbf{F_c}, \delta_{1c}$ and δ_{1s} are known, the solution for the separation phase power can readily be determined in closed form as:

$$\bar{a}_1 = \frac{\mathbf{F_c}}{\mathrm{IWR}} (\delta_{1c} - \delta_{1s}) - 1 \tag{6.52}$$

A third option for the form of a power law separation phase model is a horizontally and vertically shifted model.

$$\mathbf{F} = \overline{\mathbf{F}}_0 + \overline{a}_0\left(\delta_1 - \delta_{1c}\right)^{\overline{a}_1} \tag{6.53}$$

At $\delta_1 = \delta_{1c}$:

$$\mathbf{F}_c = \overline{\mathbf{F}}_0 + \overline{a}_0\left(\delta_{1c} - \delta_{1c}\right)^{\overline{a}_1} \rightarrow \overline{\mathbf{F}}_0 = \mathbf{F}_c \tag{6.54}$$

At $\delta_1 = \delta_{1s}$:

$$\mathbf{F} = 0 = \overline{\mathbf{F}}_c + \overline{a}_0\left(\delta_{1s} - \delta_{1c}\right)^{\overline{a}_1} \rightarrow \overline{a}_0 = -\frac{\overline{\mathbf{F}}_c}{\left(\delta_{1s} - \delta_{1c}\right)^{\overline{a}_1}} \tag{6.55}$$

Substitution of the results from Equations 6.54 and 6.55 into Equation 6.53 leads to the following result:

$$\mathbf{F} = \mathbf{F}_c\left(1 - \frac{\left(\delta_1 - \delta_{1c}\right)^{\overline{a}_1}}{\left(\delta_{1s} - \delta_{1c}\right)^{\overline{a}_1}}\right) \tag{6.56}$$

The IWR for this formulation is:

$$\begin{aligned}
\text{IWR} &= -\int_{1C}^{\delta_{1S}} \mathbf{F} \cdot d\delta_1 \\
&= -\int_{\delta_{1c}}^{\delta_{1s}} \left(\mathbf{F}_c\left(1 - \frac{\left(\delta_1 - \delta_{1c}\right)^{\overline{a}_1}}{\left(\delta_{1s} - \delta_{1c}\right)^{\overline{d}_1}}\right)\right) \cdot d\delta_1 \\
&= \mathbf{F}_c\left(\frac{\overline{a}_1}{\overline{a}_1 + 1}\right)\left(\delta_{1c} - \delta_{1s}\right)
\end{aligned} \tag{6.57}$$

For this model, when the IWR, $\mathbf{F}_c$, δ_{1c} and δ_{1s} are known, the solution for the separation phase power can be determined as:

$$\overline{a}_1 = \left(\frac{\mathbf{F}_c}{\text{IWR}}(\delta_{1c} - \delta_{1s}) - 1\right)^{-1} \tag{6.58}$$

For the first formulation, substitution of $\{\delta_{1c}, \mathbf{F}_c\}$ into Equation 6.46 leads to the result of $1=1$. For the second formulation, substitution of the same data point into Equation 6.50 leads to the result of $\mathbf{F}_c = \mathbf{F}_c$. The same result is obtained by substitution of the same data point into Equation 6.56 in regard to the third formulation. Thusly, if a power law model is used for the closure phase followed by the use of another power law model for the separation phase, one must find a different method of relating the models outside of the force balance that must be present at the contemporaneous terminus of closure and start of separation. The approach taken herein is to use the square of the coefficient of restitution, which, for the subject FRMB impact case, is the ratio of the IWR to the IWA. For the first model, the ratio of Equation 6.47 to Equation 6.29 results in the following relationship between the terminus of closure and terminus of separation deflection values:

$$\delta_{1c} = \delta_{1s}\left(\frac{a_1+1}{a_1-\varepsilon^2\bar{a}_1+1-\varepsilon^2}\right)^{(\bar{a}_1+1)^{-1}} \tag{6.59}$$

For the second model, the ratio of Equation 6.51 to Equation 6.29 leads to the following:

$$\delta_{1c} = \delta_{1s}\left(1-\varepsilon^2\left(\frac{\bar{a}_1+1}{a_1+1}\right)\right)^{-1} \tag{6.60}$$

For the third model, the ratio of Equation 6.57 to equation 6.29 leads to the following:

$$\delta_{1c} = \delta_{1s}\left(1-\varepsilon^2\left(\frac{\bar{a}_1+1}{\bar{a}_1(a_1+1)}\right)\right)^{-1} \tag{6.61}$$

The results of each of the last three equations can be substituted into Equation 6.19 written at $\{\delta_{1c}, \mathbf{F}_c\}$. For the first model:

$$\mathbf{F}_c = a_0\left(\frac{a_1+1}{a_1-\varepsilon^2\bar{a}_1+1-\varepsilon^2}\right)^{a_1(\bar{a}_1+1)^{-1}}\delta_{1s}^{a_1} \tag{6.62}$$

For the second model:

$$\mathbf{F}_c = a_0\left(1-\varepsilon^2\left(\frac{\bar{a}_1+1}{a_1+1}\right)\right)^{-a_1}\delta_{1s}^{a_1} \tag{6.63}$$

For the third model:

$$\mathbf{F}_c = a_0\left(1-\varepsilon^2\left(\frac{\bar{a}_1+1}{\bar{a}_1\left(a_1+1\right)}\right)\right)^{-a_1}\delta_{1s}^{a_1} \tag{6.64}$$

For each of these three relationships, it can readily be seen that the form is of a constant multiplied by the terminus of separation deflection raised to the a_1 power. Thus, these relationships are log-linear as was the relationship given by Equation 6.19.

6.2.5 Power Law Kinematic Response

It was previously noted that the differential equation of motion for this model, given by Equation 6.27, is nonlinear and not amenable to being solved for in closed form. We may, however, determine an approximate solution using a numerical method. Direct time integration, using the explicit central difference method, is used herein. We start with the Taylor series expansion of a function $f(x)$ at $x = a$, which can be written as:

$$f(x) = \sum_{n=0}^{\infty}\frac{f^{(n)}(a)}{n!}(x-a)^n \tag{6.65}$$

Where $f^{(n)}(a)$ is the nth derivative of $f(x)$ evaluated at $x = a$. Expanding the summation leads to the following:

$$f(x) = f(a) + \left.\frac{df}{dx}\right|_{x=a}(x-a) + \frac{1}{2}\left.\frac{d^2 f}{dx^2}\right|_{x=a}(x-a)^2 + \cdots \tag{6.66}$$

Replacing x with the displacement **u**, replacing a with t_i, which denotes the time at the ith time step and replacing x with t leads to the following form:

$$\mathbf{u}(t)=\mathbf{u}(t_i)+\left.\frac{du}{dt}\right|_{t=t_i}(t-t_i)+\frac{1}{2}\left.\frac{d^2\mathbf{u}}{dt^2}\right|_{t=t_i}(t-t_i)^2+\cdots \quad (6.67)$$

When $t=t_i+\Delta t$, Equation 6.67 becomes:

$$\mathbf{u}(t_i+\Delta t)=\mathbf{u}(t_i)+\left.\frac{du}{dt}\right|_{t=t_i}\Delta t+\frac{1}{2}\left.\frac{d^2\mathbf{u}}{dt^2}\right|_{t=t_i}\Delta t^2+\cdots \quad (6.68)$$

When $t=t_i-\Delta t$, equation 6.67 becomes:

$$\mathbf{u}(t_i-\Delta t)=\mathbf{u}(t_i)-\left.\frac{du}{dt}\right|_{t=t_i}\Delta t+\frac{1}{2}\left.\frac{d^2\mathbf{u}}{dt^2}\right|_{t=t_i}\Delta t^2+\cdots \quad (6.69)$$

Switching to the overdot notation, truncating Equations 6.68 and 6.69 to the first two terms followed by the subtraction of the former from the latter leads to the following:

$$\dot{\mathbf{u}}(t_i)=\frac{\mathbf{u}(t_i+\Delta t)-\mathbf{u}(t_i-\Delta t)}{2\Delta t} \quad (6.70)$$

Truncating the same two equations to their first three terms followed by addition leads to the following:

$$\ddot{\mathbf{u}}(t_i)=\frac{\mathbf{u}(t_i+\Delta t)-2\mathbf{u}(t_i)+\mathbf{u}(t_i-\Delta t)}{\Delta t^2} \quad (6.71)$$

Substitution of Equation 6.71 into Equation 6.27 followed by rearrangement leads to the following solution:

$$\mathbf{u}(t_i + \Delta t) = 2u(t_i) + \frac{a_0}{m}\Delta t^2 \left(\mathbf{u}_1(t_i)\right)^{a_1} - \mathbf{u}(t_i - \Delta t) \tag{6.72}$$

For the first timestep, the solution for the displacement at the second timestep, requires the solution for the previous timestep. This can be determined by solving Equation 6.70 for the displacement $\mathbf{u}(t_i + \Delta t)$, substituting the result into Equation 6.71 and rearranging (for this, $i = 1, t = t_o = 0$).

$$\mathbf{u}(-\Delta t) = \mathbf{u}(t_o) - \Delta t\dot{\mathbf{u}}(t_o) + \frac{\Delta t^2}{2}\ddot{\mathbf{u}}(t_o) \tag{6.73}$$

For each time step, we first solve for the displacement at the next time step using Equation 6.72 and then solve for the velocity and acceleration at the current time step using Equations 6.70 and 6.71, respectively. Equation 6.72 is the correct equation for the closure phase. Once the velocity of the vehicle becomes negative, the form of this equation changes based upon the separation phase model of choice. For the first separation phase model, the displacement solution becomes:

$$\mathbf{u}(t_i + \Delta t) = 2u(t_i) + \frac{F_c \Delta t^2}{m\delta_{1c}^{\bar{a}_1}}\left(u_1(t_i)\right)^{\bar{a}_1} - u(t_i - \Delta t) \tag{6.74}$$

For the second separation phase model, the displacement solution becomes:

$$\mathbf{u}(t_i + \Delta t) = 2\mathbf{u}(t_i) + \frac{F_c \Delta t^2}{m\left(\delta_{1c} - \delta_{1s}\right)^{\bar{a}_1}}\left(\mathbf{u}_1(t_i) - \delta_{1s}\right)^{\bar{a}_1} - \mathbf{u}(t_i - \Delta t) \tag{6.75}$$

For the third separation phase model, the displacement solution becomes:

$$\mathbf{u}(t_i+\Delta t)=2\mathbf{u}(t_i)+\frac{F_c\Delta t^2}{m}\left(1-\frac{\left(\mathbf{u}(t_i)-\delta_{1c}\right)^{\bar{a}_1}}{\left(\delta_{1s}-\delta_{1c}\right)^{\bar{a}_1}}\right)-\mathbf{u}(t_i-\Delta t) \tag{6.76}$$

It should be readily apparent that only the first model does not require a priori knowledge of the terminus of separation deflection.

6.3 Methods and Materials

The models developed above were evaluated, on a preliminary basis, using data generated from a pair of controlled collision tests. The first test was NHTSA test number v03196, conducted as a baseline test, involving a frontal impact between a 1995 Chevrolet Lumina LS APV minivan (VIN: 2G1WN52XS9243954, transverse 3.4-liter six-cylinder engine, four speed automatic front wheel drive, mass =1781kg) and an instrumented FRMB (36 load cells arranged in four rows and nine columns). The second test was NHTSA test number v01990, conducted as a NCAP test, involving a frontal impact between a 1994 Pontiac Trans Sport minivan (VIN: 1GMDU06D5RT202095, transverse 3.1-liter six-cylinder engine, three speed automatic front wheel drive, mass =1962 kg) and an instrumented FRMB (configuration as per the previous). This pair of tests was chosen secondary to the former being a lower speed impact test (impact speed of 24.0KPH) and the latter being a higher speed impact test (impact speed of 56.5KPH) for the same vehicle platform.

The platform determination was based upon an examination of the components of the salient subsystems as documented by the parts catalog information produced by Mitchell International, Inc. (San Diego, California, USA). The structural components, between the platform year range of 1994 and 1996, were the same for the front inner structure, side structure (including the rails) and subframe. The components comprising the front suspension were substantially similar. Differences were noted with respect to the front bumper system. The part numbers differed for the impact absorber (referenced as such for the Chevrolet and referenced as a reinforcement for the Pontiac) and the impact bar. The part numbers for the front bumper mounting brackets were the same (referenced as impact bar reinforcements for the Chevrolet and as impact bar plates for the Pontiac).

For each test, the instrumentation data in NHTSA EV5 ASCII X-Y format, was imported directly from the NHTSA website. For each test, the EV5 file was imported into a symbolic mathematics software package (Mathematica v. 12.0; Wolfram Research, Inc.; Champaign, Illinois, USA). The same software package was used for all data reductions. The EV5 file was parsed using a custom written program that utilized the standardized EV5 data element designations. The load cell barrier instrumentation file names were extracted using string pattern matching. Each file was individually imported and filtered using a custom written Society of Automotive Engineers (SAE) channel frequency class (CFC) 60 filter. The data prior to time $t = t_0 = 0$ was discarded followed by transposing 100 milliseconds of data, at the start and end of the signal, about $(0,0)$, for signal padding. This padded signal was passed through the digital filter forward and then in reverse followed by discarding of the padding.

The filtered load cell data was summed, at each time point, to generate the total barrier force time history. The discrete time-deceleration history for the test vehicle was determined by dividing the total barrier force, at each time point, by the mass of the test vehicle. The discrete time velocity and displacement of the test vehicle, with the displacement equating to the deflection for the FRMB impact case, was determined by numerically integrating the time deceleration history. As expected, the velocity did not reach a zero value at a sampled data point but instead reached that value between a pair of immediately adjacent data points. This was also the case for the acceleration in regard to the separation phase analysis. For both the velocity and the acceleration, the data points that bounded the zero value were used to generate a linear interpolation function and determine the time at which the abscissa was crossed. The same indices for the other kinematic responses were then linearly interpolated and solved at the time values at which the abscissa was crossed from the previous step.

The linear model for the closure phase was evaluated in accordance with the four methods described in Section 6.2.1. The linear model for the separation phase was evaluated in accordance with the three methods described in Section 6.2.3. The power law model for the closure phase consisted of using Equation 6.30 to determine the power value and using Equation 6.28 to determine the coefficient value. The power law model for the separation phase was implemented for each of the three methods detailed in Section 6.2.4. Finally, the numerically integrated kinematic response, for the power law model, was determined using Equation 6.72

for the closure phase displacement and Equation 6.74 for the separation phase displacement.

6.4 Results

The data reduction for both collision tests, as expected, produced total barrier force time histories that were indicative, even under the modeling constraints of uniaxiality, of a multiple degree of freedom (MDOF) system response. This is clearly evidenced by multiple, interval, substantive, extrema rather than a singular extremum. The total barrier force time history for both tests is shown in Figure 6.2. For the lower speed test (i.e. v03196), the closure phase parameters were determined to be the following: $t_c = 85.83\text{msec}, \mathbf{u}_{1c} = \delta_{1c} = 0.3732\,\text{m}, \mathbf{a}_{1c} = -122.1\,\text{m}/\text{sec}^2, \mathbf{F}_c = 2.17410^5\,\text{N}$ and $\text{IWA} = 3.95810^4\,\text{J}$. The closure phase parameters for the higher speed test (i.e. v01990) were determined to be the following: $\text{t}_c = 99.90\text{msec}, \mathbf{u}_{1c} = \delta_{1c} = 0.8244\,\text{m}, \mathbf{a}_{1c} = -96.40\,\text{m}/\text{sec}^2, \mathbf{F}_c = 1.89110^5\,\text{N}$ and $\text{IWA} = 2.41610^5\,\text{J}$.

The separation phase parameters for the lower severity collision test were determined to be the following: $t_s = 179.2\text{msec}\left(\tau_s = 93.34\text{msec}\right)$, $\mathbf{u}_{1s} = \delta_{1s} = 0.2186\text{m}, \mathbf{v}_{1s} = -1.943\text{m}/\text{sec}$ and $\text{IWR} = 3.36110^3\,\text{J}$. The separation phase parameters for the higher severity collision test were determined to be the following: $t_s = 181.6\text{msec}\left(\tau_s = 81.71\,\text{msec}\right)$, $\mathbf{u}_{1s} = \delta_{1s} = 0.6952\text{m}, \mathbf{v}_{1s} = -2.024\text{m}/\text{sec}$ and $\text{IWR} = 4.01810^3\,\text{J}$. The coefficient of restitution for the lower severity test was -0.2914 and for the higher severity test was -0.1290. The acceleration, velocity and displacement

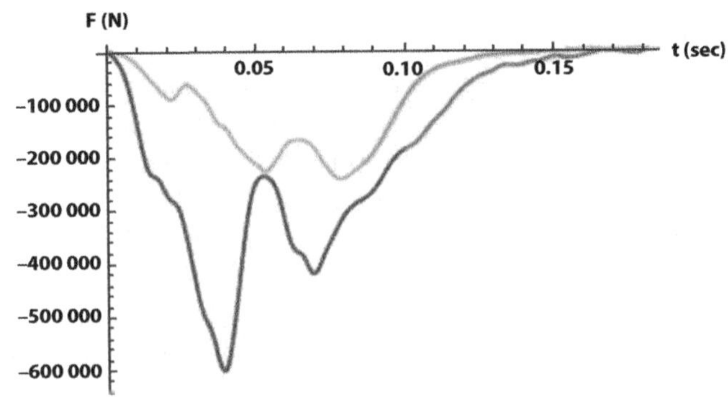

Figure 6.2 Total barrier force time histories for test v01990 (blue for closure, red for separation) and test v03196 (orange for closure, green for separation).

(deflection) time histories, for both tests, are shown in Figures 6.3 to 6.5, respectively.

The acceleration time histories mirror the total barrier force time histories, as expected, given that the former are merely the latter scaled, along the ordinate, by the inverse of the mass of the corresponding test vehicle. The responses for both collision severities were similar. The initial increase in the response magnitude was followed by a slight drop in the lower severity test and a region of reduced slope in the higher severity test. This was then followed by a double peak response, with an interposed local minimum, followed by a relatively lengthy tail response. The peak force

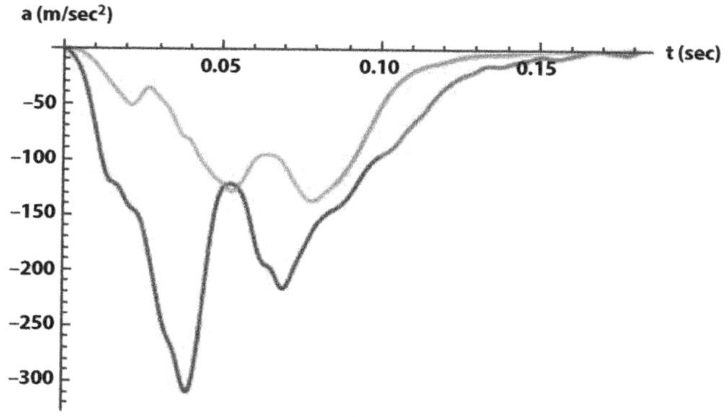

Figure 6.3 Acceleration time histories for test v01990 (blue for closure, red for separation) and test v03196 (orange for closure, green for separation).

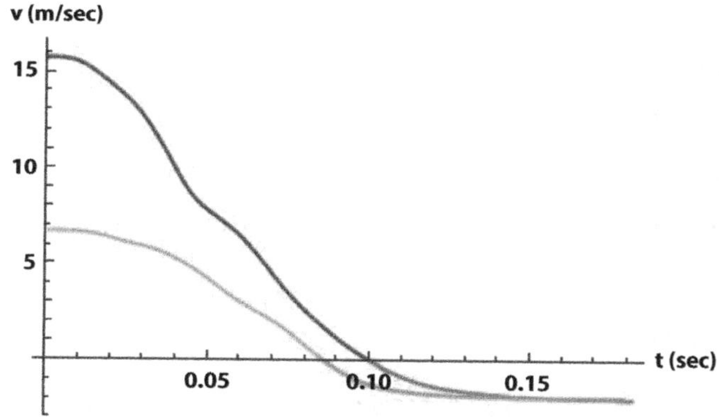

Figure 6.4 Velocity time histories for test v01990 (blue for closure, red for separation) and test v03196 (orange for closure, green for separation).

magnitude, for both cases, occurred during closure rather than at the terminus of closure. The smoothing effect of integration can readily be seen in the velocity time histories shown in Figure 6.4 and the displacement (deflection) responses shown in Figure 6.5. For both tests, the peak deflection occurred at the terminus of closure. The force deflection response for the two tests is shown in Figure 6.6.

The force-deflection response for both tests is quite similar, but not an exact overlay, over approximately the first 0.130 meters of deflection. The local minimum seen in the acceleration response for the lower severity test and the region of reduced slope seen in the higher severity test are

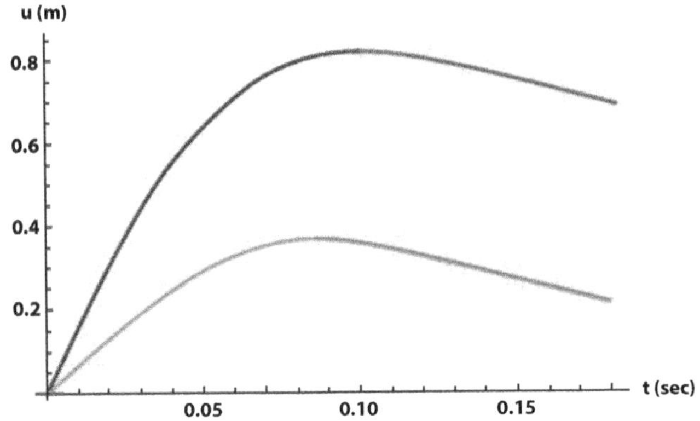

Figure 6.5 Displacement (deflection) time histories for test v01990 (blue for closure, red for separation) and test v03196 (orange for closure, green for separation).

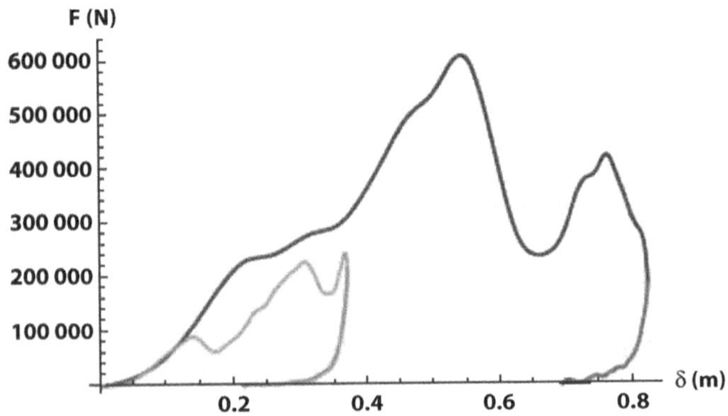

Figure 6.6 Force-deflection responses for test v01990 (blue for closure, red for separation) and test v03196 (orange for closure, green for separation).

both manifested in the force-deflection response. For the lower severity test, the peak force magnitude occurs with the second peak of the double peak response. For the higher severity test, the peak force magnitude occurs with the first peak of the double peak response. The peak deflection, for the lower severity case, occurs much closer to the peak collision force, when compared to the higher severity test.

The linear model fits for the closure phase force-deflection response for the higher severity collision test are shown in Figure 6.7. The first model, based upon the known values for δ_{1c} and $\mathbf{F}_c$, resulted in values for k, ω, t_c and the IWA of $2.294\ 10^5\ N/m, 10.81 sec^{-1}, 145.3 msec$ and 7.79610^4 J, respectively. The second model, based upon the known values for δ_{1c} and the IWA resulted in values for k, ω, t_c and $\mathbf{F}_c$ of $7.11010^5\ N/m, 19.04 sec^{-1}, 82.52 msec$ and 5.86210^5 J. The third model, based upon the known time at which the closure phase terminates, resulted in values for $k, \omega, \delta_{1c}, \mathbf{F}_c$ and IWA of $4.85110^5\ N/m, 15.72 sec^{-1}, 9.98110^{-1}\ m, 4.842\,10^5\ N$ and 2.41610^5 J, respectively.

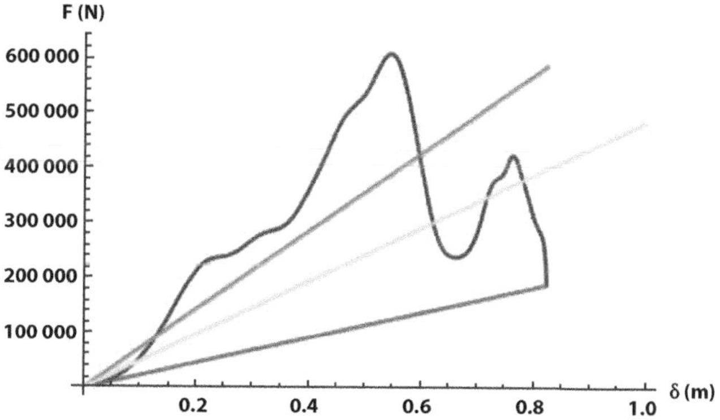

Figure 6.7 Closure phase force-deflection response for test v01990 (blue) with the first, second and third models, as per the text, shown by the red, green and yellow curves, respectively. The linear model fits for the closure phase force-deflection response for the lower severity collision test is shown in Figure 6.8. The first model, based upon the known values for δ_{1c} and $\mathbf{F}_c$, resulted in values for k, ω, t_c and the IWA of $5.827\ 10^5\ N/m, 18.09 sec^{-1}, 86.84 msec$ and 4.05710^4 J, respectively. The second model, based upon the known values for δ_{1c} and the IWA resulted in values for k, ω, t_c and $\mathbf{F}_c$ of $5.68410^5\ N/m, 17.87 sec^{-1}, 87.92 msec$ and 2.12110^5 J. The third model, based upon the known time at which the closure phase terminates, resulted in values for $k, \omega, \delta_{1c}, \mathbf{F}_c$ and IWA of $5.96510^5\ N/m, 18.30 sec^{-1}, 3.64310^{-1}\ m, 2.173\,10^5\ N$ and 3.95810^4 J, respectively.

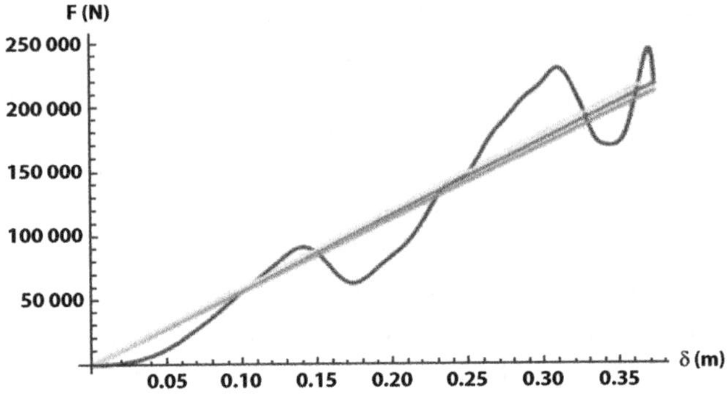

Figure 6.8 Closure phase force-deflection response for test v03196 (blue) with the first, second and third models, as per the text, shown by the red, green and yellow curves, respectively.

For the separation phase of the lower severity test, the three linear models consisted of (1) using δ_{1s} from t_s, (2) using the IWR and (3) using τ_s. For the first case, the modeled values for the stiffness, circular frequency, τ_s and IWR are 1.40710^6 N/m, 28.10sec^{-1}, 55.90msec and 3.36010^4 J, respectively. For the second case, the modeled values for the stiffness, circular frequency, δ_{1s} and τ_s are 7.03310^6 N/m, 62.84sec^{-1}, 3.42210^{-1} m and 25.00msec, respectively. For the third case, the modeled values for the stiffness, circular frequency, δ_{1s} and IWR are 5.04310^5 N/m, 16.83sec^{-1}, -5.79610^{-2} m and 4.68710^4 J, respectively. These results are shown in Figure 6.9.

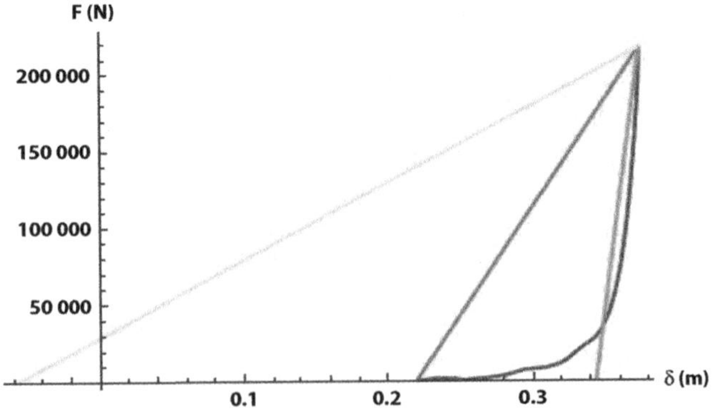

Figure 6.9 Separation phase force-deflection response for test v03196 (blue) with the first, second and third models, as per the text, shown by the red, green and yellow curves, respectively.

For the higher severity test, the modeled values generated by the first case, for the stiffness, circular frequency, τ_s and IWR are $1.46310^6 \, N/m, 27.31 sec^{-1}, 57.52 msec$ and $3.53610^5 \, J$, respectively. For the second case, the modeled values for the stiffness, circular frequency, δ_{1s} and τ_s are $4.45110^6 \, N/m, 47.63 sec^{-1}, 7.82010^{-1} \, m$ and $32.98 msec$, respectively. For the third case, the modeled values for the stiffness, circular frequency, δ_{1s} and IWR are $7.25110^5 \, N/m, 19.22 sec^{-1}, 5.636\,10^{-1} \, m$ and $2.46710^4 \, J$, respectively. These results are shown in Figure 6.10.

The power law model, as a singular model for the closure phase of the higher severity collision test, based upon the data, failed to meet the required criterion of $(F_c\delta_{1c})/IWA > 1$. The value of the evaluated term on the left of the inequality was determined to be 0.6453. For the lower severity collision test, the value of this term was determined to be 2.050, which resulted in a value of $a_0 = 6.12310^5$ (units of N per meter raised to the a_1 power) and an a_1 value of 1.050. The overlay of this model, upon the closure phase data, is shown graphically in Figure 6.11.

For the lower severity test, the first model produced a power term of 23.14 and with a residual force magnitude of $9{,}147\,10^{-1} \, N$. The second model produced a power term of 9.001. The third model produced a power term of 1.11110^{-1}. The three model fits to the separation phase force-deflection response are shown in Figure 6.13.

For the lower severity collision test, the modeled kinematic response, based upon the power law model for the closure phase followed by a power law model for the separation phase, was evaluated by means of numerical integration. Because there was only one model for the closure phase,

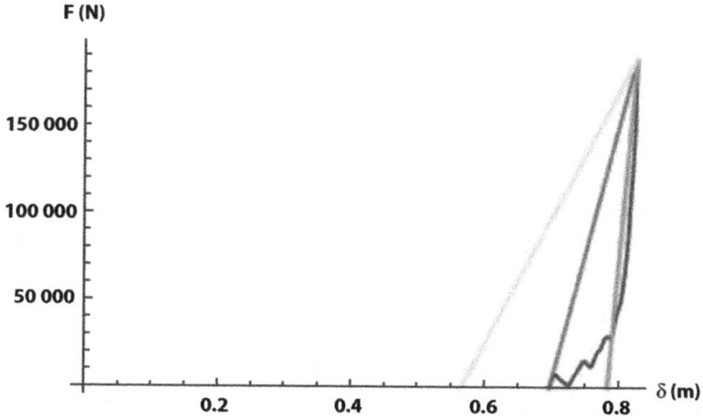

Figure 6.10 Separation phase force-deflection response for test v01990 (blue) with the first, second and third models, as per the text, shown by the red, green and yellow curves, respectively.

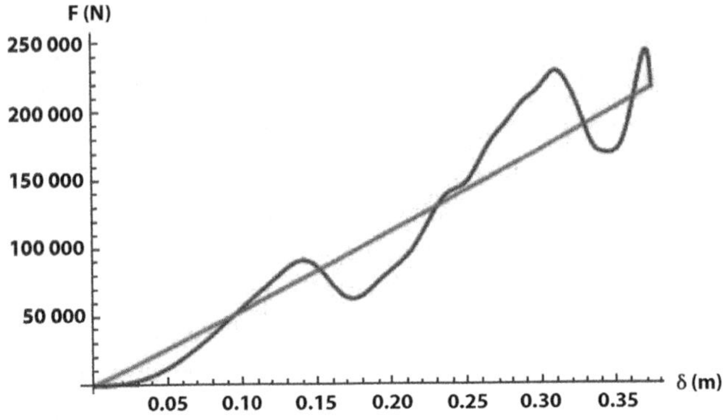

Figure 6.11 Closure phase force-deflection response for test v03196 (blue) with the power law model fit overlayed (red). For the higher severity collision test, the separation phase power law model exemplified by Equation 6.46 resulted in a power term of 37.75 and with a residual force magnitude, at the terminus of separation, of 302.5 N. The second model, for this test, exemplified by Equation 6.50 resulted in a power term of 5.084. The third model, for this test, exemplified by Equation 6.56 resulted in a power term of 1.96710^{-1}. The three models fit to the separation phase force-deflection response are shown in Figure 6.12.

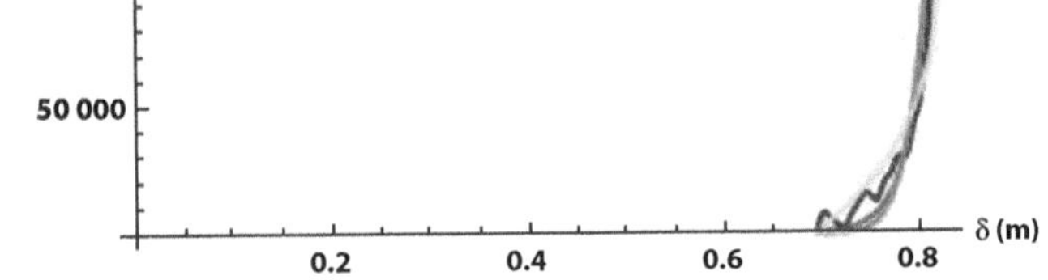

Figure 6.12 Separation phase force-deflection response for test v01990 (blue) with the first, second and third models, as per the text, shown by the red, green and yellow curves, respectively.

the differences in the modeled kinematics were due to the three different power law models for the separation phase. The models are referenced as before. For the first model, the values of t_s,δ_{1s}, velocity at separation and acceleration at separation are $177.8\text{msec}, 2.18210^{-1}\,\text{m}, -1.943\,\text{m/sec}$

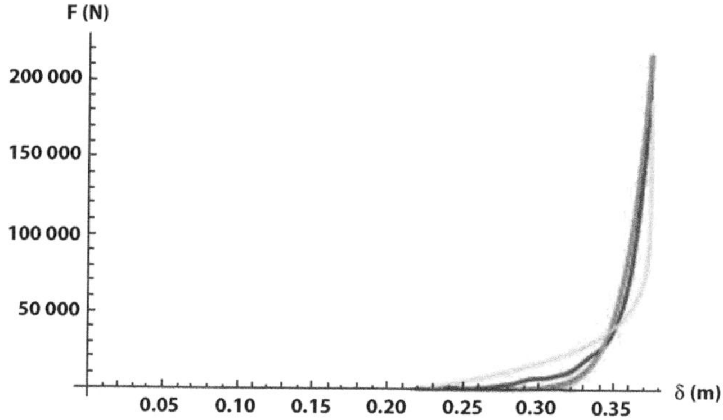

Figure 6.13 Separation phase force-deflection response for test v03196 (blue) with the first, second and third models, as per the text, shown by the red, green and yellow curves, respectively.

and $4.93510^{-4}\,\text{m}/\text{sec}^2$, respectively. The values for the second model are $182.9\text{msec}, 2.07810^{-1}\,\text{m}, -1.943\,\text{m}/\text{sec}$ and $0\,\text{m}/\text{sec}^2$, respectively. Finally, for the third model, the values are $194.6\text{msec}, 2.18610^{-1}\,\text{m}, -1.943\,\text{m}/\text{sec}$ and $0\,\text{m}/\text{sec}^2$. The results are shown, graphically, for the acceleration, velocity and displacement, in Figures 6.14 to 6.16, respectively.

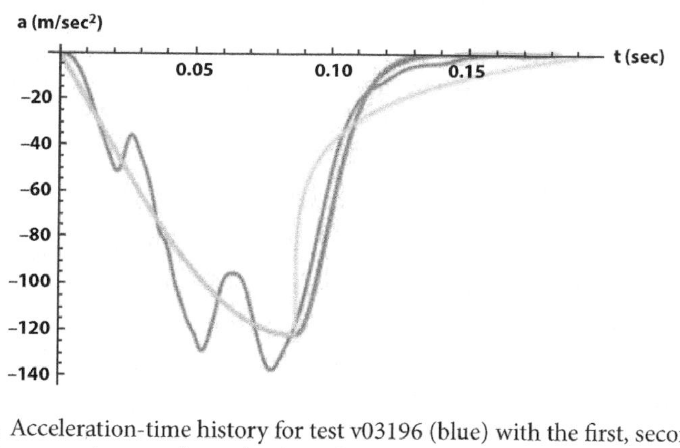

Figure 6.14 Acceleration-time history for test v03196 (blue) with the first, second and third models, as per the text, shown by the red, green and yellow curves, respectively.

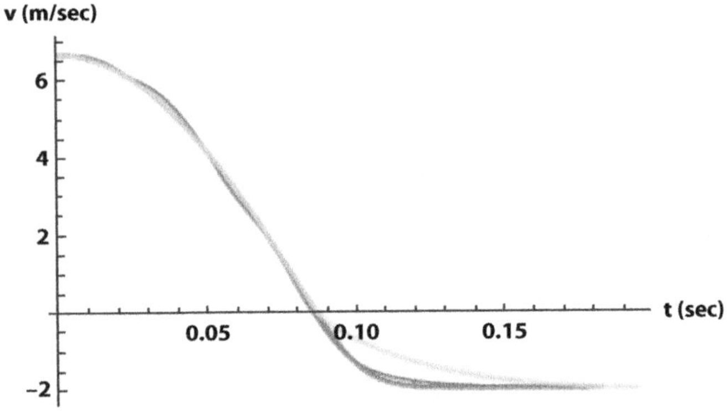

Figure 6.15 Velocity-time history for test v03196 (blue) with the first, second and third models, as per the text, shown by the red, green and yellow curves, respectively.

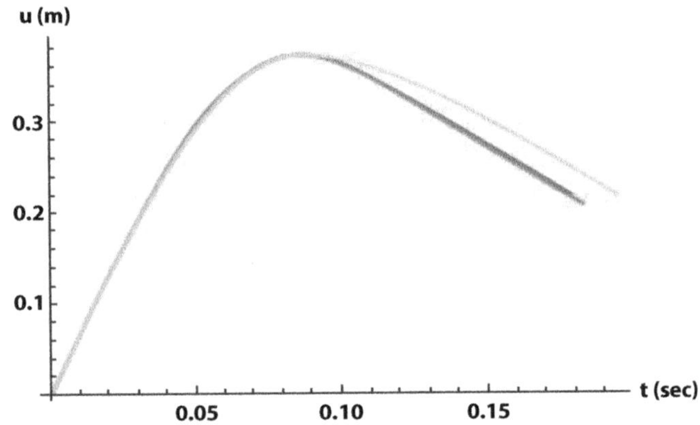

Figure 6.16 Displacement-time history for test v03196 (blue) with the first, second and third models, as per the text, shown by the red, green and yellow curves, respectively.

6.5 Discussion

Residual damage-based methods can readily be viewed as one of the simplest approaches for determining quantitative estimates for motor vehicle collision severity. For model parameter quantification from controlled collision test data, the data reduction process does not require the evaluation of any of the dynamic instrumentation data that is generated during the collision test. In contrast, even the simplest dynamic modeling approaches require significant, albeit readily implementable, data reduction. The SDOF models presented in this work fall within this classification. This statement is made because of the use of ubiquitous uniaxiality coupled with a single lumped mass for the test vehicle. The first condition, as noted previously, greatly simplifies the analysis by removing the necessity for determining the time-varying DCM for each local frame of reference that is salient to the analysis. The second condition reduces the number of second order differential equations of motion to unity.

The MDOF nature of the system response during closure, even for the uniaxial approximation, can readily be seen by simple examination of Figure 6.6. This is exemplified by the local extrema and lack of a ubiquitous monotonic response. These local responses are due to frontal subsystems such as the front bumper system, front frame, engine, front wheels, and suspension. The impact of these subsystems, within the context of a SDOF modeling approach, is variable. For the lower severity collision test, as shown in Figure 6.8, the deviation of the response from the case of a purely monotonically increasing function is limited and the force at the terminus of the closure phase is close in magnitude to the peak force. Thus, the three linear fits are closely approximated to each other, as well as the actual response (when compared with the higher collision severity test). This was clearly not the case for the closure phase of the higher severity collision test. Visual inspection of Figures 6.2 and 6.3 shows that the peak force and acceleration occur relatively early during the closure phase. This is then manifested with a peak force that occurs prior to the peak deflection as seen in Figures 6.6 and 6.7. From the latter, it can readily be seen that the three linear closure phase models diverge. Furthermore, none of the models provides a good fit for the data.

One of the findings of the subject work, which is a novel finding with respect to the application context, is that the power law model, as a single model for the entirety of the closure phase, has a limitation based upon the inequality $\mathbf{F}_c\delta_c / \mathrm{IWA} > 1$. This inequality did not hold for the higher severity collision test considered in the subject work. One may readily make the statement that collision tests with closure phase force-deflection responses that are similar to the response of the subject higher severity collision test, in regard to an early peak force magnitude and relatively low force magnitude at the terminus of closure, would also result in the inequality not holding. This statement is based upon deterministic considerations. One may further state that the set of characteristics found in the closure phase response of the higher severity collision test represent one class, but not necessarily the only class, of response for which the inequality would not hold. The lower severity collision test, on the other hand, provided data for which the inequality was held. The closure phase power law fit, however, was very close to being linear. It is unclear if this approximate linear fit represents a limitation on the use of a single power law function for modeling the closure phase.

Two additional points regarding the closure phase response are worthy of discussion. The first point is that the force deflection response for the approximate first 0.130 meters of deflection is quite similar between the higher and lower severity collision tests. That such similitude exists over a non-trivial deflection magnitude is more germane than the magnitude itself. The finding shows that the initial portion of the response follows a very similar path for the two collision severities in question. The slight differences can be attributed to differences between the test vehicles, variations associated with the implementation of the testing protocols and response contributions, albeit minor, from other load paths or a combination. The contributions of these other load paths become more substantial in the higher severity collision test, following the initial portion of similitude. The second point is that it is highly unlikely that there would be a substantially different response for a lower severity collision, for the deflection regime starting at zero and terminating at the appropriate value before 0.130 meters of deflection. This statement holds due to the fact the subject lower severity collision test must 'pass through' the same response regime, engaging the same vehicle frontal systems, in the same manner, for impacts with a lower severity.

For both tests, the linear modeling approach faired quite poorly, as expected, for the separation phase. This was most apparent for the third model, for the higher severity collision test, as shown in Figure 6.9. Qualitatively, the separation phase response for both tests can be characterized as being biphasic. The first phase of the response consists of a steep drop in the force magnitude with a minimum but finite decrement in the deflection. The second phase of the response consists of a steep decrease in the deflection with a minimum but finite decrement in the collision force. The transition between the two phases is relatively smooth (rather than abrupt). For both tests, the power law modeling approach provided a substantially better fit to the separation response when compared with the linear model fits. For the higher severity collision test, as evidenced by Figure 6.12, the first and second separation phase power law models were essentially overlayed and provided a better fit to the actual data than the third model. Again, it should be noted that the first model, by its design, does not predict a zero valuation for the force at the terminus of the separation phase. These findings are also apt for the lower severity collision test, as per Figure 6.13.

For the lower severity collision test, the first two models for the separation phase, again, were virtually overlayed in regard to kinematic responses shown in Figures 6.14 to 6.16. Both models provide a better fit to the actual data when compared to the fit provided by the third model. With respect to the terminus of the closure phase for the collision test, the modeled responses lag the actual response secondary to the former falling between the time steps of the latter. The impact of this is most apparent on the acceleration response as shown in Figure 6.14. The differences between the actual data and the first two models, in regard to the acceleration response, as expected, are minimized for both the velocity and displacement responses (as per Figures 6.15 and 6.16, respectively).

While only two tests were considered in the subject work, there are a number of findings that are of utility when one considers future development. The first, which retains both the SDOF approach and ubiquitous uniaxiality, is the consideration of a multistep power law formulation for the separation phase. This consideration derives from the fact that the model coefficients, for each power law formulation, for the two tests, differed. Ideally, for a given platform and a given model, the model parameters should be the same across all salient collisions that traverse the same severity domain. The second consideration for future development is the development of a MDOF model while retaining ubiquitous uniaxiality. Such an approach would be most useful for collision tests with a closure phase similar to the higher severity test considered in the subject work. This consideration requires evaluation of test vehicle fixed accelerometer data. The third consideration for future development is the relaxation of ubiquitous uniaxiality. This consideration requires one or both of the following two approaches. The first is the use of vehicle fixed accelerometer data. For a typical test, the configuration of the vehicle fixed accelerometer array allows for the determination of biaxial motion, in the $\mathbf{x}-\mathbf{z}$ plane, for the body of the test vehicle. The second approach for determining the kinematic response of the test vehicle is by means of videogrammetry. In theory, the process can be undertaken using video from a single fixed position camera. However, it is likely that the analysis of video data from multiple camera locations would be the most appropriate for accurately quantifying the response in three dimensions.

References

1. Sharma, D., Stern, S., Brophy, J., Choi, E.-H., An overview of NHTSA's crash reconstruction software WinSMASH. *Proceedings: 20th International Technical Conference on the Enhanced Safety of Vehicles*, Lyon, France, June 18-21, 2007, Paper number 07-0211.

2. Campbell, K.L., Energy as a basis for accident severity - A preliminary study, Doctoral dissertation, Automotive Engineering, University of Wisconsin, 1972.
3. Campbell, K.L., Energy basis for collision severity. Society of Automotive Engineers technical paper number 740565, 1974.
4. McHenry, R.R., A comparison of results obtained with different analytical techniques for reconstruction of highway accidents. Society of Automotive Engineers technical paper number 750893, 1975.
5. Emori, R.I., Analytical approach to automobile collisions. Society of Automotive Engineers technical paper number 680016, 1968.
6. Singh, J., A fundamental reconsideration of the CRASH3 damage analysis algorithm: the case against uniform ubiquitous linearity between BEV, peak collision force magnitude and residual damage depth. *Traffic Inj. Prev.*, 14, 7, 18–24, 2013.
7. Strother, C.E., Woolley, R.L., James, M.B., Warner, C.Y., Crush energy in accident reconstruction. Society of Automotive Engineers technical paper number 860371, 1986.
8. McHenry, R.R. and McHenry, B.G., A revised damage analysis procedure for the CRASH computer program. Society of Automotive Engineers technical paper number 861894, 1986.
9. McHenry, R.R. and McHenry, B.G., Effects of restitution in the application of crush coefficients. Society of Automotive Engineers technical paper number 970960, 1997.
10. Neptune, J.A., Crush stiffness coefficients, restitution constants and a revision of CRASH3 and SMAC. Society of Automotive Engineers technical paper number 980029, 1998.
11. Kerkhoff, J.F., Husher, S.E., Varat, M.S., Busenga, A.M., Hamilton, K., An investigation into vehicle frontal impact stiffness, BEV and repeated testing for reconstruction. Society of Automotive Engineers technical paper number 930899, 1993.
12. Woolley, R.L., Non-linear damage analysis in accident reconstruction. Society of Automotive Engineers technical paper number 2001-01-0504, 2001.
13. Singh, J. and Perry, J., Multilinear and nonlinear power low modeling of motor vehicle force-deflection response for uniaxial front impacts. *Accid. Reconstr. J.*, 18, 6, 30–38, 62, 2008.
14. Singh, J., Further developments regarding the dynamic modeling of motor vehicle collision response using the SDOF approach. *Collision*, 8, 1, 10–31, 2013.
15. Carpenter, N.J. and Welcher, J.B., Stiffness and crush energy analysis for vehicle collision and its relationship to barrier equivalent velocity (BEV). Society of Automotive Engineers technical paper number 2001-010500, 2001.

7

Key Matrix Generation Techniques for Hill Cipher Cryptosystem – A Comparative Study

Maharshi S. Pandya[1], Vrajesh S. Brahmbhatt[1], Arvik J. Shah[1], Rajeev Kumar Gupta[1*] and Abhijit Kumar[2]

[1]*Department of Computer Science and Engineering, Pandit Deendayal Energy University, Gandhinagar, Gujarat, India*
[2]*School of Computer Science, University of Petroleum and Energy Studies (UPES), Dehradun, Uttarakhand, India*

Abstract
Hill cipher cryptosystem is a linear algebra-based classical polygraphic substitution cipher-based technique. If the encryption key matrix (also called the key matrix) is not invertible, obtaining the de- crypted text from the encrypted text is not possible. This is because the key matrix must follow some criteria for decryption to be possible: The encryption key matrix must be invertible with respect to the modulo number. If the key matrix is generated randomly, there is a possibility that the key matrix's inverse does not exist. This paper attempts to compare two new techniques for generating the key matrix for the hill cipher cryptosystem. The proposed algorithm has been developed keeping consideration of security aspects, performance of the generated key matrix, ease of implementation, and limitations. A comparative study has been performed by utilizing a key matrix generation for Hill Cipher using Magic Rectangle (KMGHCMR)" and "Novel Methods of Generating a Self-Invertible Matrix for Hill Cipher (NMGSIMHC)."

***Keywords*:** Hill cipher, key matrix generation, self-invertible matrix, computational complexity, magic rectangle, cryptanalysis, encryption, decryption

**Corresponding author*: rajeevmanit12276@gmail.com

Tanupriya Choudhury, Abhijit Kumar, Ravi Tomar, S. Balamurugan and Ankit Vishnoi (eds.) Cyber-Physical Systems for Innovating and Transforming Society 5.0, (161–174) © 2025 Scrivener Publishing LLC

7.1 Introduction

In the realms of information security and cryptography, the processes of encryption and decryption are two of the most fundamental operations. They play a crucial part in the protection of sensitive data and the maintenance of confidentiality, integrity, and authenticity in the realm of information security. In this article, we try to compare and analyze two unique approaches to producing the key matrix for the Hill cipher cryptosystem [1, 2]. The two techniques that will be compared are: "Generation of Key Matrix for Hill Cipher using Magic Rectangle (KMGHCMR)" and "Novel Methods of Generating a Self-Invertible Matrix for Hill Cipher" (NMGSIMHC). The development of a definitive algorithm for generating the key matrix is important to address the limitation associated with adopting a random key matrix in the encryption process of the Hill cipher algorithm. This limitation arises from the potential inability to decrypt the encrypted message when the matrix lacks invertibility. The comparison is based on four factors:

- Security Aspect: Which method is more secure computationally?
- Quality of the techniques: Which method has a lesser computational cost?
- Implementation ease: Which method can be more easily implemented?
- Limitations: What are the tradeoffs of both methods?

7.2 Literature Review

In [1], a deterministic approach for creating key matrices in Hill cipher encryption was given by K. Mani and M. Viswambari, which assured greater security by generating higher-order key matrices based on m using a magic rectangle of order mn. The suggested approach increases computational efficiency while resolving the issue of acquiring adequate key matrices in a single run. It is not necessary to compute matrix inverses during decryption thanks to the methods Acharya *et al.* provided in [2] for creating self-invertible matrices for Hill cipher encryption. Since inverse computation is not necessary for Hill cipher decryption, they placed a strong emphasis on creating encryption matrices that are their own inverse. Their approaches intended to overcome the drawback of the classic Hill cipher requiring nonsingular matrices for unique decryption. Using a modified version of the Hill Cipher algorithm (HCA), Jilna NT and N. Mangathayaru devised a safe method for transferring medical data in [3]. To find data leakage, they concentrated on channel security and proposed the Agent Guilt model. The publication also included an implementation example, discussed relevant research, and addressed algorithms. K. Mani and R. Mahendran proposed a method for producing a self-invertible matrix for the Hill cipher encryption algorithm in [4]. They generated the key matrix using traditional ciphers such as Playfair and ADFGVX, avoiding the requirement for matrix inversion during decryption. Their method was designed to reduce computational complexity. Acharya, Patra, and Panda presented a permuted matrix formulation in [5] that randomly permutes the key matrix's columns and rows to generate distinct keys for each block of data encryption. This permutation approach expands the key space while improving security against crypt analysis. They also presented a reiterative matrix creation approach that generates a key matrix that leads to the identity matrix after exponentiation. The authors aimed to improve the security of the Hill cipher by producing different key matrices in this manner. Using the Hill cipher algorithm, Shanmugam and Loganathan in [6] suggested techniques for producing self-invertible matrices. They emphasized the benefit of decryption having less processing complexity because matrix inversion was no longer necessary. The study concentrated on methods to raise the level of security and reliability of encryption and decryption operations. Using a randomized technique, N. Krishna and K. Madhuravani devised a robust Hill cipher algorithm in [7]. By creating numerous ciphertexts for a single plaintext, the change attempted to increase security and counter known plaintext assaults. The strategy used a probabilistic key generator, which created more difficulty in obtaining the decryption key for attackers.

In [8], Adi Narayana Reddy *et al.* proposed a variation to the HCA that makes use of circulant matrices. They concentrated on lowering computing complexity by creating self-invertible matrices, which eliminates the requirement for matrix inversion during decryption. Their strategy attempted to improve the Hill cipher's security while keeping its efficiency. Rahul R. Ravan and Atul R. Nigavekar introduced a modified HCA in [9] to overcome the non-invertible issue matrices utilized for encryption. They developed a method for adjusting the encryption key for each block encryption, resulting in increased security. They also demonstrated a method for producing self-invertible matrices, which eliminates the computational cost associated with determining the inverse during decryption. For the encryption and decryption of images Prerna *et al.* [10] suggested a modified Hill cipher approach. To avoid the requirement for matrix inversion during decryption and lessen computing complexity, they developed a technique for creating self-invertible key matrices. With the exception of photographs with uniform backgrounds, their approach was effective for both encrypting and decrypting grayscale and color images. Elliptic curve cryptography (ECC) and the Hill cipher were proposed by Komal Agrawal and Anju Gera in as a way to increase the security and effectiveness of encryption techniques [11]. Along with the Hill Cipher's linearity, they emphasized the use of ECC's smaller key size and faster computations. The authors emphasized the benefit of the self-invertible matrix used in the Hill Cipher, which decreased computational complexity by requiring no matrix inversion during decryption.

In [12], N. Thangarasu and A. SelvaKumar presented a Lester HCA-based encryption method with an optional key matrix with the goal to solve the original Hill cipher algorithm's non-invertible key matrix issue, which prevents decryption. By using their method, an involutory key ma trix was created, allowing encryption and decryption to be performed on the same matrix without the need to find the inverse. As a result, the calculation was made simpler and more effective. Andysah Putera Utama Siahaan proposed using genetic algorithms in [13] to optimize key generation for Hill cipher encryption, with the goal of minimizing computation time spent searching for keys with a determinant of one, minimizing the requirement to compute matrix inverses during decryption. Rotondwa Munzhelele and Colin Chibaya proposed in [14, 15] presented a methodology for the creation of sets of invertible matrices with high orders, which can be utilized as keys in the encryption process of the Hill cipher. Their goal was to improve security through increasing matrix order, dynamically generating one-time pad keys, and randomly selecting a dif ferent key from the pool for each encryption. The method generates high order invertible matrices above order 4, stores them in a pool, and selects one as the encryption key. This prevents repeated use of the same key and renders brute- force attacks harder to execute. When compared to low order keys, randomly chosen high order keys increase security.

Hasoun, Rajja *et al.* [16] proposed a new approach for the classical Hill cipher based on public key cryptography. They aimed to improve security by avoiding the linearity of the original Hill cipher using RSA and securely and dynamically generating the Hill cipher matrix rather than using a static matrix. The proposed method generates an involutory key matrix, employs RSA encryption on the Hill cipher output, and requires both private and public keys for decryption. This makes this modification of the traditional Hill cipher cryptosystem more secure against known plain-text attacks than the original. Regarding an alternative approach aimed at mitigating known-plaintext attacks, a distinctive technique was introduced by Barrieta, Raymond *et al.* [17]. Their proposition involved a novel adaptation of the Hill cipher algorithm, incorporating Myszkowski transposition. They used partitioned keys from the Hill cipher matrix to perform multiple rounds of Myszkowski transposition before and after the Hill cipher encryption. This added complication was intended to mitigate known-plain-text attacks. Their method generated invertible Hill cipher keys and passed statistical tests, demonstrating greater security and a 25.7 percent faster runtime than previous modifications.

7.3 Hill Cipher

In today's information age, there is an utmost need to protect communications between parties from malicious threats. Cryptography is the study of encryption and decryption. It also plays an instrumental role to secure the transactions, correspondence, etc., that take place between two parties. Be it mobile communication, sending private messages or emails, financial transactions, or sharing secret information between government entities, communication can be made secure by using cryptographic methods. Nowadays, cryptography is recognized as a subfield in both computer science and mathematics. Furthermore, it exhibits a strong correlation with the disciplines of engineering, computer security and information theory. The main aim of these cryptographic methods is to encrypt a meaningful original message, called the plaintext, into an unintelligible form named as ciphertext in such a way like ciphertext appears as anonymous garbage without any meaning. The act of transforming a plaintext message into a ciphertext message is referred to as encryption. However, the cryptographic methods should also be able to convert the ciphertext back to its original form (plaintext) and that process is called decryption. A cryptographic encryption/decryption algorithm can both encrypt and decrypt the plaintext and the ciphertext respectively.

Symmetric encryption, also known as single-key encryption, is a cryptographic technique that employs one single key for encryption and decryption both. Both entities utilize a common key for the purpose of ensuring secure transmission and communication. Encryption algorithms can be categorized into two distinct groups named classical approaches and another one is modern techniques. A substitution cipher is a prevalent illustration of a classical methodology. A substitution cipher is a form of encryption where units of plaintext are replaced with corresponding units of ciphertext according to a certain method. The "units" might consist of either a single character or a mixture of two or more characters. The recipient deciphers the text through an inverse replacement method to obtain the original message. Substitution ciphers can be likened to transposition ciphers, in which the elements of the plaintext are reorganized in an intricate sequence while the elements themselves remain unchanged. In simple substitution ciphers, single letters of the plaintext are replaced to form a ciphertext. In polygraphed substitution ciphers, a block of letters is substituted at once instead of individual letters. A monoalphabetic cipher uses a consistent replacement for the whole message, while a polyalphabetic cipher uses different substitutions at various positions within the message. Essentially, a unit of plaintext can be mapped to numerous alternative units of ciphertext.

The Hill cipher is a monoalphabetic polygraphic substitution cipher that is based on linear algebra. The Hill cipher is a classical encryption system that was created by Lester S. Hill in 1929. It is a multi-letter cipher, as explained in his paper "Cryptography in an Algebraic Alphabet" [15]. In this paper, Hill introduced the concept of using matrix operations as the foundation of the Hill cipher. The Hill cipher employs a key matrix, consisting of numerical values, for encryption. Conversely, for decryption, the decryption matrix is utilized, which is the modular arithmetic inverse of the encryption matrix. The substitution is determined by linear equations in which each character is encoded either using alphabetical encoding between a-z where a=1, b=2 ----z=26 or using American Standard Code for Information Interchange (ASCII) encoding as a= 97, b=98,. . . , z=122 with modulus p=26 or 256 respectively.

In order to encrypt the message using an n Xn × Hill cipher, assuming n be the pairs of plaintext-ciphertext, having length n, the pairs $P_j = (p_{1j}, p_{2j}, . . ., p_{nj})$, $C_j = (c_{1j}, c_{2j}, . . . , c_{nj})$ can be labeled as plaintext and ciphertext respectively, such that $C_j = \leq KP_{j\leq}$ for 1 j n and for some unknown key matrix K [2]. In general, the Hill cipher encryption and decryption are given by $C = KP \bmod p$ and $P = K^{-1}C \bmod p$, where P, C, K, K^{-1} represent plaintext, ciphertext, encryption key matrix, and decryption key matrix respectively. In order to encrypt data, an algorithm takes m consecutive plaintext letters and replaces them with m cipher letters.

It may be defined by the following system of equations for m=3:

$$C_1 = (K_{11}P_1 + K_{12}P_2 + K_{13}P_3) \bmod 26$$

$$C_2 = (K_{21}P_1 + K_{22}P_2 + K_{23}P_3) \bmod 26$$

$$C_3 = (K_{31}P_1 + K_{32}P_2 + K_{33}P_3) \bmod 26$$

The K^{-1} be the inverse matrix of a matrix K such that $KK^{-1} = K^{-1}K = I$, here I will be the Identity matrix. However, not all matrices have inverses, and if they do, they may not be eligible to serve as key matrices for Hill ciphering. The encryption key must satisfy two important criteria, namely, the key matrix ought to be invertible, and the value of the determinant obtained from the corresponding key matrix is also odd, such that $\gcd(\det[K], p) = 1$.

7.4 Key Generation Methods for Hill Cipher

7.4.1 Magic Rectangle Method for the Generation of Key Matrix for Hill Cipher

The Hill cipher encryption technique is unsuccessful if the encryption key matrix does not meet the following criteria: it must be invertible, and the determinant of the corresponding key matrix must be an odd number. Additionally, because the key matrix in the original technique is selected randomly, it is highly challenging to find the right key matrix in a single run otherwise may fail sometimes.

The process of resulting in the key matrix K for Hill cipher using the Magic Rectangle methodology, as described in [1], employs a deterministic approach to ensure that the matrix fits both conditions. For this, it considers a magic rectangle of order $m \times n$ denoted as $MR_{m\times n}$. First, $MR_{m\times n}$ is converted into a square matrix of order $m \times m$ denoted as $SM_{m\times m}$. After converting into $SM_{m\times m}$, for each element in $SM_{m\times m}$, the modulus value p is taken based on the encryption encoding procedure. From SM, the required key matrix is generated based on rules, yielding K of order k as an output.

K' is initially chosen from the magic rectangle, possibly not meeting the criteria. Alterations can be made to K' to obtain a valid K using the provided rules up to 10 [1].

The key matrix K of higher order k for Hill cipher encryption is thought of and successfully created using this deterministic approach. Several rules are proposed to extract the correct k from K' as shown in Figure 7.1.

K	Rule
4	*$\forall i$, if MS(i, i), i = 1, ..., k is already even, leave as it is.* *Otherwise, MS(i, i) $\leftarrow$ MS(i, i) + 1*
5 9	*$\forall i$, if MS(i, i) is already even, leave as it is.* *Otherwise, MS(i, i) $\leftarrow$ $\begin{cases} MS\ (i, i) + 1,\ i = 1,2, \ldots, (k-1) \\ MS\ (n, n) \leftarrow MS\ (n, n) + 1 \end{cases}$*
6 8	*$\forall i$, if MS(i, i) i = 1,2, ..., n.* *− 3, n is already even, leave as it is.* *Otherwise, MS(i, i) $\leftarrow$ $\begin{cases} MS\ (i, i) + 1, \\ when\ i = (n-2), (n-1) \end{cases}$*
7	*$\forall i$, i = 2, ... ,6* *if MS(i, j) is already even, leave as it is.* *Otherwise, MS(i, i) $\leftarrow$ MS(i, i) + 1*
10	*$\forall i$, if MS(1,1), MS(n, n) is already odd. leave as it is.* *Otherwise, MS(i, i) $\leftarrow$ MS(i, i), MS(n, n) + 1*

Figure 7.1 Rules for obtaining k from K'.

7.4.2 A Generation of Self-Invertible Matrix for Hill Cipher Algorithm

The Hill cipher encryption technique is unsuccessful if the encryption key matrix does not adhere to the following criteria: it must be invertible, and the determinant of the corresponding key matrix must be an odd number. Furthermore, due to the random selection of the key matrix in the original method, it is exceedingly difficult to locate the correct key matrix in a single attempt and there is a possibility of failure.

The "*Novel Methods of Generating Self-Invertible Matrix for Hill Cipher Algorithm*" approach focuses on obtaining a self-invertible key matrix, eliminating the requirement to calculate the matrix's inverse during decryption.

A general method of generating an even self-invertible matrix

Let "A_{11}, A_{12}, A_{21}, A_{22} of order $q/2 \times q/2$" be part of self-invertible matrix A_n of order n.

Algorithm:

1. Select q/2 × $q/2$ matrix M_{22}.arbitrary)
2. Find $M_{11} = -M_{22}$.

3. Select $M_{12} = k(I - M_{11})$ or $k(I + M_{11})$ for k as a scalar coefficient.
4. Set $A_{21} = 1/k(I + M_{11})$ or $1/k(I - M_{11})$.
5. Complete the matrix.

7.4.3 A Generation of Self-Invertible Matrix Using Generic Approach

Let M_{11}, M_{12}, M_{21}, M_{22} of order $q/2 \times q/2$ be part of self-invertible matrix M_n of order q.

Algorithm:

1. Select A_{22}, a non-singular (q − 1) $(q - 1)$ matrix with $(n - 2)$ eigenvalues of +1 or -1 or both.
2. Compute the other eigenvalue λ of A_{22}.
3. Set $A_{11} = -\lambda$.
4. Obtain consistent solutions of A_{12} and A_{21} elements using equations.
5. Formulate the matrix.

7.4.4 Alternate Approach for a Generation of Self-Invertible Matrix

Consider A be an arbitrary non-singular matrix and E be its corresponding eigen matrix. This implies $AE = E\lambda$, where λ is a diagonal matrix obtained from the eigen values. The eigen matrix E is non-singular.

Algorithm:

1. Consider any non-singular matrix E.
2. Design a diagonal matrix λ with $\lambda = \pm 1$, distinct values.
3. Compute $E\lambda E^{-1} = A$.

7.5 Methodology for Comparative Study

This section undertakes a comprehensive comparative analysis between the works discussed in 'Novel Methods of Generating Self-Invertible Matrix for Hill Cipher Algorithm' [2] and 'Generation of Key Matrix for

Hill Cipher using Magic Rectangle' [1]. The analysis encompasses dimensions such as security considerations, efficacy of techniques, implementation feasibility, and inherent limitations. By considering these aspects, we proposed to provide a holistic evaluation of the two papers, shedding light on their respective strengths and weaknesses.

7.5.1 Background and Overview

Firstly, we thoroughly researched and analyzed the two methods by hand in order to understand the internal working of both techniques. In the paper "*Generation of Key Matrix for Hill Cipher using Magic Rectangle*", the key matrix of order K x K is extracted from an even larger matrix called the "*Magic Rectangle*" of order M x (M + 2). If the extracted key matrix is invertible, it is directly returned to the user. In contrast, "*Novel Methods of Generating Self-Invertible Matrix for Hill Cipher*" proposes various methods to generate a self-invertible key matrix, including both even-ordered and odd-ordered matrices. Finally, a general method is described that can find a self-invertible matrix of any order and size. This self-invertible matrix is returned to the user as the key matrix for encryption. It significantly minimizes the computational time to compute the inverse of a matrix during the decryption process.

7.5.2 Security Aspect

After numerous thought experiments and thorough fact-checking, we conclude that the "*Generation of Key Matrix for Hill Cipher using Magic Rectangle*" method is more secure and harder to break than the generating self-invertible matrix for Hill cipher method.

A magic rectangle formed using three variables that can be random integers adds an additional layer of security for cryptographic algorithms. The variables include *m* (number of rows), *MRS* (starting and minimum number), and *Magic Sum* (magic sum of columns). The generation process, along with various orientations, adds complexity for potential eavesdroppers. In contrast, generating a self-invertible matrix requires finding a matrix with specific eigen- value constraints, making it potentially vulnerable to modern parallel computing methods.

7.5.3 Quality of the Techniques

Both methods were programmed and analyzed for time, space, and computational complexity in Python using modules like Numpy. Using big-O notation, we analyzed the complexities of the techniques:

Time Complexity: We present the time complexities of the two methods as follows:

- Magic Rectangle: $O(m\ n + k^2)$
- Self-invertible matrix: $O(n^3)$

Space Complexity: We present the space complexities of the two methods as follows:

- Magic Rectangle: $O(m\ n)$
- Self-invertible matrix: $O(n^2)$

For computational complexity, finding a matrix satisfying eigenvalue constraints is more challenging than generating a magic rectangle of the same size.

7.5.4 Implementation Ease

After fact checking the implementation of both methods, we conclude that the "*Generation of Key Matrix for Hill Cipher using Magic Rectangle*" is easier to implement compared to the generating self-invertible matrix for Hill Cipher. This is due to the complexity of matrix operations in the latter.

7.5.5 Limitations

Both methods have limitations. In the magic rectangle technique, the proposed rules are only valid for key matrix sizes from 4 to 10. In the self-invertible matrix technique, generating odd-ordered matrices is computationally complex and less secure than the magic rectangle technique.

7.6 Conclusion and Future Prospects

From the above comparative and contrastive study, we essentially conclude that the technique "*Generation of Key Matrix for Hill Cipher using Magic Rectangle*" is better than the method of generating self-invertible matrix for Hill cipher in terms of security aspect, quality of the technique, and the implementation ease. This is due to the fact that matrix operations are computationally more complex than simple matrix modifications.

In the future, this paper could be improved by combining both algorithms to generate key matrices of any order, rather than just those with sizes ranging from 4 to 10. Additionally, using randomized matrix operations to improve the security of both methods is a possibility. Furthermore, by leveraging the power of parallel computing to find matrices with eigenvalues that satisfy some constraints, the time complexity of generating a self-invertible matrix can be reduced.

References

1. Mani, K. and Viswambari, M., Generation of key matrix for hill cipher using magic rectangle, 10, 1081–1090, 2017.
2. Acharya, B., Rath, G.S., Patra, S.K., Panigrahy, S.K., Novel methods of generating self-invertible matrix for hill cipher algorithm, 2007.
3. Nt, J. and Mangathayaru, N., A Secure Approach for Medical Data Transmission, in: *Proceedings of the The International Conference on Engineering & MIS*, pp. 1–9, 2015, September2015.
4. Mahendran, R. and Mani, K., Generation of key matrix for hill cipher encryption using classical cipher, in: *2017 World congress on computing and communication technologies (WCCCT)*, IEEE, pp. 51–54, 2017, February.
5. Acharya, B., Patra, S.K., Panda, G., Involutory, permuted and reitera- tive key matrix generation methods for hill cipher system. *Int. J. Recent Trends Eng.*, 1, 4, 106–108, 2009.
6. Shanmugam, P. and Loganathan, C., Involuntory Matrix in Cryptography. *IJRRAS*, 6, 4, 81–89, 2011.
7. Krishna, A.V.N. and Madhuravani, K., A modified Hill cipher using randomized approach. *Int. J. Comp. Netw. Inf. Secur.*, 4, 5, 56–62, 2012.
8. Adi Narayana Reddy, K., Vishnuvardhan, B., Durga Prasad, K., Generalized Affine Transformation Based on Circulant Matrices. *Int. J. Distrib. Parallel Syst. (IJDPS)*, 3, 5, 159–165, September 2012.
9. Ravan, R.R. and Nigavekar, A.R., Secured Data Communication using Novel Modification to Hill Cipher Algorithm with Self Repetitive Matrix.
10. Prerna, U., Kumara, M., Shrivastava, J.N., Image encryption and de- cryption using modified Hill Cipher technique. *Int. J. Inf. Comp. Tech. (IJICT)*, 4, 17, 1895–1901, 2014.
11. Agrawal, K. and Gera, A., Elliptic curve cryptography with hill cipher generation for secure text cryptosystem. *Int. J. Comput. Appl.*, 106, 1, 18–24, 2014.
12. Thangarasu, N. and SelvaKumar, A.L., Encryption using lester hill cipher algorithm. *Int. J. Innov. Res. Adv. Eng. (IJIRAE)*, 2, 12, 13–17, 2015.
13. Siahaan, A.P.U., Genetic algorithm in hill cipher encryption. *Am. Int. J. Res. Sci. Technol. Eng. Math*, 15, 1, 84–89, 2016.
14. Hill, L.S., Cryptography in an algebraic alphabet. *Am. Math. Mon.*, 36, 6, 306–312, 1929.

15. Munzhelele, R. and Chibaya, C., Generation of invertible high order matrix keys for the hill cipher, in: *2020 2nd International multidisciplinary information technology and engineering conference (IMITEC)*, IEEE, pp. 1–4, 2020, November.
16. Hasoun, R.K., Khlebus, S.F., Tayyeh, H.K., A new approach of classical Hill Cipher in public key cryptography. *Int. J. Nonlinear Anal. App.*, 12, 2, 1071–1082, 2021.
17. Barrieta, R.G., Canlas, A.S., Cortez, D.M.A., Mata, K.E., Modified Hill Cipher Algorithm using Myszkowski Transposition to address Known-Plaintext attack. *Int. J. Res. Appl. Sci. Eng. Technol.*, 10, 4, 3242–3249, 2022.

8

Machine Learning-Based Spotify Song Prediction

Meenakshi Jha[1*], Devansh Vyas[1], Dhruv Mehta[1], Jai Maru[1], Abhijit Kumar[1] and Rajeev Kumar Gupta[2]

[1]*School of Computer Science, University of Petroleum and Energy Studies (UPES), Dehradun, Uttarakhand, India*
[2]*Department of Computer Science & Engineering, Pandit Deendayal Energy University, Gujarat, India*

Abstract
Online streaming stages are now one of the greatest music consumption channels where most streaming platforms offer a variety of tools and indicators, such as scores and rankings, to gauge a song's popularity. Through our analysis, we address two issues identified with a song. Collaborative filtering is presently the most successful and extensively used for the recommendation engine. It is found to be rapid in theoretical studies. It selects records and similarity relationships based on the consumer's available records and collects others that are similar to the consumer's interest. To start with, we anticipate whether a generally famous melody might draw in higher-than-normal public intrigue and become "viral." Second, we foresee whether abrupt spikes and open interest will convert into long-haul prevalence development. We base our discoveries on information from the streaming stage Spotify and think about appearances in its "Generally Popular" list as characteristic of notoriety, and appearances in its "Viral" list as demonstrative of interest development. We approach the problem as a project and use a support vector machine model based on prevalence data to predict interest and the other way around. We likewise check in case acoustic data can give helpful elements to the two errands. Our outcomes show that the notoriety data alone is adequate to anticipate future interest development, accomplishing an F1-score above 90% at foreseeing whether a melody will be included in the "Viral" list after being seen in the "Most Popular".

**Corresponding author*: meenakshijha076@gmail.com

Tanupriya Choudhury, Abhijit Kumar, Ravi Tomar, S. Balamurugan and Ankit Vishnoi (eds.) Cyber-Physical Systems for Innovating and Transforming Society 5.0, (175–192) © 2025 Scrivener Publishing LLC

***Keywords*:** Song prediction, time series analysis, recommendation system, collaborative filtering

8.1 Introduction

Music is one of the most famous media used for enjoyment purposes in today's world. It is considered as the paintings of human creativity to express thoughts and feelings in the shape of sounds that consist of melody, concord, and rhythm. Music can be labeled into numerous genres, such as pop, rock, jazz, blues, and folk [4, 5]. Listening to any track in this virtual age is easy, because of smartphones that play music offline and online. Nowadays, listening to songs could be very abundant in comparison to the previous generation, therefore the intention to categorize out all this virtual music available may be very time consuming and results in information fatigue. Therefore, it is very beneficial to create a song recommender algorithm that can seek song libraries routinely and propose songs that are similar to the consumers' taste. Music streaming services have gained in popularity over the last decade, owing to the growing availability of internet services around the world and the proliferation of mobile phones. Users can also share their favorite songs, artists, playlists, and other information on these channels [6, 7].

Recommender System is software that uses an algorithm that gives recommendations on various datasets that are most exciting to a consumer. Recommendations are related to various real-life applications, along with what commodities are purchased, which song is trending, or related to the latest breaking news. On the other hand, there is a transition in the field of recorded commodity track, mainly after Apple offered Beats Music in 2014. Recently, the commercialization of the music industry is converting from being dependent on commodity sales to a model based totally on subscriptions and streaming. With the new version of the music industry, the supply of digital tracks is currently abundant compared to previous generations. Therefore, the position of a recommender mechanism is very crucial. It can provide the preferred songs to their customers, and consequently, the song companies can enhance user experience and promote different types of songs [8, 9].

Collaborative filtering uses the collaborative power of the available evaluation by customers to make recommendations. It is based on the assumption that if distinctive customers prefer same music or possess similar behaviors, their preference on other music items will also be similar. The foremost challenge in collaborative filtering methods is the sparse assessment matrix because most users access only a small part of all song libraries, consequently most evaluation cannot be done.

It computes similarity on the basis of two important aspects:

- User
- Item

This is accomplished through the usage of Cosine and Pearson correlation similarities. The cosine similarity, cos (θ), of two vectors of attributes, A and B, is:

$$\text{similarity} = \cos(\theta) = \frac{\mathbf{A} \cdot \mathbf{B}}{\|\mathbf{A}\| \, \|\mathbf{B}\|} = \frac{\sum_{i=1}^{n} A_i B_i}{\sqrt{\sum_{i=1}^{n} A_i^2} \sqrt{\sum_{i=1}^{n} B_i^2}}$$

We have taken (x, y) as data objects, and N as the total number of attributes to calculate Pearson correlation similarity.

$$Pearson(x, y) = \frac{\sum xy - \frac{\sum x \sum y}{N}}{\sqrt{\left(\sum x^2 - \frac{(\sum x)^2}{N}\right)\left(\sum y^2 - \frac{(\sum y)^2}{N}\right)}}$$

Spotify has around 75 million active users, over 30 million songs plus 20,000 new songs every day, and about 1TB of consumption data generated per day among streaming music providers.

Despite being the world's largest streaming service, Spotify did not have an official recommendation system until July 2015, when Spotify's Discover Weekly was launched. Furthermore, the quantity and quality of data available through Spotify's application programming interface (API) makes developing a recommendation engine difficult. As a company, Spotify wants to keep their users interested in their platform. One way to achieve this is by continuously providing them with fresh and preferred content (songs and artists).

This keeps the user happy by providing new interesting content. With this approach, we can aim to increase Spotify listeners at a very rapid rate. The creation of a recommendation engine, which not only provides users with the latest and most popular songs, but also with the best suited songs from the preferences of a user, can help enhance the user experience on a very large scale.

With the rise of streaming services like Prime and Spotify in recent years, recommender systems have become increasingly important. The popularity of Spotify's Discover Weekly, a music recommender system that sends listeners new songs every week, demonstrates the need for similar systems to be implemented. These suggestions are made by looking for commonalities between different songs or by favoring one feature over another. One of the most difficult challenges in designing a recommendation system is creating an algorithm that can constantly uncover new music that is interesting and can understand the users' preferences. As a result, we must strive to create an algorithm that can generate tailored recommendations for a variety of audiences. As a result, making music that is unique to you is a must.

To reach the objective, our study method is based on evaluating the similarity of the consumer's records available and other data collected that are similar to the consumer's interest. This technique is considered a collaborative approach. Our research focuses on two fundamental challenges:

1. To predict popularity rating on the basis on the audio data set collected.
2. The impact of different features that help us to predict the most preferred playlist for the user.

This paper is organized into six sections. The first section focuses on the introduction of problem statements, followed by background studies in the literature reviews section. The third section explores the different approaches and exploits the relevant algorithms applied. Furthermore, a detailed discussion on experimental setups and results has been established. Finally, the conclusion is discussed followed by detailed bibliography and references.

8.2 Literature Review

This segment helps in assessing and interpreting the contents of similar papers and research in this field.

It also helped to decide the right approach for our experiment and overcome the shortcomings of similar models.

Carlos Vicente S. *et al.* [1], the objective of the experiment is to use classifiers based on historical data to anticipate the song's popularity.

They used previous editions of the "Top 50" in their methodology. The ranking entries were then converted into instances in the next phase. Then, in order to broaden the prediction horizon, numerous rounds of prediction were conducted, with the results from one round serving as a feature in subsequent rounds. The authors have applied support vector machine (SVM) classifier with RBF kernel and obtained AUC of more than 80%, about two months ahead of time. The disadvantages of this strategy are that it only serves a tiny part of the recommendations and is reliant on previous "Top 50" editions.

Elena Georgieva *et al.* [2], the experiment's goal is to forecast whether a song will chart on the Billboard Hot 100. Logistic Regression, expectation maximization, SVMs, Gaussian Discriminant analysis, decision trees, and neural networks are the six machine learning algorithms they employed in their methodology. To build support vectors, they employed SVM to create a decision boundary based on the data points nearest to the decision boundaries. Finally, they employed the notion of neural networks to improve the prediction module. The overfitting nature of the SVM and DT modules when defining decision boundaries is a flaw in this approach. There was also a lot of variation in the outcomes.

According to Apoorva Shete *et al.* [3], the objective of the experiment is to assess the various parameters that determine the success of an artist on the Spotify platform. They have used the WMG database to access the streaming dataset of Spotify. Their methodology focuses on three machine-learning algorithms: KNN, decision tree, and random forest. The focus is on developing a predictive model where the various factors can be transformed into measurable quantities [11]. They have plotted the DT classifier, the confusion matrix, and ROC curve to compare the accuracies of different algorithms. However, the best results were obtained using DT classifiers [17]. The shortcoming of this approach is that there are great chances of prediction of 'failure' rather than a success due to the dataset used.

The authors of [13–16] proposed an improved system recommendation method and compared its performance results to those of another method.

8.3 Methodology

There are a variety of works in the Spotify Recommendation system, including artist recommendations via Twitter's hashtag, merging Spotify's history and Facebook likes to generate recommendations and even artist visualization tools [10, 12, 13]. The suggestions in all the cited works are based on third-party data, implying reliance on the availability of such data.

Our research suggests a filtering-based recommendation system that is fully based on data provided by Spotify via its API.

Towards this goal, we want to develop a methodology to interpret the various factors, which are important to engage users by making the most preferable playlist.

The following features have been provided to help us predict the preferred playlist:

- **Acousticness** - the value which describes how acoustic a song is.
- **Artists** - the artist preferred by the user.
- **Danceability** - the value that describes the probability of dancing on the audio.
- **Duration_ms** - length of the song.
- **Energy** - the value representing the sense of forwarding motion of music in song
- **Explicit** - use of strong language/offensive opinions in song.
- **Id** - song id in the database.
- **Instrumentalness** - the value representing the number of vocals in the song.

Acousticness. It has a range from 0.0 to 1.0 that determines if it is acoustic or not. 0.0 indicates a poor match, while a score of 1.0 indicates the probability that the audio is acoustic. Figure 8.1 (a).

Danceability. It ranges from 0.0 to 1, with 0.0 being the least and 1.0 being the most danceable. Figure 8.1 (b).

Duration. The tracks' duration is measured in milliseconds. The vast collection of 1,75,000 songs does not appear to reach the 10,000 milliseconds range. Figure 8.1 (c).

Energy. It is a scale that spans from 0.0 to 1.0 in terms of perceived intensity and activity. The feel of typical energetic music is rapid, loud, and boisterous. This property is influenced by perceptual parameters like dynamic range, and perceived loudness. Figure 8.1 (d).

Instrumentalness. It determines whether there are no vocals in a piece of music. The closer the score is to 1.0, the probability of it being vocal-free is more. Figure 8.1 (e).

Speechiness. The more proximate the value is to 1.0, the recording is more likely to be more speech-like. Figure 8.1 (f).

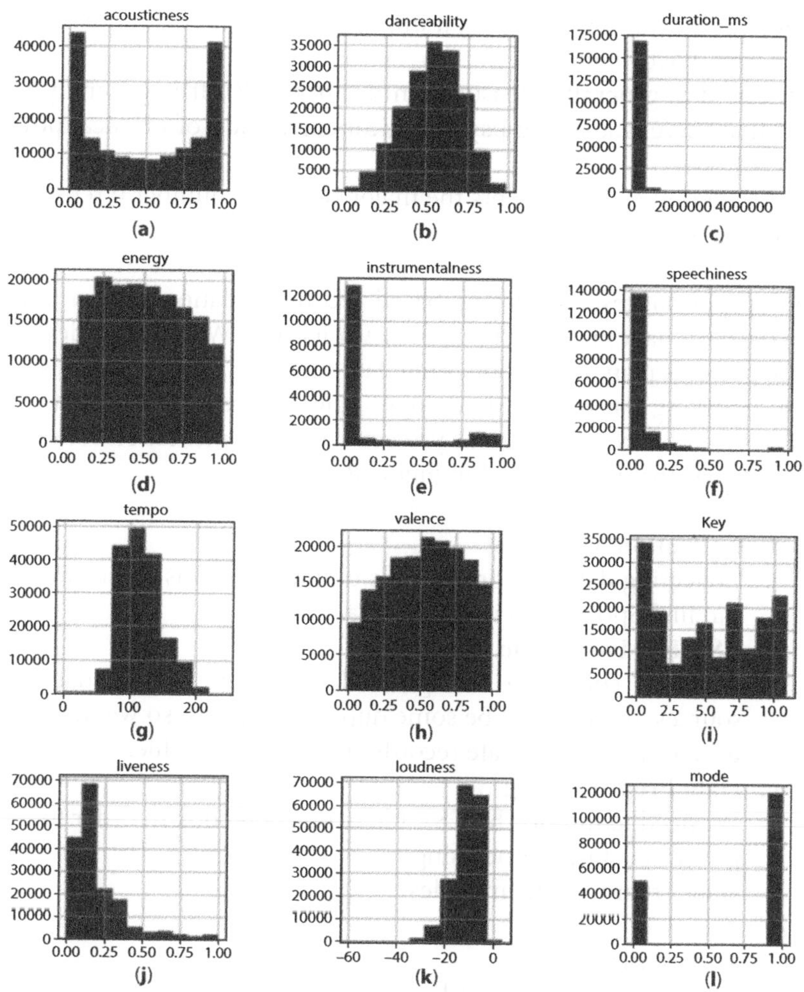

Figure 8.1 Pair plot graph across various parameters.

Tempo. A track's overall estimated tempo is stated in beats per minute. Tempo is said to be the speed or pace of a composition in musical terms, and it is determined by the average beat duration. Figure 8.1 (g).
Valence. It can be measured on a span ranging from 0.0 to 1.0 that describes an audio sample's musical positivity. Songs with high value sounds convey positivity through happy, bright, and euphoric emotions, while tracks with low valence sounds convey more negative emotions such as despair, depression, and rage. Figure 8.1 (h).
Key. It denotes that the track is in the correct key. Using standard pitch class notation, the integers are converted to music pitches. Here, 0 = C, 1 = C#/Db, 2= D, and so on till 9 = A, 10 = A#/Bb, and 11 = B. Figure 8.1 (i).

Liveness. If the number is higher, it implies that the track is more likely to be performed live. Figure 8.1 (j).
Loudness. It is generally measured in decibels (dB). It is generally perceived that there is a strong psychological correlation of physical power. Figure 8.1 (k).
Mode. The number 1 represents the major while the number 0 represents the minor. Figure 8.1 (l).

Our paper suggests a filtering-based recommendation system that is fully based on data provided by Spotify via its API. We finished developing the project's plan, began obtaining data sets from various sources, and began analyzing various methodologies, algorithms, and concepts that could be useful in completing this project. Our implementation consists of several stages, that is illustrated in Figure 8.2:

a. **Collection of Dataset**
Collecting dataset from various online platforms where we can find Spotify and its user's data.
b. **CSV File Formation**
After the collection of a given dataset from various data sources, there would be some duplicate records, so we need to remove the duplicate records and form a CSV file.
c. **Data Preprocessing**
We need to import the CSV file in our notebook in order to perform data-preprocessing.
Data Preprocessing includes:

- Tokenization
- Removal of stop-words
- Removal of special characters
- Calculating occurrence of each word in a dataset
- Removal of punctuations

d. **Time Series Analysis**
Performing clustering and analysis of collected data with the help of python libraries like Numpy, Pandas, Matplotlib, Seaborn, etc.
e. **Data Visualization**
Applying data visualization technique used for representing text data in a graph to understand and conceptualize data better.

f. Popularity Rating

Using the audio dataset collected, we will apply machine learning algorithms to predict popularity rating of songs and artists.

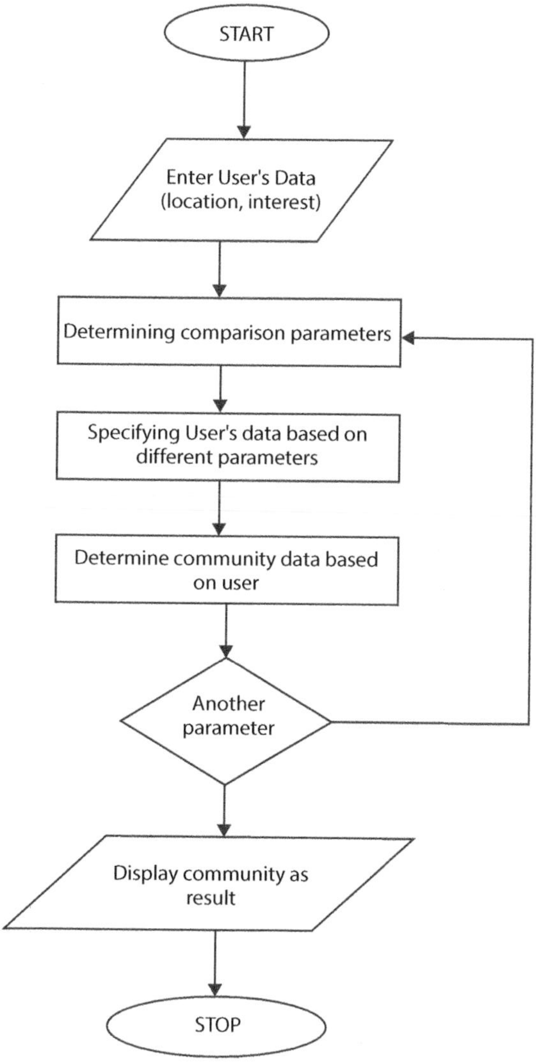

Figure 8.2 Workflow diagram.

8.4 Experimental Results

8.4.1 Task 1: Time Series Analysis

The time series has been depicted using the Figure 8.3 and Figure 8.4 depicts the year wise graph plots and Figure 8.5 depicts the graph plots in terms of popularity wise.

```
In [21]: df = pd.read_csv("Downloads/data.csv", index_col= ["tempo"], parse_dates = ["tempo"])

In [22]: df.head()
```

Out[22]:

	acousticness	artists	danceability	duration_ms	energy	explicit	id	instrumentalness	key	liveness	loudness	m
tempo												
118.469	0.995	['Carl Woitschach']	0.708	158648	0.1950	0	6KbQ3uYMLKb5jDxLF7wYDD	0.563	10	0.1510	-12.428	1
83.972	0.994	['Robert Schumann', 'Vladimir Horowitz']	0.379	282133	0.0135	0	6KuQTIu1KoTTkLXKrwlLPV	0.901	8	0.0763	-28.454	1
107.177	0.604	['Seweryn Goszczyński']	0.749	104300	0.2200	0	6L63VW0PibdM1HDSBoqnoM	0.000	5	0.1190	-19.924	0
108.003	0.995	['Francisco Canaro']	0.781	180760	0.1300	0	6M94FkXd15sOAOQYRnWPN8	0.887	1	0.1110	-14.734	0
62.149	0.990	['Frédéric Chopin', 'Vladimir Horowitz']	0.210	687733	0.2040	0	6N6tiFZ9vLTSOIxkj8qKrd	0.908	11	0.0980	-16.829	1

Figure 8.3 Time series analysis.

```
In [26]: plt.figure(figsize-(15,7))
         plt.plot(df.year)
         plt.grid(True)
         plt.title("Related to year")
         plt.show()
```

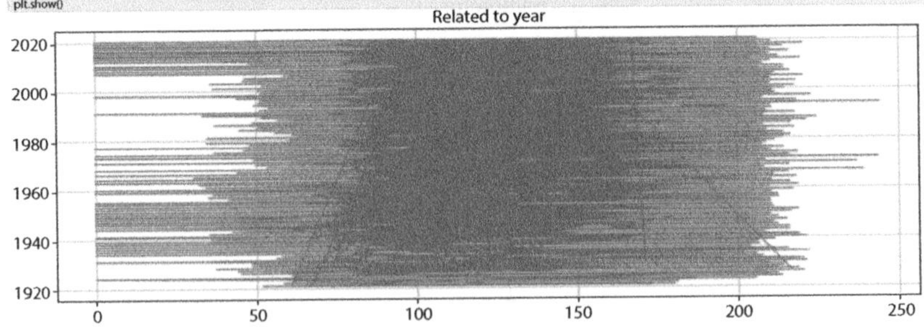

Figure 8.4 Graph plots across year.

```
In [28]: plt.figure(figsize=(15,7))
         plt.plot(df.popularity)
         plt.grid(True)
         plt.title("related to popularity")
         plt.show()
```

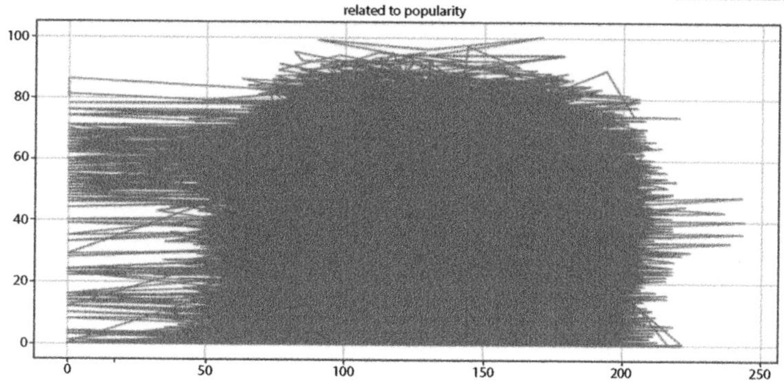

Figure 8.5 Graph plot across the popularity.

8.4.2 Task 2: Recommended Artists

```
In [22]: rating = pd.read_csv('Downloads/data_by_artist.csv',usecols=['artists','count','popularity'])
```

```
In [23]: song= pd.read_csv('Downloads/data_w_genres.csv',usecols=['artists','genres'])
```

```
In [24]: song.head()
```

Out[24]:

	artists	genres
0	"Cats" 1981 Original London Cast	['show tunes']
1	"Cats" 1983 Broadway Cast	[]
2	"Fiddler On The Roof" Motion Picture Chorus	[]
3	"Fiddler On The Roof" Motion Picture Orchestra	[]
4	"Joseph And The Amazing Technicolor Dreamcoat"...	[]

```
In [25]: rating.head()
```

Out[25]:

	artists	popularity	count
0	"Cats" 1981 Original London Cast	38.000000	12
1	"Cats" 1983 Broadway Cast	33.076923	26
2	"Fiddler On The Roof" Motion Picture Chorus	34.285714	7
3	"Fiddler On The Roof" Motion Picture Orchestra	34.444444	27
4	"Joseph And The Amazing Technicolor Dreamcoat"...	42.555556	9

```
In [26]: data=pd.merge(song,rating,on='artists')
```

```
In [27]: data.head()
```

Out[27]:

	artists	genres	popularity	count
0	"Cats" 1981 Original London Cast	['show tunes']	38.000000	12
1	"Cats" 1983 Broadway Cast	[]	33.076923	26
2	"Fiddler On The Roof" Motion Picture Chorus	[]	34.285714	7
3	"Fiddler On The Roof" Motion Picture Orchestra	[]	34.444444	27

```
In [31]: data["average rating"] = data["popularity"] * data["count"]

In [32]: data.sort_values('average rating',ascending=False,inplace=True)

In [33]: data.head()
```

Out[33]:

	artists	genres	popularity	count	average rating
23446	The Beatles	['beatlesque', 'british invasion', 'classic ro...	48.060753	823	39554.0
24542	The Rolling Stones	['album rock', 'british invasion', 'classic ro...	34.573913	1035	35784.0
8103	Frank Sinatra	['adult standards', 'easy listening', 'lounge']	26.004383	1369	35600.0
2924	Bob Dylan	['album rock', 'classic rock', 'country rock',...	30.860806	1092	33700.0
7142	Elvis Presley	['rock-and-roll', 'rockabilly']	33.391919	990	33058.0

```
In [34]: #recommended artist

         data["artists"].head(1)

Out[34]: 23445    The Beatles
         Name: artists, dtype: object
```

8.4.3 Task 3: Popularity Rating

The results has been depicted using the Figure 8.6, Figure 8.7, and Figure 8.8.

```
In [14]: data3["popularity"]= [ 1 if i>=66.5 else 0 for i in data3.popularity ]
         data3["popularity"].value_counts()

Out[14]: 0    162612
         1      7297
         Name: popularity, dtype: int64

In [15]: a=data3[data3["popularity"]==1]
         a.describe()
```

Out[15]:

	acousticness	danceability	duration_ms	energy	explicit	instrumentalness	key	liveness	loudness	mode	popularity	speechiness	tem
count	7297.000000	7297.000000	7297.000000	7297.000000	7297.000000	7297.000000	7297.000000	7297.000000	7297.000000	7297.000000	7297.0	7297.000000	7297.000
mean	0.248213	0.635226	217523.299712	0.627288	0.308209	0.040169	5.192545	0.178443	-7.272764	0.636426	1.0	0.101923	120.6714
std	0.265867	0.167081	54806.874777	0.201137	0.461785	0.167650	3.584400	0.141956	4.291995	0.481061	0.0	0.102930	30.3941
min	0.000000	0.000000	37640.000000	0.000020	0.000000	0.000000	0.000000	0.000000	-54.376000	0.000000	1.0	0.000000	0.000
25%	0.034600	0.538000	185093.000000	0.505000	0.000000	0.000000	2.000000	0.094100	-8.372000	0.000000	1.0	0.037300	97.387
50%	0.146000	0.654000	211666.000000	0.649000	0.000000	0.000000	5.000000	0.121000	-6.319000	1.000000	1.0	0.056800	119.958
75%	0.384000	0.754000	241371.000000	0.777000	1.000000	0.000151	8.000000	0.215000	-4.821000	1.000000	1.0	0.121000	140.053
max	0.996000	0.979000	713192.000000	1.000000	1.000000	1.000000	11.000000	0.965000	0.175000	1.000000	1.0	0.903000	220.099

```
In [16]: data3.hist(figsize=(15, 15), color='black')
         pit.show()
```

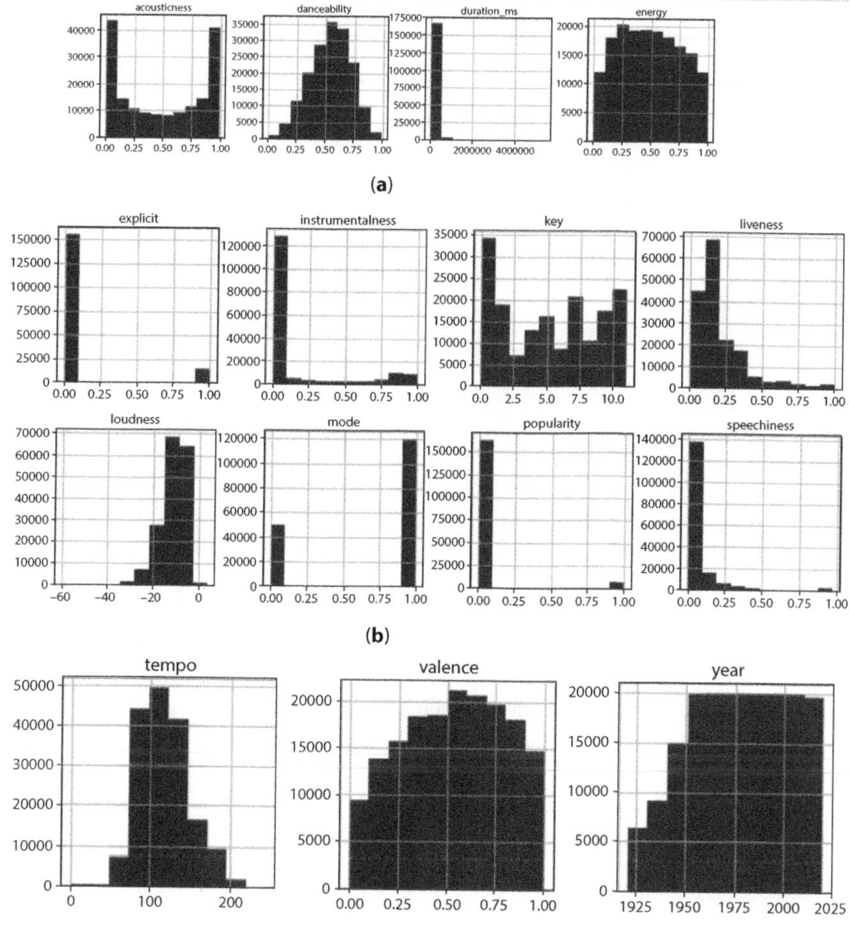

Figure 8.6 (a) Graph plots across various parameters. (b) Graph plots across various parameters. (c) Graph plots across various parameters.

```
In [17]: plt.figure(figsize=(20, 10))
         sns.heatmap(data3.corr(), annot=True)

Out[17]: <matplotlib.axes._subplots.AxesSubplot at 0x12a9b2b5828>
```

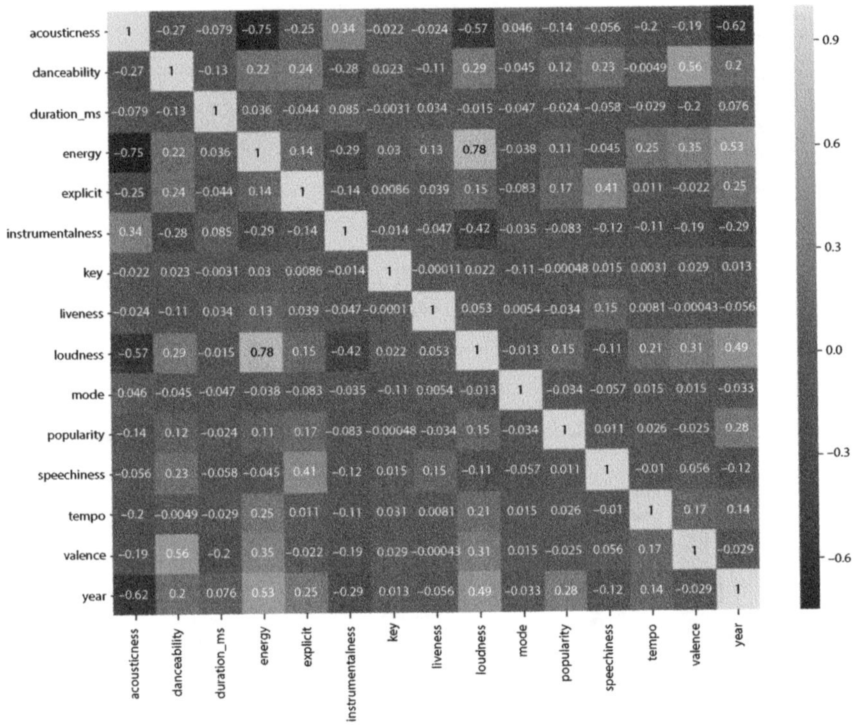

Figure 8.7 Heat map plot across various parameters of artists in years.

In [25]:
```
fig, ax = plt.subplots(figsize = (12, 10))
lead_artists = data3.groupby('artists')['popularity'].sum().sort_values(ascending=False).head(10)
ax = sns.barplot(x=lead_artists.values, y=lead_artists.index, palette="Greys", orient="h", edgecolor='black', ax=ax)
ax.set_xlabel('Sum of Popularity', fontsize=12)
ax.set_ylabel('Artist', fontsize=12)
ax.set_title('10 Most Popular Artists in Dataset', fontsize=14, weight = 'bold')
plt.show()
```

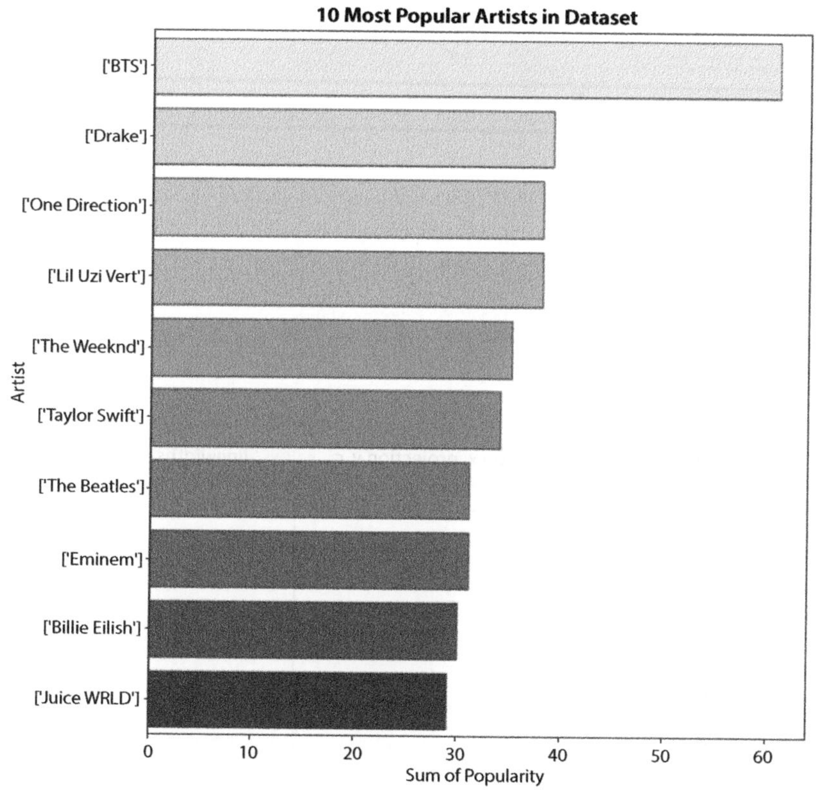

Figure 8.8 A histogram of artists and the sum of their popularity.

8.4.4 Task 4: Differentiate Genres

The results has been plotted using dispersion plot in Figure 8.9.

```
In [61]: cluster_pipeline = Pipeline([('scaler', StandardScaler()), ('kmeans', KMeans(n_clusters=10, n_jobs=-1))])

In [62]: X = df1.select_dtypes(np.number)

In [63]: cluster_pipeline.fit(X)

C:\Users\dell\anaconda3\lib\site-packages\sklearn\cluster\_kmeans.py:938: FutureWarning: 'n_jobs' was deprecated in version 0.23 and will be removed in 0.25.
  warnings.warn("'n_jobs' was deprecated in version 0.23 and will be"
Out[63]: Pipeline(steps=[('scaler', StandardScaler()),
                ('kmeans', KMeans(n_clusters=10, n_jobs=-1))])
```

```
In [64]: df1['cluster'] = cluster_pipeline.predict(X)

In [65]: tsne_pipeline = Pipeline([('scaler', StandardScaler()), ('tsne', TSNE(n_components=2, verbose=2))])

In [66]: genre_embedding = tsne_pipeline.fit_transform(X)

[t-SNE] Computing 91 nearest neighbors...
[t-SNE] Indexed 2664 samples in 0.145s...
[t-SNE] Computed neighbors for 2664 samples in 0.452s...
[t-SNE] Computed conditional probabilities for sample 1000 / 2664
[t-SNE] Computed conditional probabilities for sample 2000 / 2664
[t-SNE] Computed conditional probabilities for sample 2664 / 2664
[t-SNE] Mean sigma: 0.792505
[t-SNE] Computed conditional probabilities in 0.311s
[t-SNE] Iteration 50: error = 80.6410141, gradient norm = 0.0031250 (50 iterations in 2.058s)
[t-SNE] Iteration 100: error = 75.5284271, gradient norm = 0.0090969 (50 iterations in 1.437s)
[t-SNE] Iteration 150: error = 75.0547485, gradient norm = 0.0039558 (50 iterations in 1.372s)
[t-SNE] Iteration 200: error = 74.9820404, gradient norm = 0.0005662 (50 iterations in 1.571s)
[t-SNE] Iteration 250: error = 74.9772339, gradient norm = 0.0010004 (50 iterations in 1.502s)
[t-SNE] KL divergence after 250 iterations with early exaggeration: 74.977234
[t-SNE] Iteration 300: error = 1.7339339, gradient norm = 0.0009797 (50 iterations in 1.233s)
[t-SNE] Iteration 350: error = 1.5234519, gradient norm = 0.0003601 (50 iterations in 1.194s)
[t-SNE] Iteration 400: error = 1.4483689, gradient norm = 0.0002049 (50 iterations in 1.507s)
[t-SNE] Iteration 450: error = 1.4130844, gradient norm = 0.0001453 (50 iterations in 1.240s)
```

```
In [74]: fig = plt.scatter (projection.x, projection.y, c='yellow', linewidths=0.1)
```

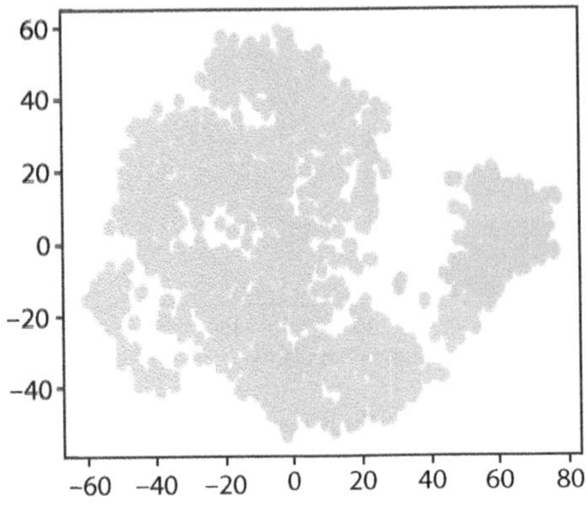

Figure 8.9 Dispersion plot.

8.5 Conclusion

Based on numerous variables and their impact, this article offered a Recommendation System for Spotify's users based on time series analysis based on exploratory data analysis. This method generates suggestions based on an ordered list of the most frequently played songs throughout time. Spotify only offers a fraction of all songs played for the engine to provide recommendations based on these characteristics. Based on the acoustic data set collected, we projected the popularity rating. Based on the audio data set provided, we have also identified genres.

In the future, we will strive to develop an algorithm that only plays the parts of the music that are repeatedly played by consumers. Furthermore, there is room for improvement in the current model to enhance the accuracy of the predictions.

Our primary focus is on the popularity of the songs, and a beta model with random effects is constructed to provide a fundamental solution to questions like: what are the determinants of popularity?

References

1. Araujo, C.S., Cristo, M., Giusti, R., Predicting Music Popularity on Streaming Platforms, pp. 141–148, May 2020, doi: 10.5753/sbcm.2019.10436.
2. Georgieva, E., Suta, M., Burton, N., Hitpredict : Predicting Hit Songs Using Spotify Data, pp. 2–6, 2018, [Online], Available: http://cs229.stanford.edu/proj2018/report/16.pdf.
3. Apoorva Shete, N.M.S.G., IRJET- Prediction of an Artist's Success on Spotify. *IRJET*, 8, 10, 286–291, 2021.
4. https://developer.spotify.com/web-api/tutorial/
5. http://spotipy.readthedocs.io/en/latest/#installation
6. Zheng, E., Kondo, G.Y., Zilora, S., Yu, Q., Tag-aware dynamic music recommendation. *Expert Syst. Appl.*, 106, 244–251, 2018.
7. Zhao, D., Zhang, L., Zhao, W., Genre-based Link Prediction in Bipartite Graph for Music Recommendation. *Procedia Comput. Sci.*, 91, Itqm, 959–965, 2016.
8. Sánchez-Moreno, D., Gil González, A.B., Muñoz Vicente, M.D., López Batista, V.F., Moreno García, M.N., A collaborative filtering method for music recommendation using playing coefficients for artists and users. *Expert Syst. Appl.*, 66, 1339–1351, 2016.
9. Deng, S., Wang, D., Li, X., Xu, G., Exploring user emotion in microblogs for music recommendation. *Expert Syst. Appl.*, 42, 23, 9284–9293, 2015.
10. Su, J.H., Chang, W.Y., Tseng, V.S., Personalized music recommendation by mining social media tags. *Procedia Comput. Sci.*, 22, 303–312, 2013.
11. Bogdanov, D., Haro, M., Fuhrmann, F., Xambó, A., Gómez, E., Herrera, P., Semantic audio content-based music recommendation and visualization based on user preference examples. *Inf. Process. Manage.*, 49, 1, 13–33, 2013.
12. Lee, K., Hyung, Z., Lee, K., Music recommendation using text analysis on song requests to radio stations. *Expert Syst. Appl.*, 41, 5, 2608–2618, 2014.
13. Mao, K., Chen, G., Hu, Y., Zhang, L., Music recommendation using graph based quality model. *Signal Process.*, 120, 806–813, 2016.
14. Xiong, R., Wang, J., Zhang, N., Ma, Y., Deep hybrid collaborative filtering for Web service recommendation. *Expert Syst. Appl.*, 110, 191–205, 2018.

15. Ha, T. and Lee, S., Item-network-based collaborative filtering: A personalized recommendation method based on a user's item network. *Inf. Process. Manage.*, 53, 5, 1171–1184, 2017.
16. Choi, I.Y., Oh, M.G., Kim, J.K., Ryu, Y.U., Collaborative filtering with facial expressions for online video recommendation. *Int. J. Inf. Manage.*, 36, 3, 397–402, 2016.
17. Girsang, A.S., Wibowo, A., Edwin, Song Recommendation System Using Collaborative Filtering Methods. *ICDTE 2019*, Yamanashi, Japan, October 25–27, 2019.

9

Artificial Intelligence and Sentiment Analysis in Political Campaigns

Amit Das* **and Sanjeev Malaviya**

The ICFAI University, Dehradun, Uttarakhand, India

Abstract

Sentiment analysis, a data-driven approach to understanding public opinion, has gained prominence in contemporary political campaigns. This paper explores its role in shaping campaign strategies, from targeted messaging to crisis management. We examine methods, case studies, and ethical implications, highlighting sentiment analysis as a powerful tool for political engagement and decision-making. Artificial intelligence (AI) is revolutionizing political campaigns by optimizing voter targeting, enhancing messaging, and improving campaign strategies. From predictive analytics to personalized engagement, AI empowers campaigns to make data-driven decisions and engage with voters more effectively. The advanced AI algorithms and sentiment analysis tools are creating different political theories in the era of digital politics.

Keywords: Artificial intelligence (AI), sentiment analysis, political campaigns, voter analytics, microtargeting, predictive analytics, social media engagement, digital politics

9.1 Introduction

In the realm of modern politics, staying attuned to the pulse of public sentiment has become both a challenge and an imperative. As political landscapes evolve, so do the tools and technologies available to campaigns and candidates seeking to connect with voters. Among these tools, Artificial

**Corresponding author*: amitdas01@gmail.com; amitdas@iudehradun.edu.in;
ORCID: https:// orcid.org/0000-0001-5164-7486

Tanupriya Choudhury, Abhijit Kumar, Ravi Tomar, S. Balamurugan and Ankit Vishnoi (eds.) Cyber-Physical Systems for Innovating and Transforming Society 5.0, (193–210) © 2025 Scrivener Publishing LLC

Intelligence (AI) and sentiment analysis have emerged as powerful allies in the strategic arsenal of political campaigns [2].

The convergence of AI and sentiment analysis offers unprecedented opportunities for understanding and influencing public opinion, optimizing campaign strategies, and navigating the intricacies of contemporary political discourse. In this era of data-driven decision-making, political campaigns are increasingly turning to AI to harness the vast reservoirs of information available in the digital age. The capacity of AI to process, analyze, and derive insights from massive datasets has revolutionized the way campaigns operate.

Coupled with sentiment analysis, which deciphers the emotional nuances embedded in textual and visual content, AI empowers campaigns to navigate the complex and dynamic landscape of public sentiment effectively [1].

This paper embarks on a comprehensive exploration of the symbiotic relationship between AI and sentiment analysis in political campaigns. It delves into the methodologies, applications, and implications of employing AI-driven sentiment analysis to inform campaign strategies.

By examining real-world case studies and ethical considerations, we aim to shed light on the multifaceted role AI plays in shaping modern political discourse and campaigning [1, 3].

This chapter would try to intercept the mechanism of AI and sentiment analysis enable campaigns to understand the electorate on a deeper level, identify key issues, personalize messaging, and optimize resource allocation. We will also address the ethical dimensions of AI in politics, including concerns related to data privacy, transparency, and fairness [3].

In an era where the digital realm serves as a battleground for hearts and minds, the fusion of AI and sentiment analysis stands as a testament to the transformative power of technology in shaping the democratic process. This paper seeks to unravel the intricacies of this transformative force, ultimately contributing to a more nuanced understanding of how AI and sentiment analysis are reshaping political campaigns in the digital age [4].

9.2 Artificial Intelligence and Sentiment Analysis in Modern Politics

In the ever-evolving landscape of modern politics, the fusion of AI and sentiment analysis has become a defining feature of political campaigns, policy-making, and public discourse. This dynamic pairing of technologies holds the potential to reshape the way political actors engage with constituents, understand public opinion, and formulate strategies. In this era of data abundance and digital connectivity, AI and sentiment analysis have emerged as essential tools, offering politicians and campaigns invaluable insights into the thoughts, emotions, and preferences of the electorate.

9.3 Artificial Intelligence: A Catalyst for Political Transformation

Artificial Intelligence (AI), with its capacity for data processing and predictive analytics, has ushered in a new era of political decision-making. Campaigns and politicians now leverage AI-driven algorithms to navigate the vast sea of voter data, identifying trends, correlations, and predictive patterns. This enables them to tailor their outreach, craft policy agendas, and allocate resources with unprecedented precision. Machine learning models can predict voter behavior, helping campaigns prioritize their efforts and focus on issues that resonate most with the electorate.

9.4 Sentiment Analysis: Deciphering the Public Pulse

At the heart of this transformation lies sentiment analysis, a branch of AI that deciphers the emotional undercurrents of public discourse. Sentiment analysis algorithms can scour social media platforms, news articles, and other textual sources to gauge public sentiment on a variety of issues, candidates, and policies. By categorizing sentiments as positive, negative, or neutral, campaigns gain a real-time understanding of how the public perceives them and their opponents.

9.5 Applications AI and Sentiment Analysis in Modern Politics

Artificial intelligence and sentiment analysis (Figure 9.1) offer a plethora of applications in modern politics [5, 7]:

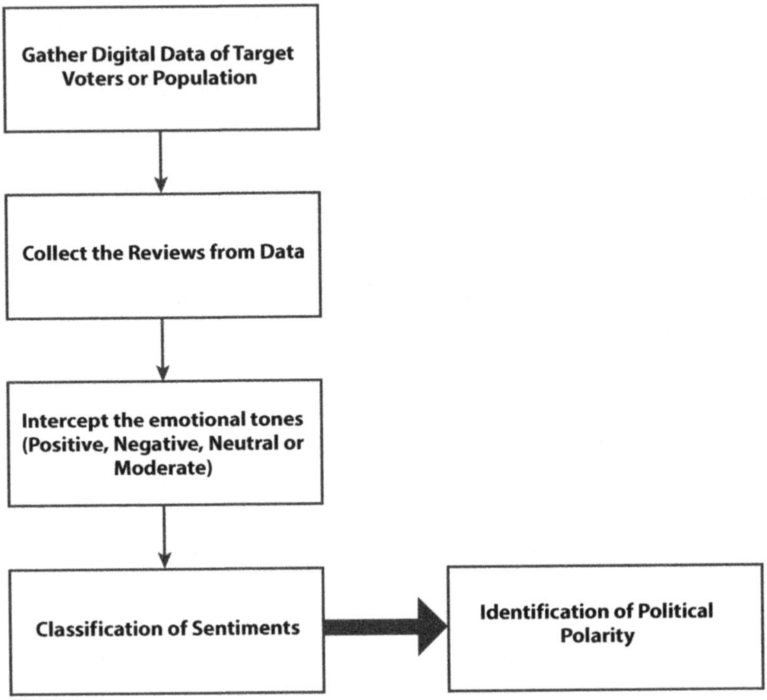

Figure 9.1 Sentiment analysis in political campaign.

- Personalized Messaging: AI allows campaigns to craft personalized messages that resonate with individual voters, based on their preferences and sentiment.
- Issue Prioritization: Sentiment analysis helps identify trending issues, enabling campaigns to address the concerns that matter most to voters.
- Real-time Feedback: AI-driven sentiment analysis provides campaigns with immediate feedback on the effectiveness of their messaging, allowing for quick adjustments.
- Crisis Management: Rapid sentiment analysis can detect and mitigate crises by identifying negative sentiment spikes related to a candidate or issue.
- Voter Engagement: AI-powered chatbots and automated outreach tools engage with voters in real-time, addressing their questions and concerns.

9.6 Ethical Considerations

While the intersection of AI and sentiment analysis brings immense potential, it also raises ethical concerns. Issues of data privacy, bias in algorithms, and the responsible use of voter data are paramount [12]. Striking the balance between harnessing the power of AI and protecting democratic values and individual rights remains a critical challenge.

As modern politics continues to evolve in the digital age, the role of AI and sentiment analysis will likely expand. Campaigns, policymakers, and citizens must grapple with the ethical and practical implications of these technologies, striving for a future where data-driven decision-making serves the interests of democracy, transparency, and civic engagement.

9.7 Artificial Intelligence in Political Campaigns

The use of AI in political campaigns has been growing in significance in recent years. These AI technologies offer various advantages for political campaigns, candidates, and parties. There are some ways in which AI is utilized in political campaigns:

- **Voter Analytics:** AI can analyze vast amounts of voter data to identify trends, preferences, and potential swing voters. Predictive analytics can help campaigns target specific demographics more effectively, allocate resources efficiently, and tailor messages to resonate with different voter groups.
- **Microtargeting:** AI-driven microtargeting enables campaigns to deliver highly personalized messages to individual voters based on their demographics, past voting behavior, and interests. This can improve the efficiency of advertising spending and increase the likelihood of voter engagement.
- **Sentiment Analysis:** AI-powered sentiment analysis, as discussed earlier, can assess public sentiment toward candidates, policies, and campaign events. This information helps campaigns adjust their strategies and messaging to align with public opinion.
- **Social Media Engagement:** AI chatbots and algorithms are used to engage with voters on social media platforms. They can answer questions, provide information, and encourage voter participation, enhancing a campaign's online presence.

- **Fundraising and Donation Prediction:** AI algorithms can predict potential donors and their likelihood of contributing to a campaign. This helps campaigns optimize fundraising efforts and tailor donation requests [21].
- **Campaign Strategy Optimization:** AI can assess campaign strategies in real-time, adjusting ad spending, messaging, and targeting based on performance data. This dynamic approach can maximize the impact of campaign resources.
- **Speech and Debate Preparation:** AI tools can analyze past speeches and debates, providing candidates with insights into their strengths and weaknesses. This helps them refine their messaging and debate strategies.
- **Issue Identification:** AI can identify emerging issues and trends by analyzing news articles, social media discussions, and other sources. Campaigns can then address these issues promptly.
- **Robo-Polling:** AI-powered robo-polling systems can conduct surveys and gather voter opinions quickly and cost-effectively. These surveys provide valuable data for understanding public sentiment.
- **Campaign Security:** AI can enhance campaign cybersecurity by identifying and mitigating potential threats, such as phishing attacks and data breaches, which can be detrimental to campaigns.
- **Automated Content Generation:** AI can assist in generating campaign content, such as press releases, social media posts, and email newsletters, saving time and resources.
- **Voter Outreach:** AI-driven communication tools, like automated text messages and chatbots, can facilitate voter outreach and encourage voter registration and turnout.

While AI offers numerous benefits in political campaigns, there are also ethical and privacy concerns to consider, including data protection, transparency, and the potential for misuse. Balancing the advantages of AI with these ethical considerations is a critical aspect of its responsible use in political campaigns.

9.8 Use of Sentiment Analysis in Political Campaigns

Sentiment analysis is a valuable tool that has been increasingly used in political campaigns to gain insights into public opinion and tailor campaign strategies. Here are some ways sentiment analysis is employed in political campaigns [8, 9]:

- **Understanding Public Opinion**: Sentiment analysis can help political campaigns gauge public sentiment on various issues. By analyzing social media posts, news articles, and other online content, campaigns can gain real-time insights into how the public feels about specific policies, candidates, or political events.
- **Targeted Messaging:** Campaigns can use sentiment analysis to identify key issues that resonate with specific voter demographics. This information allows campaigns to craft messages and policies that align with the sentiments of their target audience, increasing the likelihood of winning their support.
- **Crisis Management:** Sentiment analysis can be used to detect and manage potential crises. Campaigns can monitor social media and news outlets for negative sentiment spikes related to their candidate or party, enabling them to respond quickly and mitigate damage.
- **Candidate Image Management:** Political campaigns use sentiment analysis to assess the public's perception of their candidate. By tracking sentiment over time, campaigns can adjust their messaging and branding to improve the candidate's image and appeal.
- **Competitor Analysis:** Sentiment analysis can help campaigns understand how their competitors are perceived. This knowledge can be used to highlight differences between candidates or parties and exploit weaknesses in their opponents' messaging.
- **Identifying Swing Voters:** Sentiment analysis can help identify undecided or swing voters. By analyzing their online interactions and sentiments, campaigns can target these individuals with personalized messages and outreach efforts.
- **Tracking Campaign Effectiveness:** Sentiment analysis can be used to measure the impact of campaign events, advertisements, and speeches. Campaigns can assess whether their messaging is resonating with the intended audience and adjust as needed.

- **Issue Prioritization:** Sentiment analysis can assist campaigns in prioritizing campaign issues. By analyzing sentiment data, campaigns can determine which issues are most important to voters and allocate resources accordingly.
- **Geographic Targeting:** Sentiment analysis can be used to identify regions or constituencies with specific sentiment patterns. Campaigns can then allocate resources and tailor their messages to better appeal to these areas [18].
- **Debates and Speech Preparation:** Sentiment analysis can provide insights into the topics and issues that are top-of-mind for voters. This information can be used to prepare candidates for debates and speeches, ensuring they address the issues that matter most to the audience [19].

It is important to note that while sentiment analysis can be a powerful tool in political campaigns, it has limitations. Sentiment analysis algorithms may not always accurately capture the nuances of human emotions and can be influenced by factors like sarcasm or irony in online communication. Additionally, ethical considerations regarding privacy and data usage should be considered when employing sentiment analysis in political campaigns [20].

9.9 Interrelated Variable Matrix for AI and Sentiment Analysis in Modern Politics

The interrelated variable matrix illustrates various factors associated and correlated with AI and sentiment analysis in modern politics are interconnected (Table 9.1):

Table 9.1 Interrelated variables in politics.

Interrelated variables	Description
AI Applications in Politics	The use of AI technologies in political campaigns, governance, and decision-making processes.
Sentiment Analysis	The application of sentiment analysis techniques to assess public opinion, emotions, and trends.

(Continued)

Table 9.1 Interrelated variables in politics. (*Continued*)

Interrelated variables	Description
Data Privacy and Ethics	The ethical considerations and data privacy concerns related to the collection and use of voter data.
Algorithmic Bias	The potential for biases within AI models and sentiment analysis algorithms, affecting analysis outcomes.
Resource Allocation Strategies	The allocation of campaign resources and budget based on AI-driven insights from sentiment analysis.
Campaign Strategy Formulation	The development of political campaign strategies, messaging, and policy positions informed by AI analysis.
Personalized Messaging	The customization of political messages and advertisements based on sentiment analysis and voter profiles.
Voter Engagement and Mobilization	The use of AI-driven tools, such as chatbots and automation, to engage with voters and boost turnout.
Issue Prioritization	The identification of emerging political issues through sentiment analysis, influencing campaign priorities.
Data Security and Compliance	Ensuring the security of AI systems and data used in political applications, while complying with regulations.
Regulatory Environment	The influence of government regulations and policies on AI and sentiment analysis practices in politics.

This interrelated variable matrix underscores the complexity of AI and sentiment analysis integration in modern politics (Figure 9.2). These variables interact and influence each other in various ways, and understanding these relationships is crucial for policymakers, political campaigns, and researchers to effectively harness these technologies while addressing ethical concerns and regulatory compliance (Table 9.2).

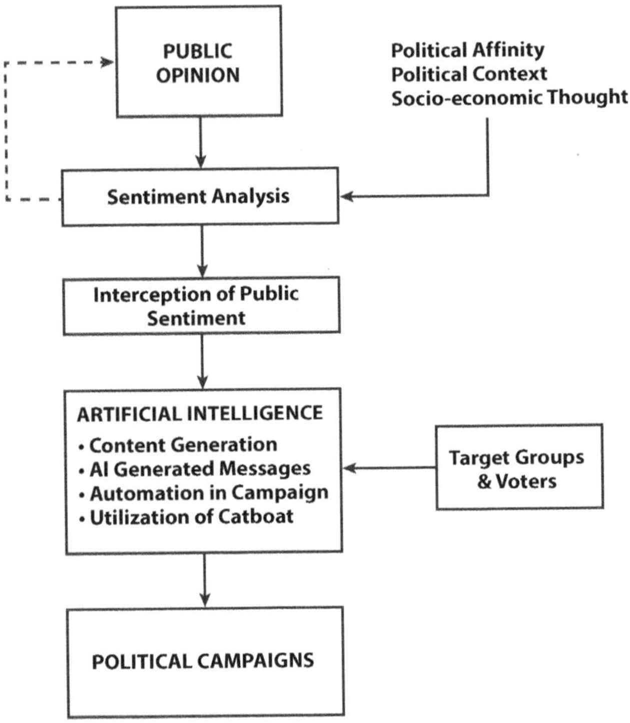

Figure 9.2 Artificial intelligence and political campaign.

Table 9.2 Variable type.

Variable type	Variable	Effect
Independent variable	Public Sentiment	Public sentiment towards a political candidate or party
Dependent variable	Use of AI in Campaigns	Level of automation in social media content generation, Chabot utilization, AI-generated political messages
Mediating variable	Exposure to AI Generated Content	• Public exposure to AI-generated political content • Level of trust in AI-generated messages
Moderating variable	Political Context	Influence of the political climate or environment on the impact of AI on public sentiment
	Socio-economic Statues	The socio-economic factors moderate the relationship between AI use and public sentiment

9.10 Cambridge Analytica: Data Scandal of Digital Politics

The Cambridge Analytica case in the USA refers to a significant data scandal that came to light in 2018, revealing the misuse of Facebook user data for political purposes during the 2016 United States presidential election [10]. There are some key points about the case:

- **Data Acquisition:** Cambridge Analytica, a British data analytics firm, obtained personal data (Table 9.3) from millions of Facebook users without their explicit consent [17].
- **Data Usage:** Cambridge Analytica used this data to create detailed psychological profiles of Facebook users, aiming to understand individual personalities, preferences, and susceptibilities. These profiles were then used to target users with personalized political content and advertisements.
- **Influence on the 2016 Election:** The firm's alleged involvement was primarily associated with Donald Trump's presidential campaign. It was reported that Cambridge Analytica worked

Table 9.3 Data types.

Data types	Data sets
Social Media Data	Twitter API, Tweet datasets
News Articles	News API, datasets from news organizations
Public Opinion Survey	Surveys from research organization and government agencies
Speech Transcripts	Official campaign websites, government archives, debate transcripts
Political Advertisement	Political Ad monitoring services, political research organizations
Demographic Data	Census data, voter registration records, demographic datasets
Election Results	Election commission data, government election databases
Campaign Finance Data	Campaign finance regulatory bodies, government datasets

with the campaign to tailor digital advertising messages to specific voter segments, potentially influencing voter behavior.

- **Whistleblower:** The scandal was exposed by Christopher Wylie, a former Cambridge Analytica employee, who revealed information about the data breach and how the company had used Facebook data.
- **Investigations and Legal Consequences:** Regulatory authorities, including the U.S. Federal Trade Commission (FTC) and the U.K. Information Commissioner's Office (ICO), launched investigations into whether Facebook and Cambridge Analytica had violated data privacy laws. Both companies faced legal action and fines.
- **Facebook's Response:** Facebook faced significant public backlash for its role in the data breach. The company's CEO, Mark Zuckerberg, testified before the US Congress, and Facebook implemented changes to its data privacy policies and platform access to prevent similar incidents.
- **Impact on Public Perception:** The scandal raised awareness about data privacy, the potential for data misuse, and the role of social media in political campaigns. It led to discussions about data protection, ethical considerations in digital politics, and regulatory reforms [10].
- **Global Implications:** The Cambridge Analytica scandal had implications beyond the USA, prompting discussions about data privacy and protection worldwide. It contributed to debates on the responsible use of personal data in digital politics.

Overall, the Cambridge Analytica case was a watershed moment in the world of digital politics. It was an intersection of computational technology, data privacy, and politics, highlighting the need for greater transparency, ethical considerations, and regulatory oversight in the digital age of campaigning and elections.

9.11 Digital Politics

At present, technology is working as a thought engine for global citizens; it created the borderless globalization and has been observed that the technology is undermining democracy up to some extent [11]. The digital politics (Figure 9.3) occurs due to intersection between information and communication technologies (ICT), intelligent algorithms, and political

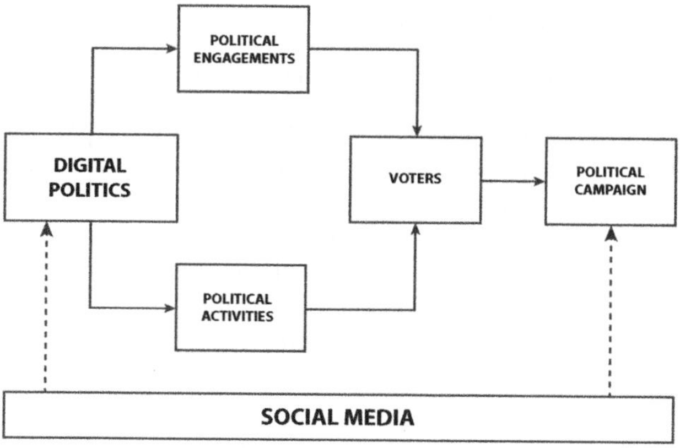

Figure 9.3 Digital politics.

practices and capable to control various political activities such as political campaigning, optimization and scheduling of political resources, and an analysis of political information gathered from various sources [14]. These technologies are useful for governance and policymaking. Digital politics is the resultant effect of social media and the use of AI tools in national and international level media platforms [6]. The incarnation of technology and social media has created a major gap between the real-life politics and virtual politics with exponential countereffects [15, 16].

The dynamics of actors of politics have been completely changed due to various catalytic in the form of technology and algorithms (Table 9.4) [13].

The key factors of *Digital Politics* are as follows:

Table 9.4 Key factors of digital politics.

Key-factors	Impact	Interactions	Example
Technology Platforms	• Access of Global and local political information. • Fabrication of political communication and discourse. Facilitating micro-targeting groups. • Voter manipulation.	• Influence data privacy. • Intrude political transparency of state. • Distraction of political engagements of citizens. • Plug-in of misinformation with traditional campaign strategies.	Social media, Search engines

(*Continued*)

Table 9.4 Key factors of digital politics. (*Continued*)

Key-factors	Impact	Interactions	Example
Data and Algorithms	• Personalization of political campaigns, messaging, and advertising. • Automated decision-making in elections • Major risk of algorithmic biasness and discrimination.	• Data monopolies influence political power dynamics. • Enhances voter targeting and campaign efficiency. • Intertwined with technical platform architecture and content moderation policies.	AI, machine learning, deep learning, big data
Political Actors	• Adapt political campaign strategies for online environments. • Use digital tools for political mobilization and fundraising. • Potential for online political polarization.	• Drive political content creation and broadcasts. • Influence platform algorithms. • Shape and influence the public opinion and political agendas. • Interact with voters directly through the digital channels.	Political candidates, political parties, political activists political affinity groups
Citizens and Voters (e.g., online engagement, misinformation)	• Access political information and news. • Participate in online political discussions and political activities. • Sensitivity towards disinformation and fake news.	• Drive the political contents and political trends on platforms. • Political behaviors of voters and perceptions are shaped and influenced by digital campaigns and information.	Misinformation and disinformation, online engagements

(*Continued*)

Table 9.4 Key factors of digital politics. (*Continued*)

Key-factors	Impact	Interactions	Example
Legal and Regulatory Frameworks	• Attempt to govern online political activity and data uses. • Address issues of online hate speech, misinformation, and disinformation. • Potential for censorship and restriction of freedom of expression of voters and activists.	• Impact online platform policies and content moderation practices. • Shape the use of data and algorithms in political practices. • Influenced by political actors and political lobbying efforts.	Data conditionality, data privacy, data protection acts, regulations for online political campaign, financial regulations

9.12 Conclusion

In summary, AI and sentiment analysis are powerful tools in reshaping the landscape of political campaigns. They provide unprecedented insights into public sentiment, enabling campaigns to personalize messaging, allocate resources efficiently, and engage with voters effectively. However, their ethical use, potential for bias, and data privacy considerations must be carefully addressed to maintain public trust and the integrity of democratic processes. As technology advances, striking a balance between innovation and responsible AI and sentiment analysis practices will be crucial in modern political campaigns.

References

1. Sangle, S.S. and Sedamkar, R.R., NLP-Based Sentiment Analysis with Machine Learning Model for Election Campaign—A Survey, in: *Congress on Intelligent Systems*, pp. 595–612, Springer Nature Singapore, Singapore, 2022.
2. Cambria, E., Das, D., Bandyopadhyay, S., Feraco, A., Affective computing and sentiment analysis, in: *A practical guide to sentiment analysis*, pp. 1–10, 2017.

3. Valle-Cruz, D., Lopez-Chau, A., Sandoval-Almazan, R., How much do Twitter posts affect voters? Analysis of the multi-emotional charge with affective computing in political campaigns, in: *DG. O2021: The 22nd Annual International Conference on Digital Government Research*, pp. 1–14, 2021.
4. Bartlett, J., Smith, J., Acton, R., *The future of political campaigning*, Demos, UK, 2018.
5. Bose, R., Dey, R.K., Roy, S., Sarddar, D., Analyzing political sentiment using Twitter data, in: *Information and Communication Technology for Intelligent Systems: Proceedings of ICTIS 2018*, Volume 2, pp. 427–436, Springer Singapore, 2019.
6. Sharma, P. and Moh, T.-S., Prediction of Indian election using sentiment analysis on Hindi Twitter. *2016 IEEE International Conference on Big Data (Big Data)*, Washington, DC, USA, pp. 1966–1971, 2016, doi: 10.1109/BigData.2016.7840818.
7. Chen, H. and Zimbra, D., AI and opinion mining. *IEEE Intell. Syst.*, 25, 3, 74–80, 2010.
8. Sandoval-Almazan, R. and Valle-Cruz, D., Sentiment analysis of facebook users reacting to political campaign posts. *Digital Gov.: Res. Pract.*, 1, 2, 1–13, 2020.
9. Sandoval-Almazan, R. and Valle-Cruz, D., Facebook impact and sentiment analysis on political campaigns, in: *Proceedings of the 19th annual international conference on digital government research: governance in the data age*, pp. 1–7, 2018.
10. Isaak, J. and Hanna, M.J., User data privacy: Facebook, Cambridge Analytica, and privacy protection. *Computer*, 51, 8, 56–59, 2018.
11. Barber, B.R., The uncertainty of digital politics. *Harv. Int. Rev.*, *23*, 1, 42, 2001.
12. Das, A., Malaviya, S., Singh, M., The Impact of AI-Driven Personalization on Learners' Performance. *Int. J. Comput. Sci. Eng.*, 11, 8, 15–22, 2023, www.ijcseonline.org.
13. Das, A., AI-Enabled Adaptive Learning for Special Needs Students. *IUP J. Inf. Technol.*, *19*, 3, 45–61, 2023.
14. Elmer, G., Live research: Twittering an election debate. *New Media Soc.*, 15, 1, 18–30, 2012.
15. Koc-Michalska, K., Lilleker, D.G., Surowiec, P., Baranowski, P., Poland's 2011 Online Election Campaign: New Tools, New Professionalism, New Ways to Win Votes. *J. Inf. Technol. Polit.*, 11, 2, 186–205, 2014.
16. Fominaya, C.F., *Social movements and globalization: how protests, occupations and uprisings are changing the world*, Palgrave Macmillan, New York, 2014.
17. Sahayak, V., Shete, V., Pathan, A., Sentiment Analysis on Twitter Data. *Int. J. Innov. Res. Adv. Eng.*, 2, 1, 178–183, 2015.

18. Wilson, Wiebe, Hoffmann, Recognizing Contextual Polarity in Phrase-Level Sentiment Analysis. *Proceedings of the 2005 Conference on Empirical Methods in Natural Language Processing (EMNLP)*, pp. 347–354, 2005.
19. Cortes, C. and Vapnik, V., Support vector machines. *Mach. Learn.*, 20, 3, 273–297, 1995.
20. Breiman, L., Random Forests. *Mach. Learn.*, 45, 1, 5–32, 2001.
21. Sepp, H. and Schmidhuber, J., Long short-term memory. *Neural Comput.*, 9, 8, 1735–1780, 1997.

10

Digital Platforms and Leveraging Technologies to Enhance Learner Engagement

Amit Das[1]* and Sanjeev Malaviya[2]

[1]*ICFAI Tech School, The ICFAI University, Dehradun, Uttarakhand, India*
[2]*ICFAI Business School, The ICFAI University, Dehradun, Uttarakhand, India*

Abstract
This article explores the role of technology in enhancing learner engagement. With the continuous advancement of digital tools and platforms, educators have new opportunities to captivate students' interest and create interactive learning experiences. The abstract highlights the potential benefits of leveraging technology to personalize instruction, foster active participation, and bridge the gap between in-classroom and remote learning. By presenting practical examples and considering ethical considerations, the article emphasizes the importance of purposeful technology integration to cultivate a dynamic and student-centric learning environment. Manuscript also intercepted the direct, indirect, moderating, and mediating variables to enhance the learner's engagement through modern technologies.

***Keywords*:** Leveraging technology, learner engagement, digital tools, interactive learning, personalized instruction, AI (artificial intelligence), variables

10.1 Introduction

In the digital era, technology has revolutionized the way we live, work, and learn. In education, the integration of technology has emerged as a powerful tool to enhance learner engagement. With the diverse array of digital tools and platforms available, educators could create dynamic and interactive learning experiences that captivate students' interest and deepen their

**Corresponding author*: amitdas01@gmail.com

Tanupriya Choudhury, Abhijit Kumar, Ravi Tomar, S. Balamurugan and Ankit Vishnoi (eds.) Cyber-Physical Systems for Innovating and Transforming Society 5.0, (211–232) © 2025 Scrivener Publishing LLC

understanding [1]. This article explores the transformative impact of leveraging technology to foster active participation, personalize instruction, and bridge the gap between in-classroom and remote learning environments, ultimately empowering students to thrive in a technology-driven world. Students today are digital natives, born into a world where smartphones, tablets, and computers are part and parcel of daily existence [7]. As such, they expect their educational journey to be enriched by the same technological advancements that have shaped their personal lives. Leveraging technology in education not only aligns with students' expectations but also capitalizes on the potential to revolutionize the traditional classroom experience [8].

In the fast-paced world of education, where attention spans are shrinking and traditional teaching methods may struggle to captivate students, the integration of technology has emerged as a game-changer. Leveraging technology to enhance learner engagement has become a focal point for educators seeking to create dynamic, interactive, and meaningful learning experiences. With the vast array of digital tools, online platforms, and educational applications available, educators have a powerful arsenal at their disposal to capture students' interest, stimulate their curiosity, and foster a genuine passion for learning [1].

By recognizing the profound impact technology can have on learner engagement, educators are reimagining their teaching approaches to create a more interactive and student-centric learning environment. Whether in traditional brick-and-mortar classrooms or in the virtual realm of remote education, technology has the power to transform passive learners into active participants, empowering students to take charge of their learning journey [2].

This article delves into the transformative potential of leveraging technology to enhance learner engagement. It explores the myriad ways in which digital tools and platforms can be harnessed to create personalized learning experiences, foster active participation, and bridge the gap between educators and learners. As we embark on this exploration, it becomes clear that the integration of technology is not simply about adopting the latest gadgets or trends; rather, it is a deliberate and purposeful effort to meet the evolving needs of modern learners and equip them with the skills necessary to thrive in an increasingly interconnected and digital world.

The modern educational technologies impacted the education (Table 10.1) in modern days as follows:

Table 10.1 Educational technologies.

Educational technologies	Impact
Interactive Learning Platforms	The use of a learning management system provides interactive learning with a high degree of learning engagements [11].
Gamification	The unique teaching pedagogy includes the digital gaming elements in teaching to make the learning experiences more enjoyable and motivated [1].
Virtual Reality (VR) and Augmented Reality (AR)	Virtual reality (VR) and augmented reality (AR) are capable of fabricating the teaching environment, making them more interactive and collaborative. Simulators and digital 3D models motivate learners to understand the knowledge more deeply [11].
Educational Video Contents	The sharing of instructional or educational videos through various social media platforms helps learners learn the concepts in an 'anytime, anywhere' approach.
Educational Podcast and Audio Resources	The educational podcasts and audio resources provide an easy approach of learning and engagements to the learners.
Integration of social media	The intensive use of social media platforms aims to collaborate, spread, and share educational and knowledge resources [3].
Adaptive Learning System	The adaptive learning systems is useful to create the personalized learning environment based on the unique learning needs of the learner.
Educational Recommender System	The educational recommender systems recommend the educational resources and contents to the learner's as per their learning needs.
Education Learning-Mobile Apps	The dense availability of mobile phones help learners to access the educational contents (audio and video) as per their convenience and availability.
Collaborative Tools for Educational Projects	Digital platforms are used for geographical borderless educational collaboration and exchange of knowledge between the learners.

(*Continued*)

Table 10.1 Educational technologies. (*Continued*)

Educational technologies	Impact
Online Simulation and Virtual Labs	The online simulators and virtual labs facilitate the hands-on learning and experimental learning to learners.
E-Books, Digital texts and E-Libraries	The digital contents and e-books are convenient to carry due to their portability. The E-libraries assures the learners to access digitally learning contents from anywhere and anytime.
Artificial Intelligence (AI), Machine Learning, Deep Learning, Transformative Learning	These AI-driven educational platforms create a personalized learning environment by using AI, machine learning, and deep learning algorithms and programs.
Educational Webinars and Virtual talks	By using digital platforms, the speakers could be invited through the virtual platforms from the diverse domains to develop a multidisciplinary approach among the learners.
Learner' Feedback and Assessment Tools	There is a use of online tools to gather instant feedback and assessment of the performances of the learners.
Learner's Data Analytics	Data analytics tools are useful to intercept the learner's profile and learning patterns.
Flipped Class-room Models	A blended model of classroom teaching uses advanced educational technologies to increase the learner's engagement.
Personal Learning Paths	By using a personalized learning environment, the learners are capable of selecting the unique learning approach as per the unique learning environment.

10.2 Personalized Instruction and Adaptive Learning

One of the most significant benefits of technology in education is the ability to personalize instruction based on individual student needs and learning styles [5]. Adaptive learning platforms utilize data-driven insights to identify each student's strengths and areas for required improvement, tailoring lessons to suit their unique learning requirements. By offering customized content at an appropriate level of difficulty and pace, technology ensures that learners remain challenged and motivated, enhancing their overall engagement in the learning process [12].

In the traditional classroom setting, teachers or educational institutions face the challenge of accommodating the diverse learning needs of their students. While some learners grasp concepts quickly and thrive in a fast-paced environment, others may require additional time and support to acquire knowledge from the same material. This variability in learning styles and paces often makes it difficult for educators to provide individualized attention to each student [11].

The facility of personalized instruction and adaptive learning made possible by the involvement of leveraging technology. It is offering a revolutionary approach to address and handle various learning challenges. Through tailoring the learning experience to suit each student's unique strengths, weaknesses, and preferences, personalized instruction aims to optimize learning outcomes and enhance learner engagement [10].

The concept of personalized learning could be achieved by using the approach of adaptive learning, a concept driven by data analytics and AI. Adaptive learning systems gather real-time data on students' performance, interactions, and progress. Through sophisticated algorithms, these systems analyze the data to identify patterns, strengths, and areas for improvement for each individual student. Based on these insights, the technology then adjusts the content, difficulty level, and learning pace to meet the student at their current skill level. For example, a learner who excels in mathematics may be presented with more challenging problems to maintain engagement and stimulate further learning growth. On the other hand, a student who struggles with certain concepts might receive additional explanations, practice exercises, or alternative learning materials to reinforce more understanding.

The resultant benefits of personalized instruction and adaptive learning are exponential towards the learning growth of the learner. Students experience a unique sense of ownership and control over their learning journey, as the content is customized to match their individual knowledge needs. This empowerment fosters a positive learning experience and encourages a growth mindset to the learner. The adaptive learning systems provide (Figure 10.1) instant feedback and progress tracking, enabling students to identify their learning strengths and weaknesses accurately. This real-time

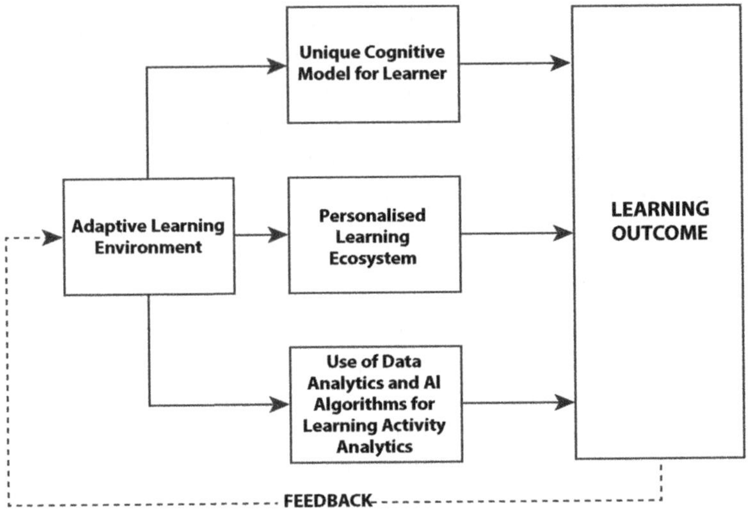

Figure 10.1 Learning outcome.

feedback loop enhances metacognition, as students gain insight into their learning strategies and adjust accordingly.

The adaptive nature of the technology ensures that students are neither uneasy by content that is too challenging nor bored by material they have already mastered. This learning process balance keeps students engaged, motivated, and continuously progressing in their academic journey [13].

Incorporating personalized instruction and adaptive learning into educational settings can occur in various ways. It may involve using educational software and digital platforms that adapt content based on individual responses [2]. Additionally, online learning management systems and educational apps can facilitate personalized learning paths for students, providing a wealth of resources and interactive activities catered to their needs.

However, it is crucial to acknowledge that technology is not a replacement for human educators; rather, it complements their efforts and empowers them to better support their students. Teachers play a pivotal role in interpreting data insights from adaptive learning systems and providing further guidance, mentorship, and encouragement to students.

Personalized instruction and adaptive learning represent a paradigm shift in education. By leveraging technology to tailor the learning experience to individual students, educators can promote engagement, foster a love for learning, and ultimately unlock each student's full potential [4]. As technology continues to advance, the potential for personalized and adaptive learning to revolutionize education and create a more equitable

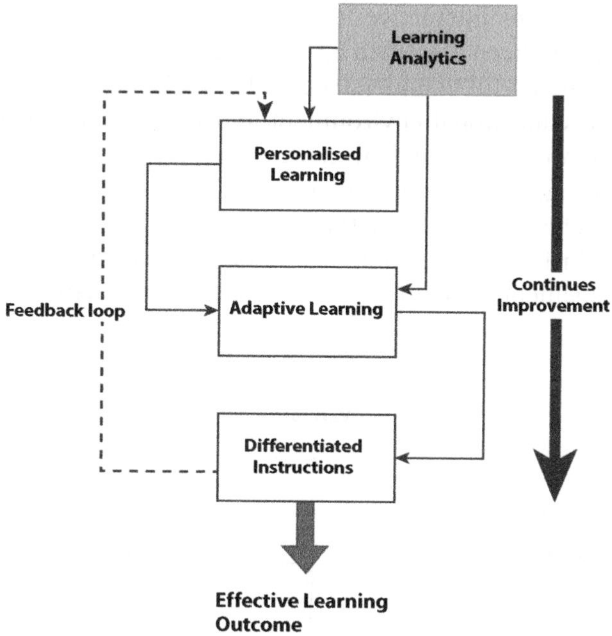

Figure 10.2 Learning analytics.

and inclusive learning environment becomes ever more promising. The efficiency of digital learning platforms is determined by the capabilities of learning analytics. Learning analytics (Figure 10.2) is the process of gathering, analysing, and reporting data on learners and their contexts to improve education. It uses data from sources like online platforms and assessments to provide insights into student performance and engagement.

10.3 Interactive Learning Experiences

Digital tools have redefined how students interact with educational content. From virtual simulations to interactive quizzes, technology brings subjects to life and transforms passive learners into active participants. Augmented reality and VR enable students to explore historical sites, dive into the depths of the ocean, or even travel to distant planets, creating immersive and memorable learning experiences. Gamification techniques, such as rewards, badges, and leaderboards, inject an element of fun and competition, motivating students to stay engaged and continuously improve their performance [15].

The fabrication of interactive learning environment involved various variables that have been identified by the researchers. Through those, multiple variables are useful to understand and visualize the complex relationships between educational environment and technologies (Figure 10.3). The identified variables could be categories under independent, dependent, moderating, and mediating variables (Table 10.2) [16, 17].

The comprehensive study of those variables gives an understanding about the intrinsic relationship between interactive learning technologies, learner's engagement, and other potential influencing factors [18].

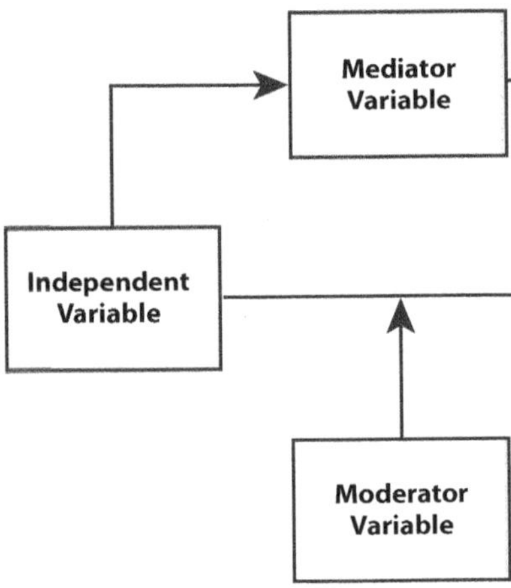

Figure 10.3 Relation between different variables.

Table 10.2 Types of variables.

Independent Variable	• The independent variable directly impacts the dependent variable. • It has been observed by the researchers that the slight variation in the independent variable affects the dependent variable. • It is the potential input or cause during the research.
Dependent Variable	• The dependent variable presents the changes that occurred due to independent variables.
Moderator Variable	• It is a factor that influences the relationship between independent and dependent variables or in other words it identifies the conditions under which the relationship between dependent and independent variable may be varied.
Mediator Variable	• This variable is responsible in explaining the process through which the independent variable affects the dependent variables.

The probable list of variables (Table 10.3) associated with the interactive learning technologies and learner's engagement are given below:

Table 10.3 Variables for digital learning.

Independent Variable	• Type of Technology Platform • Level of Gamification • Multimedia Content for Learning • Platform integration with Social Media • Mobile Learning Platform
Dependent Variables	• Learning Outcomes • Learner's Engagement • Learner's Satisfaction • Knowledge/Skill Acquisition • Retention Rates
Moderating Variables	• Prior Knowledge about the Subject • Learning Style • Technology Proficiency • Level of Instructor Support • Motivation Level of Learner
Mediating Variables	• Level of Technology Acceptance • Learner Engagement • Self-Efficacy of Learner • Collaborative Learning • Learner's Cognitive Load

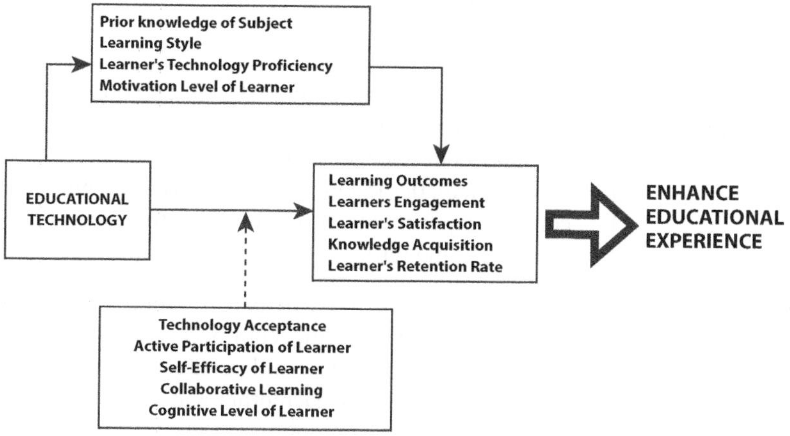

Figure 10.4 Enhanced educational experiences.

Interactive learning experiences are educational activities that require active participation and engagement from learners, going beyond passive consumption of information. These experiences (Figure 10.4) can be implemented in various learning settings, including classrooms, workshops, online platforms, and informal learning environments [19].

The learner's engagement is the crucial aspect of the online learning platforms, the level of engagement is associated with the various variables [5]. The *mathematical model* could be useful to show the relationship between different attributes of learning.

Let

E_L : Level of Engagement of the Learner

T_i : Interactive Learning Technology used for the Learning by the Learner

M : Motivation Level of the Learner

P_k : Learner's Prior Knowledge about the subject

The mathematical model could be expressed as follows: -

$$E_L = \alpha_0 + \alpha_1 T_i + \alpha_2 M + \alpha_3 P_k + \in \qquad (10.1)$$

where

α_0 : It is a constant term, representing the initial level of learner's engagement when (T_i, M, P_k) are zero.

$\alpha_1, \alpha_2, \alpha_3$: Representing the weight of variables (T_i, M, P_k) on E_L.

$\in$: This is the error term, presenting unobserved factors influencing the engagement level of the learner.

The key aspects (Table 10.4) of interactive learning experiences are:

Table 10.4 Interactive learning experiences.

Features	Experiences
Hands-on Activities	Learners directly engage with materials and objects to explore concepts and principles. This approach is common in science, technology, engineering, and mathematics (STEM) fields, where students conduct experiments or build models to deepen their understanding [20].
Group Discussions	Encouraging learners to participate in group discussions promotes critical thinking, communication skills, and the exchange of ideas and perspectives. It allows students to learn from each other and develop their viewpoints on a given topic.

(Continued)

Table 10.4 Interactive learning experiences. (*Continued*)

Features	Experiences
Simulations and Role-Playing	Simulations replicate real-life scenarios, enabling learners to apply their knowledge and skills in a controlled environment. Role-playing exercises can help students empathize with different roles and understand complex situations better [21].
Gamification	Integrating game elements and mechanics into the learning process can make it more enjoyable and motivating. Points, badges, leaderboards, and challenges can create a sense of achievement and foster a competitive spirit [4].
Interactive Multimedia	Educational videos, animations, simulations, and VR experiences immerse learners in the subject matter, making it more engaging and memorable. Visual and auditory stimuli enhance comprehension and retention [3].
Collaborative Projects	Group projects promote teamwork, collaboration, and communication skills. Learners work together to explore topics in-depth, share responsibilities, and solve problems collectively [10].
Interactive Online Platforms	Web-based tools and platforms provide interactive quizzes, exercises, and multimedia content to actively engage learners in self-paced or instructor-led courses. These platforms often track progress and offer personalized learning experiences.
Field Trips	Taking learners outside the classroom to relevant locations, such as museums, historical sites, or nature reserves, provides hands-on experiences and a deeper understanding of the subject matter in real-world contexts [11].
Problem-Based Learning	Learners are presented with real-world problems to solve, fostering critical thinking, research skills, and creative solutions. This approach prepares students for real challenges they may encounter in their careers [5].
Peer Teaching	Allowing learners to teach and explain concepts to their peers reinforces their understanding of the material. This method enhances retention and confidence in their knowledge.

The benefits of interactive learning experiences include increased learner engagement, better retention of information, improved problem-solving abilities, and enhanced critical thinking skills. By actively participating in their learning, students develop a deeper understanding of the subject matter and are better equipped to apply their knowledge in practical situations [23]. Effective implementation of interactive learning experiences can lead to more enjoyable and effective learning outcomes.

The process-map is a visual representation of the entire integrated outlines of steps and complete flow of process in the system. It provides a crystal-clear idea and systematic overview of the different elements that associate and contribute to gain the specified goal or objective. Figure 10.5 is presenting the visual outlining all the key steps and the components in the process of integrating technologies to deliver the best education with conducive learning environment [24].

10.4 Leveraging Technology: Inclusivity and Access to Education

The induction of leveraging technology in education breaks down barriers to learning, making education more inclusive and accessible to all. With remote learning platforms and online courses, geographical constraints are no longer a hindrance, allowing students from diverse backgrounds to access quality education (Figure 10.5). Additionally, technology accommodates various learning styles and preferences, ensuring that every student can engage with the content in a way that suits the learner in the best approach [25].

Inclusivity and access to education are crucial aspects of a fair and equitable society. The emerging technologies in education have created various direct and indirect benefits to the society.

The benefits could be listed as below:

- They refer to providing education to all learners, regardless of their background, abilities, gender, ethnicity, socioeconomic status, or geographic location, with equal opportunities of learning and to receive all learning benefits from the educational system.
- Inclusivity in education focuses on creating learning environments that welcome diversity, respect different perspectives, and foster a sense of belonging with the educational ecosystem for all students.

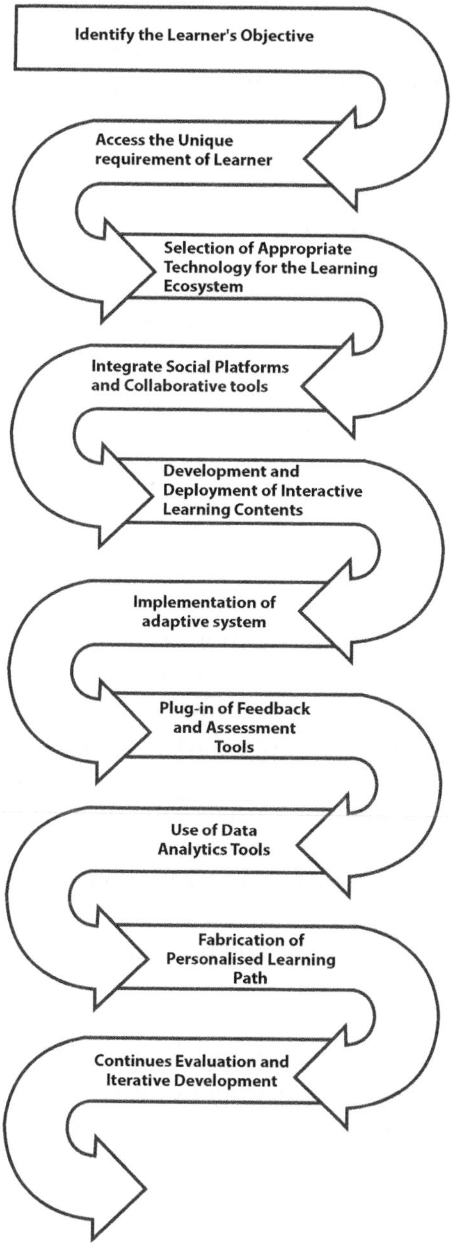

Figure 10.5 Process of digital learning.

- An inclusive education system incorporates diverse perspectives, cultures, and histories into the curriculum, promoting understanding and empathy among learners with unique learning solutions.

10.5 Seamless Learning

The flexibility of technology allows for seamless knowledge transition between in-classroom learning and remote learning. Cloud-based collaboration tools enable real-time interaction between students and teachers, fostering a sense of strong learning community and support regardless of physical location. Hybrid learning models combine the benefits of face-to-face instruction with the advantages of technology, providing a versatile and adaptive approach that caters to the changing unique needs of global learners.

Seamless in-classroom and remote learning, also known as hybrid or blended learning, refers to a modern educational approach that integrates both traditional face-to-face instruction and online learning experiences. The goal is to create a cohesive and flexible learning environment that allows students to transition smoothly between in-person and remote learning modes (Figure 10.6). The induction of information and communication technology (ICT) with the teaching pedagogies created the good number of learning facilities for learners without geographic and time zone restrictions. Seamless learning is creating frictionless learning experiences for the learners with the freedom to learn as per their learning requirements or needs.

The online learning facilities could be categories under two heads. They are as follow:

- Asynchronous online learning classes
  The *asynchronous online learning classes* facilitate learners to learn as per their own schedule within a specific time frame. Learners can finish the allocated assignments and other learning contents during the certain time calendar such as a one-week or two-week period.
- Synchronous online learning classes
  The *synchronous online learning classes* facilitate the learners to join the virtual classroom with classmates and an instructor as per the schedule timetable. The learner can join the classrooms from anywhere due to the virtual nature

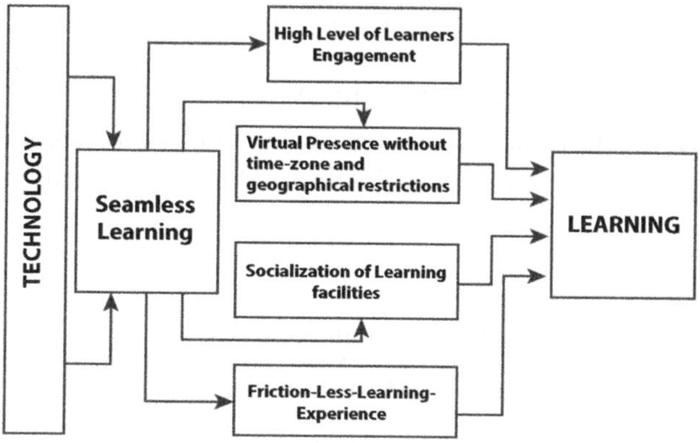

Figure 10.6 Seamless learning.

of classroom and could be actively participated with fellow classmates in real-time learning activities or discussions during the specified class time.

10.6 Ethical Considerations and Digital Citizenship

The exponential growth of internet technologies is creating enormous opportunities for the learners to enhance their engagements towards the gathering of knowledge or skills as per emerging needs. It is essential for the complete digital ecosystem to promote ethical considerations among the user for responsible digital citizenship [6]. Instructors or educators must guide learners to handle digital platforms by using technologies responsibly, ethically, and safely [27].

The digital platforms contain a very high volume of information and learning data. It is necessary for digital learners to develop the critical thinking and digital literacy to handle the digital platforms ethically. It will help learners to identify the credible source of knowledge and learning platforms. This informed approach may help the learner to expand the user experiences (UX) ethically [9, 14, 22].

In the era of IT, AI and ML, ethical considerations and digital citizenships are important aspects and required for the navigation in the online platforms [7]. The digital citizenship motivates the internet user to handle online or digital platforms in a responsible manner to engage with society. Misinformation, deepfakes, and non-ethical use of information could be addressed and stopped by the deployment of digital ethics and digital citizenships [27].

Online learners must obey the ethical consideration (Table 10.5) and strictly apply strong ethical behavior during the use of technologies for online education [26]. The matrix (Table 10.6) for the ethical use of digital learning ecosystem is as follows:

Table 10.5 Ethical consideration for online learners.

Dimensions	Ethical considerations for online learners
Academic Integrity	Avoid plagiarism and properly cite references of sources.
	Maintain honesty in the completion of assignments, exams, and other online activities.
	Honor the academic work of others and avoid cheating.
Respectful online Communication	Conduct the respectful and inclusive communication with peers and instructors.
	Avoid any type of online delivery of offensive language, discrimination, and harassment.
	Respecting diverse perspectives of thoughts and opinions.
Learner's Data Privacy & Security	Safeguarding personal information and respecting others' privacy.
	Strict security protocols for online platforms and digital tools.
	Systematic reporting of unethical behavior encountered on digital platforms.
Time Management	Meeting deadlines and manage time effectively for the completion of assignments and learning activities participation.
	Avoiding unauthorized assistance.
	Communicating with course instructors if facing digital platform challenges that may impact deadlines.

(Continued)

Table 10.5 Ethical consideration for online learners. (*Continued*)

Dimensions	Ethical considerations for online learners
Use of Technology	Using technology responsibly and ethically in the learning environment.
	Respecting software licenses and intellectual property rights.
	Handling technical issues and troubleshooting promptly.
Learner's Participation and Collative Learning	Engaging actively in online discussions and collaborative learning activities.
	Providing constructive real-time feedback to peers and respecting diverse opinions of other learners.
	Avoiding online behaviors that may disturb the learning experience of other learners.
Awareness about Digital Literacy	Developing critical thinking skills for evaluation of available online information.
	Completing fact-checking and verifying information before sharing with others.
	Recognizing and avoiding the spread of misinformation and fake information.
Digital Accessibility	Ensuring learning content and communications are accessible to all learners.
	Informing instructors of any accessibility needs and seeking accommodations.
	Respecting diverse learning styles and approach of peers.

10.7 Conclusion

Modern leveraging technologies are enhancing the learner's engagement and working as the most transformative force in education. The process of personalized instruction is increasing the learner's learning experiences and continues learning motivation. The technologies are playing an important role in making learners active for their educational activities and

Table 10.6 Digital citizenship and digital ethics.

Key factors	Digital citizenship	Digital ethics
Digital User's Responsibility	Respect for other online users	Ethical use of digital technologies and digital platforms
	Responsible sharing of authenticated information	Avoid digital content plagiarism
	Awareness of digital footprint and digital profile	Avoid infringement of Intellectual Property Rights (IPR)
Privacy of Data	Protection of personal information of users	Respect other digital users' privacy
	Understanding about online privacy settings	Avoiding unauthorized access of any digital platforms or user's data
	Safeguard of sensitive and confidential data	Transparent in data practices and data protection
User Safety	Rules for respectful conduction of online platforms	Reporting of inappropriate content to policy makers for compliances
	Prevention from Cyberbullying	Strong legal framework for online harassment
	Authentic and secure online accounts	Avoid harmful online activities
Problem Solving & Critical Thinking	Active evaluation of online information	Avoiding misinformation and deep fakes
	Analyzing of digital media critically	Continues fact-checking of available information
	Regular evaluation of online sources	Recognizing biased content or digital platforms

(*Continued*)

Table 10.6 Digital citizenship and digital ethics. (*Continued*)

Key factors	Digital citizenship	Digital ethics
Digital Literacy	Basic digital skills	Promotion of media literacy
	Information literacy	Encouragement of critical thinking
	Technological proficiency	Digital media literacy
Global Digital Citizens	Respecting diverse perspectives and digital cultures	Avoid delivering online hate speech and hate contents
	Promoting digital inclusion and cohesiveness	Understanding the global implications of digital malpractice of digital content and digital activities
	Cultural sensitivity about online contents and activities	Avoid online discrimination

promoting the inclusivity. The digital learning ecosystem and digital learning tools have created the dynamic learner-centric-learning-environment to inspire learning curiosity, learning passion and assist learners to achieve more learning goals in digital era. The quick development and delivery of digital learning platforms indicates some socio-techno challenges and such issues could be handled and abolished with the help of a strict ethical approach. It is necessary for the learners to enjoy the digital platforms required the good understanding about the advantages and disadvantages of digital platforms and probable ethical aspects.

References

1. Coates, H., Leveraging LMSs to enhance campus-based student engagement, *Educause Q., 28*, 1, 66–68, 2005.
2. Priyatno, A. and Rianita, E., Leveraging gamification into EFL grammar class to boost student engagement. *Teach. English Technol.*, 22, 2, 90–114, 2022.
3. Coates, H., A model of online and general campus-based student engagement. *Assess. Eval. Higher Educ.*, 32, 2, 121–141, 2007.

4. Campbell, M., Maridelys, D., Lucio, R., Can a digital whiteboard foster student engagement? *Soc. Work Educ.*, 38, 6, 735–752, 2019.
5. Chaka, C., Nkhobo, T., Lephalala, M., Leveraging Student Engagement through MS Teams at an Open and Distance E-Learning Institution. *J. Educ. e-Learning Res.*, 9, 3, 136–146, 2022.
6. Ribble, M.S., Bailey, G.D., Ross, T.W., Digital citizenship: Addressing appropriate technology behavior. *Learn. Leading Technol.*, *32*, 1, 6, 2004.
7. Wulandari, E. and Triyanto, W., Digital Citizenship Education: Shaping Digital Ethics in Society 5.0. *Univers. J. Educ. Res.*, 9, 5, 948–956, 2021, DOI: 10.13189/ujer.2021.090507.
8. Alagha, I., Leveraging Semantic Web Technologies to Enhance Individual and Collaborative Learning, in: *2013 Palestinian International Conference on Information and Communication Technology*, pp. 1–7, 2013, doi: 10.1109/PICICT.2013.11.
9. Koretsky, M.D. and Magana, A.J., Using Technology to Enhance Learning and Engagement in Engineering. *Adv. Eng. Educ.*, 7, 2, 2019.
10. Sarker, M.N., II, Wu, M., Cao, Q., Alam, G.M., Li, D., Leveraging digital technology for better learning and education: A systematic literature review. *Int. J. Inf. Educ. Technol.*, 9, 7, 453–461, 2019.
11. Ignatyeva, I., The Trend of Technologisation of Modern Education (the Use of Humanitarian Technologies). *Procedia – Soc. Behav. Sci.*, *214*, 606–613, 2015. doi:10.1016/j.sbspro.2015.11.766.
12. Walkington, C.A., Using adaptive learning technologies to personalize instruction to student interests: The impact of relevant contexts on performance and learning outcomes. *J. Educ. Psychol.*, *105*, 4, 932, 2013.
13. Das, A., Malaviya, S., Singh, M., The Impact of AI-Driven Personalization on Learners' Performance. *Int. J. Comp. Sci. Eng.*, *11*, 8, 15–22, 2023.
14. Das, A., AI-Enabled Adaptive Learning for Special Needs Students. *IUP J. Inf. Technol.*, 19, 3, 45–61, 2023.
15. Rafatirad, S. and , Sayadi, H., *Advancing Personalized and Adaptive Learning Experience in Education with Artificial Intelligence*, pp. 1–6, 2023, doi: 10.23919/EAEEIE55804.2023.10181336.
16. Lok Cheung, S., Rosunally, Y., Simon, S., Kamran, M., Personalised Learning through Context-Based Adaptation in the Serious Games with Gating Mechanism. *Educ. Inf. Technol.*, 28, 1–32, 2023. doi: 10.1007/s10639-023-11695-8.
17. Kamal, K., K., Personalized Education Based on Hybrid Intelligent Recommendation System. *J. Math.*, 2022, 1–9, 2022. doi: 10.1155/2022/1313711.
18. Bieliaieva, O., Skrypnikova, T., Khmil, T.A., Interactive learning technologies in higher education as a tool for training a competitive specialist. *Probl. Ekol. Med.*, 26, 5-6, 32–36, 2022. doi: 10.31718/mep.2022.26.5-6.06.
19. Leslie, A., Beverley, E., Sian, M.P., Enhancing the online learning experience using virtual interactive classrooms. *Aust. J. Adv. Nurs.*, *32*, 4, 22–31, 2015.

20. Quadir, B., Yang, J.C., Chen, N.S., The effects of interaction types on learning outcomes in a blog-based interactive learning environment. *Interact. Learn. Environ., 30*, 2, 293–306, 2022.
21. Mamolo, L.A., Students' evaluation and learning experience on the utilization of Digital Interactive Math Comics (DIMaC) mobile app. *Adv. Mob. Learn. Educ. Res., 2*, 2, 375–388, 2022.
22. Barrett, N.E., Liu, G.Z., Wang, H.C., Seamless learning for oral presentations: Designing for performance needs. *Comp. Assisted Lang. Learn., 35*, 3, 551–576, 2022.
23. Gürhan, D. and Serkan, C., Seamless Learning: A Scoping Systematic Review Study, 5, 4, 225–234, 2018, doi: 10.20448/JOURNAL.509.2018.54.225.234.
24. Shaheen, N.L., Technology accessibility: How US K-12 schools are enacting policy and addressing the equity imperative. *Comp. Educ., 179*, 104414, 2022.
25. Lambert, S.G., A tangible manipulative for inclusive quadrilateral learning. *J. Technol. Persons Disabil., 10*, 1, 66–81, 2022.
26. Capuno, R., Suson, R., Suladay, D., Arnaiz, V., Villarin, I., Jungoy, E., Digital Citizenship in Education and Its Implication. *World J. Educ. Technol.: Curr. Iss., 14*, 2, 426–437, 2022.
27. Hawamdeh, M., Altınay, Z., Altınay, F., Arnavut, A., Ozansoy, K., Adamu, I., Comparative analysis of students and faculty level of awareness and knowledge of digital citizenship practices in a distance learning environment: case study. *Educ. Inf. Technol., 27*, 5, 6037–6068, 2022.

11

Disruptive Technologies in Cyber-Physical Systems in War

Ayan Sar[1], Tanupriya Choudhury[1], Rahul Kumar Singh[2], Abhijit Kumar[2]*, Hussain Falih Mahdi[3] and Ankit Vishnoi[4]

[1]*School of Computer Sciences, University of Petroleum and Energy Studies (UPES), Dehradun, Uttarakhand, India*
[2]*School of Computer Science, University of Petroleum and Energy Studies (UPES), Dehradun, Uttarakhand, India*
[3]*Department of Computer and Software Engineering, University of Diyala, Baquba, Iraq*
[4]*CSE Department, Graphic Era Deemed to be University, Dehradun, Uttarakhand, India*

Abstract

The real-time integration of disruptive technologies within the realm of the cyber-physical systems (CPS) has been in the process of revolutionizing the intricate landscape of warfare, with particular attention and emphasis on the directed energy weapons, which are available with the developed countries, autonomous systems and the potential of artificial intelligence (AI). This research framework would delve into the rapidly transforming impact of disruptive technologies on the defense posture systems (DPS), ultimately elucidating the fact of their important role in the reshaping of the strategies that the military should acquire. The directed energy weapons (DEWs), which consisted of the laser and microwave systems, had the potential to offer rapid and more precise capabilities for targeting the enemy, which might alter the present scenario of the traditional kinetics of modern warfare. The autonomous systems, which ranged from uncrewed aerial vehicles to ground-based robots, introduced their heightened agility and ultimately reduced human risk in many operational environments. On the other hand, simultaneously, AI-driven decision-making would enhance the adaptive and strategic capabilities of the modern-day DPS systems, which would optimize the responses to more dynamically different battlefield scenarios. The integration

**Corresponding author*: ahijitkaran@hotmail.com

Tanupriya Choudhury, Abhijit Kumar, Ravi Tomar, S. Balamurugan and Ankit Vishnoi (eds.) Cyber-Physical Systems for Innovating and Transforming Society 5.0, (233–250) © 2025 Scrivener Publishing LLC

and real-time fusion of these disruptive technologies would not only amplify the lethality and accuracy of the operations done by the military but also pose many novel challenges in the perspective of ethical considerations, frameworks which would be legal, and leveraging the real potential for its adversarial exploitation. This proposed system would underscore the traditional and multifaceted implications of the disruptive technologies within the realm of CPS, specifically from the perspective of DPS, and ultimately shedding light on the strategic implications along with the ethical dimensions and the evolving nature of modern warfare.

***Keywords*:** Modern warfare, military applications, intelligent systems, responsible innovation, transparent transactions

11.1 Introduction

In this ever-evolving landscape of modern warfare, the integration and convergence of disruptive technologies and cyber-physical systems (CPS) has rapidly emerged as a transformative force, allowing to reshape the various nature of conflicts and strategic operations. This chapter delves into the field of intricate interplay between the disruptive and CPS, which unravels the implications for contemporary warfare. Cyber-physical systems, often characterized by the addition of computational elements with physical processes, have been the epicentral backbone of military operations. These intelligent systems can synchronize information technology, communication networks, and various other physical entities to enhance their human capability of decision-making, logistics, and overall efficiency on the battlefield. The fusion and integration of disruptive technologies within CPS introduce a new paradigm shift while redefining its boundaries of what is achievable in modern warfare. At the extreme forefront of this rapid evolution is artificial intelligence (AI), driving autonomous systems and their decision-making process. The role of AI in military applications extends itself from predictive analysis to that of autonomous weapon systems, accompanying a new era of efficiency and adaptability on the battlefield. Simultaneously, the deployment of various autonomous systems, including drones and uncrewed vehicles, also revolutionized the investigation, scrutiny, and tactical operations, reducing dangerous human exposure to various hazardous environments in real-time. However, this blend of disruptive technologies also raises the bar of ethical and legal concerns, prompting the need for reformation of the rules and regulations. The exploration of the intricate balance between innovation and responsibility is also important, shedding light on the potential risks and challenges associated with the integration of disruptive technologies in CPS warfare. As we move forward in this field, the understanding of various dynamics of disruptive technologies within the scope of CPS becomes a point of supreme importance for strategists, policymakers, and technocrats in ensuring the future security and stability of the world.

11.2 Cyber-Physical Systems in Modern Warfare

11.2.1 Exploring Cyber-Physical Systems: Definition and Key Characteristics

Cyber-physical systems (CPS) represent the integration and fusion of various computational algorithms and physical processes, creating an interconnected system that is capable of monitoring, controlling, as well as responding to the physical world. At the core level, CPS combines the virtual world of computer systems with the tactile aspects of the physical world, creating a symbiotic relationship where information from the physical environment is gathered, processed, and utilized to make various real-time decisions. It had its key components, which make the system intelligent and efficient, as seen in Figure 11.1. Figure 11.1 has three main pillars, but others make the system stronger.

- Computational Algorithms: CPS integrates smart advanced algorithms designed to analyze and interpret data from various sources. These algorithms are capable enough to enable the systems to derive insights, make predictions, and execute actions based on the information received.
- Communication Networks: Bilateral exchange of information is a fundamental aspect of the CPS. Robust communication networks also facilitate seamless connectivity between different elements of the military ecosystem, including sensors, vehicles, command centers, and other autonomous systems.
- Physical Entities: CPS involves the blending of various other physical entities such as sensors, uncrewed vehicles, and other military hardware. These entities also serve as the eyes and ears of the system, collecting data from the physical world and relaying it to the computational components.

The key characteristics include:

- Interconnectedness: CPS establishes an interconnected, networked environment where various components communicate and share information in real time. This interconnected network enables a holistic approach to the battlefield, fostering and promoting coordinated and synchronized military operations.
- Real-time data processing: The ability to process data swiftly is a real hallmark of CPS. Real-time data processing allows the intelligent system for rapid decision-making, which is considered a critical capability in dynamic and rapidly evolving military scenarios.
- Autonomy: Some CPS components exhibit a degree of autonomy, which implies that they can operate and make human decisions using intelligent algorithms with minimum human intervention. This autonomy enhances the efficiency and responsiveness of the military systems to a greater extent.
- Integration of Physical and Virtual Components: CPS seamlessly blends the physical and virtual realms and aspects. Physical sensors and entities generate data, which is further processed in the virtual domain for deriving valuable and actionable insights and informing decisions to policymakers.

The integration of CPS in the era of modern warfare is very transformative. It empowers military forces with various unprecedented capabilities to gather, process, and act upon information swiftly and decisively.

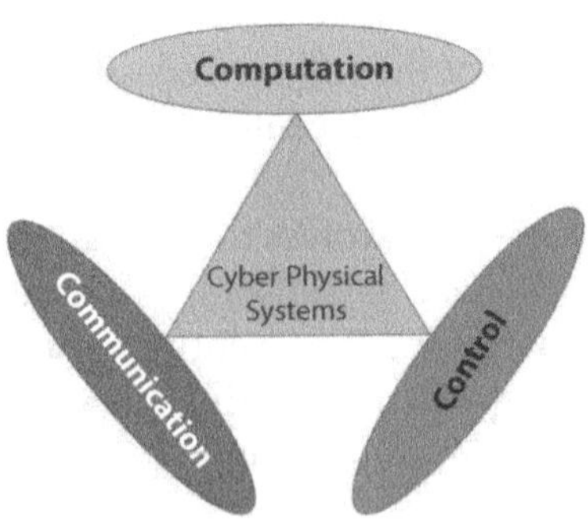

Figure 11.1 Three pillars of a cyber-physical system.

The merging of computational power with the physical environment results in the enhancement of situational awareness and logistical optimization of CPS, which ultimately contributes to the effectiveness and success of military operations.

11.2.2 Integration of CPS in Military Operations

The integration of CPS in military operations necessitates the use of advanced technologies to streamline and optimize various aspects of warfare. This fusion is characterized by:

- Real-time Data Processing: CPS enables the processing of vast amounts of real-time data in different formats generated from sensors, surveillance equipment, and other sources. This capability provides military decision-makers with up-to-the-minute information for fast and efficient decision-making.
- Command and Control Systems: CPS improves command and control systems by the interconnection of military units, vehicles, and command centers through communication networks. This network system facilitates seamless and efficient communication, coordination, and information sharing across the battlefield.
- Logistics and Supply Chain Management: In the military logistics supply, CPS optimizes the movement and distribution of resources in an efficient manner. The automated tracking systems (ATS) and the utilization of sensors and radio-frequency identification (RFID) technology ensure the efficient management of the supplies and reduce delays while improving the overall logistic performance.
- Situational Awareness: CPS strengthens situational awareness by intermingling data from various sources, such as satellites, uncrewed vehicles, and ground sensors. This consolidated information provides a very comprehensive understanding of the battlefield while enabling all military policymakers to make informed decisions.
- Unmanned systems: CPS often includes autonomous systems like drones and uncrewed vehicles to operate with a degree of autonomy, and successfully carry out tasks such as reconnaissance or surveillance without human intervention, thereby increasing the military's capabilities and reducing human hazards.

The working of CPS can be understood from the below Figure 11.2. It fully demonstrated the backend working and the way of integrating with the military operations.

11.2.3 Cyber-Physical Systems in Achieving Operational Objectives

In this realm of modern warfare, CPS play a part in reshaping the landscape of military operations through their unique mixture of various intelligent computational algorithms, communication networks, and physical entities. At the core level, CPS exemplify a holistic approach to warfare through the smooth integration of digital and physical domains. This integration is not only a technological confluence but a strategic shift that has had profound implications for how the military objectives are being visualized, planned, and executed in a planned way.

The importance of CPS in the achievement of operational objectives stems from its ability to enhance the overall efficiency and effectiveness of various military endeavors. The nature of the network of the different components of CPS would allow for a more holistic and dynamic approach to the battlefield while ultimately enabling a more efficient and accurate way of military decision-making. This network would surely extend the different facets of the military applications and operations, which would start from the strategic planning for logistical execution.

On the other hand, another key facet would be the rapid transformation of different techniques of strategic planning and decision support.

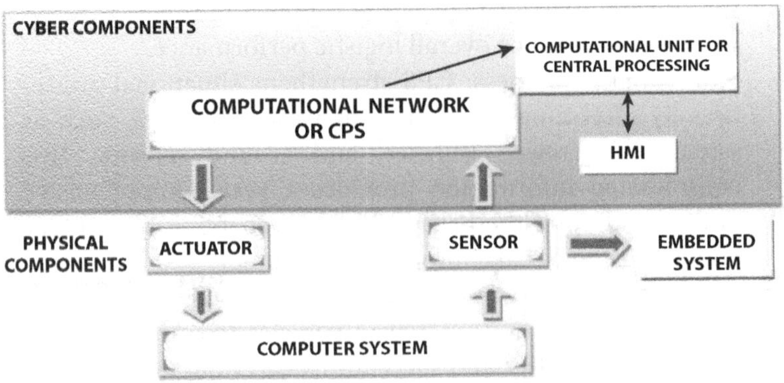

Figure 11.2 Backend working of CPS.

The CPS would rapidly smoothen the path of a comprehensive analysis of the vast datasets, ultimately offering different military policymakers and stakeholders who could strongly grasp the real-time information for the effective formulation of agile and adaptive strategies that would respond to the nature of fluidity and modern-day conflicts.

Moreover, in this field, CPS played a very important and pivotal role in the logistics and management of the supply chain, which, in turn, optimized the flow of resources and reduced the logistical burden on different military operations. The ATS, which the CPS powers in the backend, plays a pivotal role in providing the meticulous oversight of different resources. This would result in timely delivery with precision of different crucial supplies in the frontline. This resulted in the streamlining of the logistical processes but also contributed to different durability and sustainability of different military operations.

The contributions of reduction of human hazards in the different and serious military endeavors rapidly underscore the importance of CPS. The incorporation of different autonomous systems, such as autonomous aerial vehicles or specifically uncrewed aerial vehicles (UAVs) or ground-based robots, into this CPS architectural framework. Here, many tasks could be performed without any rapid exposure of human personnel to the most hazardous environments. This would not only enhance the safety of the various military forces but would also open various new possibilities for reconnaissance, along with surveillance and different kinds of interactive engagement in different challenging environments.

11.3 Artificial Intelligence in Cyber-Physical Systems

11.3.1 Autonomous Weapon Systems and AI-Driven Decision-Making

In this ultra-modern landscape of warfare, the fusion of AI into CPS has led to the development of autonomous weapon systems. These systems anchor the advanced AI algorithms to make real-time decisions on the battlefield, starting from target identification to engagement. The ability of these systems to analyze in real-time vast amounts of data at a faster pace surpasses human ability. Also, it enables a quicker and more precise response system in dynamic and complex environments. Figure 11.3 shows a detailed working of autonomous weapon systems.

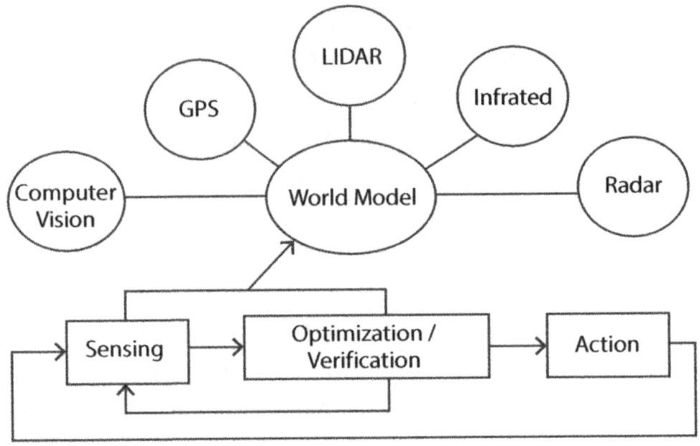

Figure 11.3 Working of an autonomous weapon system.

Artificial intelligence-driven decision-making plays an important role in the enhancement of situational awareness. Different intelligent machine learning algorithms, trained and tested on diverse datasets, enable the CPS in pattern recognition, predicting enemy movements, and in adapting to evolving scenarios. However, the deployment of various autonomous weapon systems also raises various ethical concerns, encompassing the potential for unintended consequences, accountability for various AI-driven actions, and its importance for the maintenance of human oversight to ensure adherence to international laws and ethical codes of conduct.

11.3.2 Artificial Intelligence for Predictive Analysis and Situational Awareness

The integration and efficient fusion of AI in CPS significantly improves predictive analysis, as well as situational awareness on the battlefield. Artificial Intelligence algorithms process data from various sensors, satellites, and other communication networks for the generation of real-time meaningful insights. Predictive analysis allows military policymakers to anticipate enemy movements, as well as assessing potential threats, and frame informed decisions.

Moreover, AI contributes to the development of various intelligent surveillance and investigation systems. These systems can sovereignly identify and track the targets while minimizing the risk to human operators. The different AI algorithms enable the analysis of various large datasets, which include images, videos, and sensor data from different sources, to identify different anomalies and potential security loopholes and breaches.

11.3.3 Ethical and Legal Implications of AI in Warfare

The real-time adoption of AI in this sector of CPS would rapidly prompt the hosting of different ethical and legal faces. The delegation of the decision-making authority for these autonomous or unmanned systems would raise questions about the morality of the usage of AI in modern warfare, specifically in situations where human lives could come to the verge of threat. The principle of proportionality and the differentiation between combatants and non-combatants would become more complex in the specific context of different AI-driven weapons.

Additionally, ensuring compliance with the different international humanitarian laws (IHL) and its rules for different engagements was very crucial. There is a specific need for more transparent regulations in this field along with the ethical codes of conduct for the accurate governance of the use of AI in warfare. There should also be an established monitoring agency that could emphasize the point of accountability, transparency, and preservation of human dignity and respect. Collaboration at the international level between different countries would be essential for the establishment of a framework that would balance the different benefits of using AI in the enhancement of military capabilities along with the imperativeness for upholding ethical standards and prevention of its misuse.

11.4 Autonomous Systems and Robotics

11.4.1 Drones and Unmanned Aerial Vehicles (UAVs)

The uncrewed aerial vehicles, which are specifically known as drones, are autonomous aircraft without any human intervention or any human on board. These form the key components of the autonomous systems in the various military operations. The UAVs vary in their size, along with their intricate capabilities and functionalities, which would make them widely versatile tools for the wider scope of military applications.

- Micro-UAVs: The smaller drones, which often weigh less than a few kilograms, as shown in Figure 11.4, were more often used in the exploration of short-range exploration along with surveillance. They must be easily deployable in

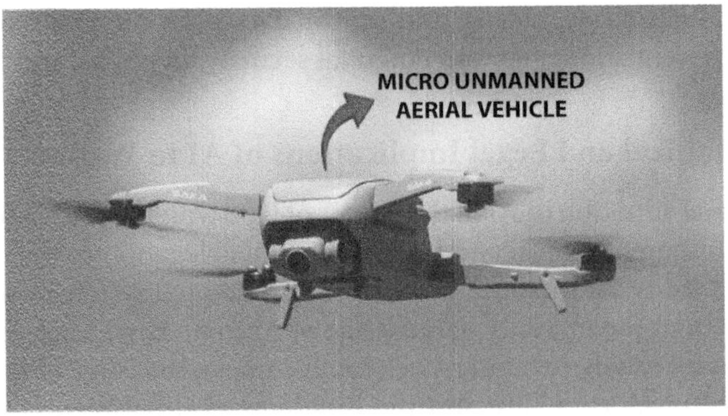

Figure 11.4 Micro UAV.

different terrains and could be able to navigate in very confined spaces.

- Fixed-Wing UAVs: These are a special type of drone that might look like traditional aircraft and are more widely known for their real potential of endurance and long-range capabilities. These UAVs could be more used in the scenario of deep exploration in situations and surveillance over different large geographic areas.
- Multi-rotor UAVs: Drones with various rotors, such as quadcopters and hexacopters, provide extremely strong stability and agility. These are widely used for close-range surveillance and aerial photography and can be equipped with various payloads.

The integration of UAVs into military operations provides many advantages strategically, such as surveillance and reconnaissance, as shown in Figure 11.5, precision strikes, logistics, and resupply. The UAVs are equipped with high-resolution cameras, sensors, and other intelligence-gathering technologies that can provide real-time situational awareness. They are used to monitor enemy movements and assess the battlefield from all angles. The differently armed UAVs, which are often referred to as unmanned combat aerial vehicles (UCAVs), would rapidly enable them to be more precise and have accurate targeted strikes on different enemy positions. This capability of the vehicles would reduce the different collateral damage to many extents and would allow for extreme surgical operations to be more successful. Besides having all these advantages of uncrewed aerial vehicles, the uses of these vehicles would also pose different threats

Figure 11.5 A UAV operated by the US Military.

and challenges, such as the confession of the airspace and misuse of different non-state actors. The boosting of the UAVs would raise concern about the congestion of the airspace, especially in times of dense environments. The effective management of air traffic technologies is much needed for the prevention of collisions and ensuring safe operations. The different technologies, which are available commercially, would also raise various concerns about the potential misuse by outside attackers for surveillance or anything possible. The ethical questions raised by the remote execution of the military operations, along with its accountability, would bring the civilians to the point of casualties.

11.4.2 Ground and Sea-Based Autonomous Systems

Uncrewed Ground Vehicles (UGVs): UGVs are more autonomously operated vehicles, which were fully designed at first for performing military operations ground-based. These might vary in their size and the point of functionality, which might range from the smallest to the largest of the platforms in terms of weaponry. These would play a pivotal role in the diversification of military applications, which would include exploration, surveillance and explosive ordinance disposal (EOD), along with logistics support.

Autonomous Combat Vehicles: The effective and accurate use of autonomous combat vehicles represented significant progress in the robotics on ground-based. These vehicles are more equipped with AI-driven systems, more sensors, and more advanced weaponry, ultimately advancing them for operating autonomously. These vehicles would always enhance the capabilities on the field by providing a more rapid and tactical response with increased firepower and their real ability to operate in various hazardous environments without any human casualties.

Uncrewed Surface Vehicles (USVs): USVs are the types of remotely operated vessels that can mainly do the work of navigation and operation on aquatic surfaces. They could be very useful in naval missions, which include the deep exploration of aquatic life, and this could be very useful in warfare using anti-submarine technologies. This could execute any type of task in the different littoral zones where the traditional vessels could face any challenges.

Autonomous Underwater Vehicles (AUVs): Autonomous underwater vehicles are mainly operated remotely, which unleashed the robotic vehicles mainly designed for underwater exploration and operations. They could also operate without any human intervention and could be equipped with better sensors and propulsion systems. These could play a critical role in naval applications, including underwater surveillance and detection of mines with environmental monitoring.

The effective collaboration between remote systems and various human operators is very important for the success of missions. This constitutes the integration of human decision-making with AI-driven capabilities to ensure a seamless flow of information and actions on the battlefield. Despite the remote nature of the systems, human oversight is crucial, especially in situations requiring complex decision-making. The development of robust communication protocols that will enable clear and reliable information exchange between humans and remote systems poses heavy threats. It is also required to ensure that human operators can intervene when necessary to maintain control and ethical standards.

11.4.3 Challenges Faced in Deploying Autonomous Systems

One of the major ethical concerns surrounding the deployment of various remote systems in warfare is the delegation of lethal decision-making. The usage of lethal force without direct human intervention raises various questions about its accountability, responsibility, and the potential for inadvertent consequences. Various autonomous systems, if not following a code of conduct, have the potential to have a severe impact on civilians. It is also important to ensure that these systems adhere to international humanitarian laws and rules of engagement to minimize collateral damage. The rapid pace of development and its deployment in real-time in autonomous systems raise concerns about augmentation. The deficiency of a clear ethical code of conduct can contribute to an arms race, with every developing nation increasing its potentially autonomous weapons.

11.5 Fifth Generation (5G) Technology and Network-Centric Warfare

11.5.1 High-Speed Data Transmission for Military Applications

Fifth generation (5G) technology represents a prototypical shift in the field of wireless communication, offering data speeds unparalleled as in Figure 11.6, with reduced latency and enhanced network capacity. In the context of the military, the real ability to transmit large volumes of data at high speeds is very crucial at the time of decision-making, intelligence gathering, and operational effectiveness. In a military operation, where UAVs with high-resolution cameras and sensors are deployed, 5G enables these

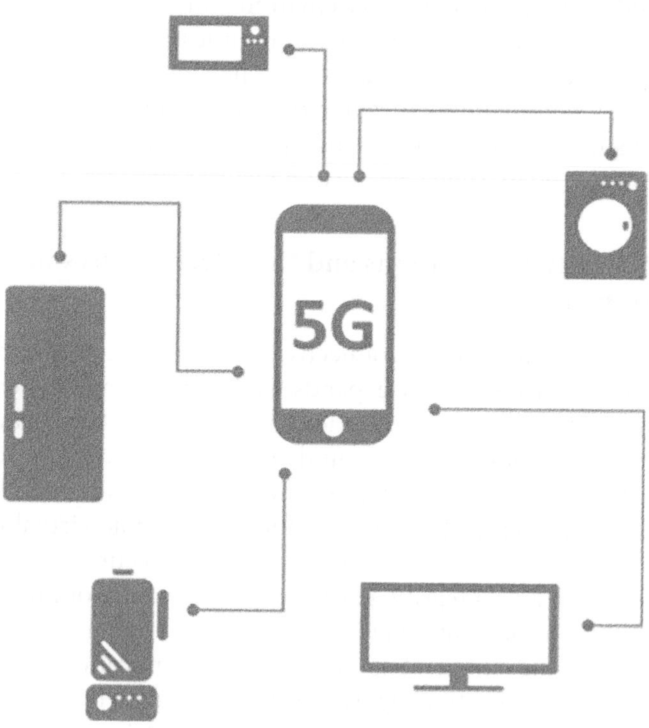

Figure 11.6 5G connectivity.

UAVs to transmit real-time high-definition video feeds and sensor data to command centers; 5G also facilitates the real-time control of these vehicles from a remote location with enhanced maneuverability and responsiveness. Special forces units that conduct covert operations in dense urban environments requiring secure and instant communication with minimal latency can take advantage of 5G networks by providing reliable and high-speed communication infrastructure.

11.5.2 Enhanced Connectivity and Communication in the Battlefield

Network-centric warfare refers to a special strategy adopted by the military that emphasizes the use of a robust interconnected network for enhancing the effectiveness of military operations. It mainly relies on the seamless flow of important information between various elements on the battlefield. With the 5G technology, military assets such as uncrewed vehicles, sensors, and surveillance systems can be integrated into a unified network. Even in the chaos of the battlefield, 5G provides enhanced reliability despite having dynamic and unpredictable military environments. The low latency of 5G networks also provides instantaneous communication. Moreover, 5G networks are designed to be highly scalable and flexible, and their adaptability allows military commanders to tailor their communication networks to customized specific requirements. The dynamic resource allocation capabilities of 5G also enable efficient use of network resources.

11.5.3 Security Implications and Countermeasures in 5G Networks

With the increased and better connectivity of devices and systems in 5G networks, the surface of attack expands while presenting new challenges for securing different communication channels. Hackers may exploit different vulnerabilities in the multitude of connected devices and infrastructure components to compromise their integrity and confidentiality. The 5G's network slicing allows the creation of multiple virtual networks tailored to different applications, and it introduces security challenges for ensuring isolation and integrity. For the sensitive nature of military communications and to prevent unauthorized access to military networks, 5G deployments should implement advanced authentication mechanisms along with robust encryption algorithms to secure data transmitted. Also, establishing a robust cybersecurity framework that involves continuous monitoring of network traffic and the implementation of advanced threat detection systems is crucial from the security point of view. Collaborative efforts between different government entities, agencies, and private sector cybersecurity experts are crucial in the interconnected nature of 5G networks.

11.6 Regulatory Frameworks for CPS Warfare

11.6.1 International Agreements on the Use of Disruptive Technologies

International agreements play a pivotal role in shaping the code of conduct and various regulations surrounding the use of disruptive technologies in warfare. This rapid advancement of CPS has prompted many discussions among developing nations to establish a regulatory body that can implement frameworks to guide its ethical and responsible deployment. Several existing international agreements and contracts touch upon aspects related to these disruptive technologies in warfare. The Geneva Conventions, in Figure 11.7, established in the aftermath of World War II, set a remarkable

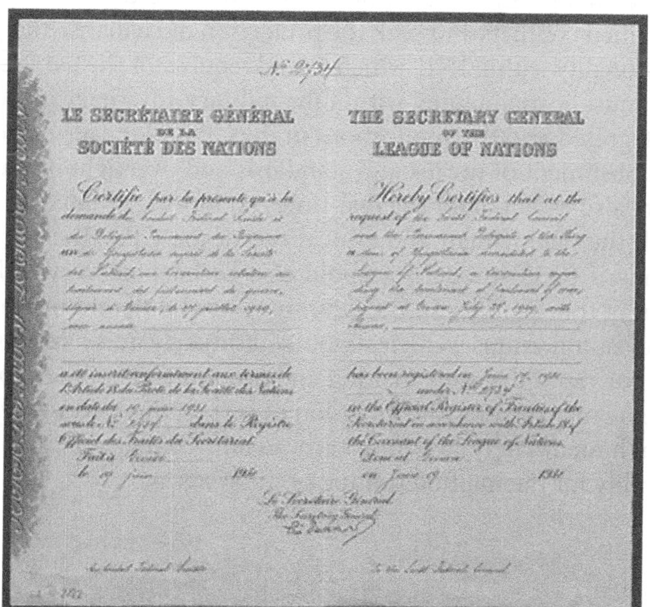

Figure 11.7 Geneva convention certificate.

standard for the humane treatment of civilians and war prisoners [5]. The Certain Conventional Weapons (CCW), also known as the Inhumane Weapons Convention, is a multilateral treaty that addresses the use of specific weapons that may be harmful to humans and can have adverse effects [4]. The discussions within the United Nations on lethal autonomous weapons systems (LAWS) [2] exemplify an opportunity for the strengthening and amendment of international agreements. Nations can enhance together through international cooperation through various collaborative platforms that will facilitate the exchange of knowledge, practices, and concerns related to disruptive technologies.

11.6.2 Establishing Norms and Standards for CPS in Warfare

The deployment of CPS raises ethical concerns, such as the potential for indiscriminate targeting and civilian harm. The Geneva Conventions can be expanded to incorporate norms specific to the ethical use of CPS. NATO's Standardization Agreements (STANAGs) provide a framework for interoperability among member nations [3]. However, an extension of these types of agreements for addressing the CPS would ultimately ensure that the technologies communicate effectively from different nations collectively. The international humanitarian law (IHL) would ultimately outline the rules along with the code of conduct that would govern these along with the armed conflicts and seek the protection of civilians. The principle of proportionality within IHL, which would require for the harm caused by the attack must be maintained within the military advantage gained, could also be integrated into the applications of the CPS [1]. Ensuring adherence to the establishment of norms and standards and oversight of the mechanisms were also essential for the real-time monitoring of the development, along with the deployment and ethical use of the CPS. The open source open standard (OSS) model [6] could also be adapted very well for the promotion of transparency in the development of different military-grade CPS. Also, autonomous vehicles would ultimately raise certain ethical questions for rapid decision-making and accountability. These principles could also be managed for the inclusion of certain directives for the prioritization of human safety, avoiding harm to non-combatants, and ensuring accountability for the malfunctioning of the systems.

11.6.3 Balancing the New Innovations with Ethical and Legal Considerations

The true development of autonomous weapons with the help of technology and AI-powered would raise various ethical concerns, which might surround their ability to make life and death decisions without any human intervention. The true balancing of this innovation of autonomous weapon systems (AWS), keeping in focus the ethical considerations, would involve the issue of accountability, along with transparency and its real potential to leverage unintended consequences. The various organizations, which are working in this sector, like the Campaign to Stop Killer Robots [7], would ultimately advocate for the preemptive ban on the overall development and use of LAWs. The IHL would, in turn, govern and conduct the armed conflicts and seek to protect the civilians and combatants who were no longer part of hostile teams and training. The use of uncrewed aerial vehicles for surveillance also raises concerns about privacy infringement, as these technologies can capture sensitive information without any consent. Balancing innovation with ethical and legal considerations in this context of disruptive technologies requires addressing specific examples and challenges. These examples illustrate the total complex interplay between technological advancement, ethical principles, and legal frameworks.

References

1. International Committee of the Red Cross, What is international humanitarian law?, International Committee of the Red Cross, 2022, April 5, https://www.icrc.org/en/document/what-international-humanitarian-law.
2. Lethal Autonomous Weapon Systems (LAWS) – UNODA, (n.d.), https://disarmament.unoda.org/the-convention-on-certain-conventional-weapons/background-on-laws-in-the-ccw/#:~:text=Autonomous%20weapons%20systems%20require%20%E2%80%9Cautonomy,could%20further%20enable%20such%20systems.
3. Nato, What is NATO?, NATO, (n.d.), https://www.nato.int/cps/en/natohq/topics_82686.htm.
4. The Convention on Certain Conventional Weapons – UNODA, (n.d.), https://disarmament.unoda.org/the-convention-on-certain-conventional-weapons/.
5. The Geneva Conventions and their Commentaries, International Committee of the Red Cross, 2021, May 20, https://www.icrc.org/en/war-and-law/treaties-customary-law/geneva-conventions.

6. What is open-source software?, IBM, (n.d.), https://www.ibm.com/topics/open-source.
7. Stop Killer Robots, Stop killer robots, (n.d.), https://www.stopkillerrobots.org/.

Index

Also of Interest

Check out these published and forthcoming titles in the "Industry 5.0 Transformation Applications" series from Scrivener Publishing

Generative Artificial Intelligence
Concepts and Applications
Edited By R. Nidhya, D. Pavithra, Manish Kumar, A. Dinesh Kumar, and S. Balamurugan
Forthcoming 2025. ISBN 978-1-394-20922-4

Intelligent Robots and Cobots
Concepts and Applications for Industry 5.0 Transformation
Edited By Ramasamy V., S. Balamurugan, and Sheng-Lung Peng
Forthcoming 2025. ISBN 978-1-394-19817-7

Optimized Computational Intelligence Driven Decision Making
Theory, Application and Challenges
Edited By Hrudaya Kumar Tripathy, Sushruta Mishra, Minakhi Rout, S. Balamurugan and Samaresh Mishra
Forthcoming 2025. ISBN 978-1-394-24253-5

Cyber-Physical Systems for Innovating and Transforming Society 5.0
Edited by Tanupriya Choudhury, Abhijit Kumar, Ravi Tomar, S. Balamurugan and Ankit Vishnoi
Forthcoming 2025. ISBN 978-1-394-19771-2

Welding Practices for Industry 5.0
Edited by Syed Quadir Moinuddin, Shaik Himam Saheb, Ashok Kumar Dewangan, Muralimohan Cheepu and S. Balamurugan
Published 2024. ISBN 978-1-394-17241-2

Metaverse and Immersive Technologies
An Introduction to Industrial, Business and Social Applications
Edited by Chandrashekhar A., Shaik Himam Saheb, Sandeep Kumar Panda, S. Balamurugan and Sheng-Lung Peng
Published 2023. ISBN 978-1-394-17454-6

www.scrivenerpublishing.com

Printed and bound by CPI Group (UK) Ltd, Croydon, CR0 4YY
19/09/2026
14965092-0001